ADVENTURES OF A MIDDLE-AGED FART

ANDY GABRIEL-POWELL

Also by the Author:

Richard Grenville and the Lost Colony of Roanoke. McFarland & Company, Inc., Publishers, 2016. (ISBN-13: 978-1476665719)

Looking for Sea Turtles *(A Romance)* Amazon Publishing, 2019 (ISBN-13: 978-1980622840)

*"Life is not what you make it,
but what you make OF it."
~ Andy Gabriel-Powell*

Adventures of a Middle-aged Fart Copyright © 2019 by Andy Gabriel-Powell All Rights Reserved.

No part of this book may be reproduced in any form or by any electronic or mechanical means including information storage and retrieval systems, without permission in writing from the author. The only exception is by a reviewer, who may quote short excerpts in a review.

Cover design by Mike Weston
Photography by the Author

The conversations in the book originate from the author's recollections, and so may not be verbatim. However, in all cases, the author has retold them in a way that evokes the feeling and meaning of what was said, the essence of the dialogue is, therefore, accurate. The stories that surround these conversations have been developed from personal (and I admit) occasionally sketchy travelogues I kept at the time. I have changed the names of people, hotels & businesses etc. where I think it prudent, and always with the best intention of avoiding embarrassment. What is related herein then, is ultimately a memoir and one written in a way intended only for literary effect.

Andy Gabriel-Powell

Printed in the United States of America

First Printing: October 2019

Amazon Publishing

ISBN-9781097101719

CONTENTS

PREFACE 1
PROLOGUE 3
TO HILL AND BACK 9
BARRAS JARPA 13
    (Day One ~ Flight Time) 13
    (Day Two ~ El Calafate) 21
    (Day Three ~ Perito Moreno) 23
    (Day Four ~ To the Torres) 26
    (Day Five ~ Vaqueroes) 31
    (Day Six ~ Refugio Dickson) 33
    (Day Seven ~ Los Perros) 36
    (Day Eight ~ The John Gardner Pass) 38
    (Day Nine ~ Lone Walk to Pahoe) 43
    (Day Ten ~ Valle Frances) 44
    (Day Eleven ~ Full Circle) 46
    (Day Twelve ~ Defeat and Victory) 47
    (Day Thirteen ~ The Pacific Ocean) 50
    (Day Fourteen ~ Adios Amigos) 51
    (Epilogue) 54
CLIPBOARD MAN 55
    (Day One ~ Departures and Arrivals) 56
    (Day Two ~ A Good Burning) 59
    (Day Three~ Becoming a Cathar) 61
    (Day Four ~ Two Groups are Better than One) 65
    (Day Five ~ Rennes-Les-Chateaux) 69
    (Day Six ~ Rennes Les Foot Spa) 71
    (Day Seven ~ All Pastis and Lavender) 73
    (Day Eight ~ C'est la Vie) 76
NIGHT ON A BARE-ARSED MOUNTAIN 79
    (Day One ~ Hyperspace) 80
    (Day Two ~ Mules and Mobile shops) 82
    (Day Three ~ The Martians have Landed) 84

(Day Four ~ "Yah-lah") 87
(Day Five ~ Discontent) 90
(Day Six ~ Incontinent) 93
(Day Seven ~ Bring Out Your Dead) 96
(Day Eight ~ The Lost Day) 97
(Day Nine ~ 'The Rescue') 98
(Day Ten ~ Two-man Sojourn) 99
(Day Eleven ~ Breaking the Rules) 103
(Day Twelve ~ Ever Downward) 104
(Day Thirteen ~ Falling off the Marrakech Express) 106
(Day Fourteen ~ My Blue Heaven) 108
(Day Fifteen ~ Freedom) 111
(Epilogue) 111

REELING IN THE BILGES 113

(Foolish Thoughts) 113
(The Call) 114
(Day One – Do You Speak Basque?) 115
(Day Two – Shore Leave) 119
(Day Three – Cast Off) 121
(Deathbed Recollections) 125
(Douarnenez) 125
(Sardines, Peaches, and Potatoes) 127
(The Longest Night, the Longest Day) 129
(Day Eight – Buoy Ahoy!) 131

HEBRIDEAN OVERTURES 134

(Day One ~ This Way to Purgatory) 135
(Day Two ~ Road to the Isles) 140
(Day Three ~ Butts & Brochs) 143
(Day Four ~ Mealaisbhal and Mangurstadh) 147
(Day Five ~ An Clisham) 150
(Day Six ~ It's All a Bit Twee'd) 153
(Day Seven ~ Uisge Gu Leor / Whisky Galore) 157
(Day Eight ~ Over the Sea to Skye) 161
(Day Nine ~ Long Road Home) 163

THE UNDISCOVERED COUNTRY 165

(Day One ~ Cultural Notes) 165
(Day Two ~ The Bears are Wearing Uniforms) 171

(Day Three ~ There's More Snow Than I thought) 175
(Day Four ~ Tripping Out) 178
(Day Five ~ A Walk on the Wild Side) 181
(Day Six ~ Pilgrimage) 185
(Day Seven ~ I Love Montenegro) 187
(Day Eight ~ Room With a View) 190
(Day Nine ~ The Tourist Trap) 192

DRINKING THE KOOL-AID 195

(One Giant Leap) 196
(Welcome to America, Well Almost) 197
(Class Actions) 202

PREFACE

These travelogues were never intended to be made public. Originally, I wanted to create a private journal, one to be read when life no longer permitted adventure. What changed my mind is something I will never fully understand, for what's in these pages is revealing, sometimes coarse, and often, quite personal. Maybe I was trying to convey a message, I don't know. Perhaps I should leave you to decide.

Andy Gabriel-Powell
Greenville, South Carolina
October 20th 2019

ANDY GABRIEL-POWELL

PROLOGUE

In England, it's a legal requirement to take your car to a garage for an annual inspection. The object of this is to ensure that it remains roadworthy and is not in danger of falling apart at a critical moment. We call it an 'M.O.T.' ~ named after the Ministry of Transport who decreed such examinations must take place. Doctors have much the same requirement of their patients, especially if you haven't been to see them for several months. It was almost three years since I'd last seen mine.

Thus, I was not surprised to receive a letter one morning, 'requesting' that I make an appointment for an 'M.O.T.' with my Doctor. I was middle-aged at the time, and thus, old enough for medical people to get encouraged by the possibility of discovering a patient with something beyond a routine case of tonsillitis. My mind raced ...

"Oh, that's a nasty looking hangnail you have there. I'm sorry, but amputation up to the elbow is the only thing we can do for you ..."

Such 'whole body' check-ups, however, also tend to involve the painful insertion of large needles; something I knew my wimpy-arsed body was not going to handle well. Against my better judgement then, I made the appointment.

As feared, when I arrived at the surgery, one of the nurses pounced. My shoulders sagged. There was no escape; besides, what if something WAS falling apart? My overactive imagination was already beginning to envisage that I had only days to live.

Fifty questions later, and after much poking, prodding, and excessive use of scales and tape measures, I had been subdued for the kill. Rolling up my sleeve, I closed my eyes and gritted my teeth, ready for the agony that was to follow.

"Relax... just a tiny scratch." She said.

Tiny it might have been, but the neat trick of attaching and detaching a succession of syringes to the needle, each capable of extracting gallons of blood, ensured my body would declare otherwise. As the nurse finally dabbed the puncture wound with a cotton pad, I sighed like a rapidly deflating balloon. My arm felt entirely devoid of blood, and my face had turned a ghostly shade of grey.

Once upon a time when you gave blood, they used to provide you with a cup of tea afterwards and allow you to chill out on a comfy sofa; not anymore. With the nurse holding my impaled arm, I was led out to the reception area like some tragic case of dementia and guided to a seat.

A few minutes later, the receptionist handed me a card and, to my relief, told me to come back in a week. This was no bad thing; if my Doctor had seen me straight away, he'd have thought my 'few days to live' prognosis somewhat optimistic...

Having fretted that my blood samples might need referring for the advancement of medical science, I duly returned to the surgery the following week. This time the Practice nurse moved no further towards me than the doorway of her lair. She did smile at me though, and in that unsettling way, only nurses can.
Rescued by the 'bing-bong' of the loudspeaker and the announcement of my name, I hurried towards the Doctor's office. Had I remained, I feared the nurse would have been twitchy enough to find a reason to drain the blood from my other arm.
After tentatively knocking on the door, I entered my Doctor's surgery and sat down. He was busy reading my notes.

"It's been a while" he declared as he finally spun round to look me straight in the eye. He was smiling too... so there WAS something wrong with me. His opening remark did nothing to dispel my fears...

"There are things we need to discuss, Mr Powell."

There it was again; that formal address only Head-teachers issue when summoning schoolchildren to their study for a beating. This was going badly.

"Your results are normal for your age. In fact, everything is normal ... for your age," he continued.

That was the second time he'd said 'for your age' and in the same breath too. Perhaps I needed to say something.

"You said 'for your age'" Doctor. Isn't that a good thing? I mean, I've led a very average life so my results should be average for my age, right? At least the results didn't say I was eighty-five years old!"

As my attempt at humour lay shredded on the floor, he gave me a withering look, took a deep breath, expelled it with a sigh, and began a short but brutal lecture.

"That's the point, Mr Powell. You ARE your age. You HAVE lived an average life, and you will probably continue to live an average life. Therefore, you will probably die around the average age for men in your condition."

I waited for the punchline. I didn't have long to wait.

"My point is Mr Powell, people who lead a more active life tend to live longer. In their retirement, they generally suffer less from illness too; illnesses that prevent them from doing the things they lament not having done when they were younger. You can grow old having that regret, or you can do something about it while you still can."

There was a pause as this sunk in. With a wary look on my face, I responded...

"Do what exactly?"

I had visions of having to join a bunch of psychotic individuals, killing themselves by attempting to lift five hundred pound weights in a gym somewhere; clearly, I was an idiot who needed further instruction.

"Go and do something scary, something that gets the heart pounding; something that overloads the senses, an adventure perhaps. It's these things that lead to a happier, healthier life, and one that allows you, in your dotage, to say, 'I did that.'"

In the stillness of the moment, he could not have been more compelling. Not knowing quite what to say next, I reached out, shook his hand, and, thanking him for the advice, left the surgery; my mind fogged by his words. 'Do something scary' he'd said...

Driving home, I began to create a list of 'scary things' in my head and then mentally cross them off one by one...

What about hang-gliding, I thought? Nope, I'd be the one who got caught by a rogue gust of wind and hit by a plane. Maybe I should try rock-climbing then? Nope,

I'd be the one that grabbed a loose rock and plunged to his death. Besides, I'm terrified of heights; so much so, that I doubt I'd make it thirty feet up a cliff-face before the poor bastard below me would suffer the fallout from my pants. There's always scuba diving, perhaps? Nope, not that either; I'd seen 'Jaws'; I'd also seen 'Deliverance', so white-water rafting was out too. What about a parachute jump? On second thoughts, I'd worked with someone who'd broken their leg in several places while doing just that, and she, unlike me, had been a professional skydiver. What about one of those 'thrill flights' then? I'd never flown before. That would be easy to arrange with someone down at the local airfield.

That idea hung around in my head until I saw a news broadcast a few nights later. It featured the image of a single-engine plane nose down in a field - the headline: 'No survivors'.

The flight idea persisted though. Reasoning that every day, millions of people flew on airliners all over the world, and mostly without any concern whatsoever; I wondered... What if I was to jump on one of these, one with at least two, or preferably, four engines, and fly somewhere I'd never been? That seemed to have less risk. Even if the idea might not quite tick the 'did something scary' box on my medical record, it was a start.

My next question was where to go. Logically, it would have to be abroad; England was far too small to make use of globetrotting jets. The problem with that was I'd never been anywhere outside my tiny island home in my entire life.

At first, I thought France could be the answer. It was only an hour's flight away, but it would be a flight nonetheless. The French also spoke an unfathomable language that my high school efforts to 'oeuvre la Porte' would find challenging at the very least. My first ever flight, and to a country with a foreign language... Here then, was something with a definite 'scary' factor.

However, there was a problem. Everybody in England went to France; I mean EVERYBODY in England went to France... With the advent of open borders, many Brits had even retired there in favour of cheap housing, and a lower cost of living. There was also the daily floodtide of Brits travelling to France on a 'Booze cruise', the aim of which was to buy as much cheap alcohol as one could hope to convince British Customs and Excise on your return, was all 'for personal consumption' *(and several friends, or liver transplants)*. Everywhere I went in fact; it seemed likely that I would encounter large numbers of Brits traipsing through the French countryside.

I sighed. Telling people you had been to France was never going to attract the kudos or gasps of awe and wonderment that I needed, nor would it signal the 'Wow! He's done something scary' response I hoped to impress my Doctor with. I had to think again.

What I would do when I got to wherever 'abroad' turned out to be, was also something I hadn't considered. I am not one to sit on a beach for a week while turning into a boiled lobster. I had to find something more stimulating.

About two weeks passed, then, while out walking the nearby coast-path one evening, the answer to my question became as plain as the shoes on my feet... literally.

I enjoyed going for a long walk, often covering fifteen miles or more. So why not take a flight somewhere and go for a long walk when I got there? It was naïve in its simplicity, but it was enough to start planning that scary thing I apparently needed to do. All I had to figure out, was where to go for a walk that wasn't in France, and (*preferably,*) didn't involve the risk of being eaten by cannibals, killed by some terrifying beast, shot, held hostage, or risk coming home with a disease that really would mean amputation...

A few days later, while searching for a reference book in the local library, I spied one of those world globes where all the countries are different colours. The thought struck me that if I spun it around and randomly stuck my finger on it, I might find the answer to my question. Squinting at the globe, the chances of hitting France using this method seemed quite small. In fact, the odds weren't that much better for landing anywhere in the whole of Europe.

Thus, much to the consternation of the librarian, I popped the globe out of its cradle, closed my eyes, spun it in all directions, and purposefully stuck my finger on its surface.

When I opened my eyes, I discovered I'd chosen to go for a walk in the Pacific Ocean, several hundred miles off the coast of southern Chile... I could have declared the result null and void and tried again, but there was something strangely appealing about the tip of South America, and it was the nearest landfall to my finger after all. Looking closer, I could see that, apart from the ridge of the Andes Mountains, the area was almost featureless; this, it turned out, was a place called Patagonia.

When I arrived home that evening, I fired up my laptop and punched 'Patagonia' into the search field. The results were encouraging:

'A temperate climate during summer months' (*check)*; potential dangers include Condors, (who apparently would only munch on me if I were dead;) and Pumas... (*check... I think)*; 'sparsely populated' - great, definitely not on the tourist routes, (*check)*; and best of all, Patagonia possessed more than its fair share of 'see before you die' places that would ensure maximum kudos with my Doctor, AND provide the 'I did that' memories for my dotage... *(Double-check!)*

So there you have it. I'd made my decision. Cue the start of a series of adventures my body has never quite forgiven me for...

TO HILL AND BACK

I'd read about the Drug Lords of Columbia and their habit of kidnapping and shooting people. To me, at least, it seemed logical to conclude this was typical behaviour for the whole of South America. Thus, I had a graphic image that those searching for me would find the remains of my body at the bottom of a ravine…Condors having carried off the missing bits. If Patagonia was to be my goal, then, I had to find someone, anyone, who had the necessary knowledge to ensure I would not become news headlines.

Truthfully I didn't even know where to start looking; the local travel agents were hopeless, unless of course I wanted to spend my money on one of those tours where people 'do' an entire country, *(or two)*, in a week, or just look at it while consuming e-coli onboard a cruise ship. They blew their last chance when one merely shrugged their shoulders at the word 'Patagonia', and declared that it was still a "white bit" on the tourism map; *(actually it was more of a beige colour.)* Disappointed, I drove home, convinced I would need to 'friend' Marco Polo or Ferdinand Magellan on social media if I were ever going to set foot on Patagonian soil…

That night, and not convinced the internet would have anything better to offer, I half-heartedly punched 'Treks to South America' into the search field and waited.

To prove my convictions wrong, there, right at the top of the list, was a company offering treks to 'remote regions' of the planet. In hope, I clicked through their homepage and discovered a trek to somewhere in South America called 'Torres Del Paine'. I knew nothing of the location, but it WAS in Patagonia, and that was all that mattered. I clicked on the link to find out more.

'This is one of the toughest treks in the world' it read. 'You should have previous experience of trekking in extreme conditions for up to eight or more hours a day' it continued.

Ignoring the 'You will be physically fit' warning, I clicked on through to the list of kit considered essential for the trek. I had not one single item on it; this trek was fast becoming a challenge in every respect. It was also a challenge that lay about as far south as one can go without freezing to death in Antarctica. This gave it considerably more kudos than France.

With the flight details confirming the plane to take us there had four engines, two more than my minimum requirement, I blithely clicked goodbye to a sizable amount of my miserable savings.

A few days later, a receipt and a detailed information pack dropped through the letterbox signalling that I was about to embark on a journey to the other end of the planet, something that was beyond any reasonable doubt, to me at least, scary in every possible way.

With the clock ticking, my next objective was to buy the recommended kit, *(at the not recommended prices,)* and push myself into a training regime my naïve mind considered would meet the 'physically fit' requirement of the information pack.

In trying to work out what level of fitness that would be, I re-read the information pack and soon discovered that the requirement to be able to walk for up to eight hours a day, meant, EVERY day, not just the ONE day I could barely manage at the moment. The trek also included a mountain pass to negotiate, one that involved a climb far more gruelling than anything I'd attempted before.

I was in trouble. With a fitness level that might at best register as 'woeful', I now knew I needed to attain something a whole lot close to 'superman' if I was going to avoid being humiliated. I had just six months in which to achieve it.

Now, I have to confess, I am not one for attending gymnasiums. Thus, and with the strangest logic, I got it into my head that the easiest way to improve my fitness would be to climb a mountain or two here in the British Isles. Unfortunately, the nearest ones I could find were at the other end of the country. Plan B then was simple; find a nearby hill that I could run up and down a few times in the hope that it would have the same impact.

Living among the hilly west of England at the time, it didn't take long to find a suitable hill; better still, the one I chose was just thirty minutes' drive from my home. On the downside, though, it was only five hundred feet high... not exactly a mountain...

Nevertheless, and for reasons, I still can't fathom the logic of, I figured that being able to climb this hill twenty times in a single day, some ten thousand feet in total, would be enough to raise my level of fitness sufficient for the entire two-week challenge that lay waiting for me in Patagonia... *(I know, right?)*

Nevertheless, when the following weekend arrived, I packed everything I'd bought for the trek into my backpack, gave myself a hernia lifting it into the car and headed off for a first attempt at climbing my 'mountain'.

For the sake of authenticity, I'd chosen to wear the 'state-of-the-art' mountaineers clothing, *(complete with fashionable motifs)* that I'd also bought for the trek. The North Devon coastline didn't exactly simulate the conditions associated with the glaciers and mountains of Patagonia, but I was certainly prepared for it if it suddenly changed its mind...

My five hundred foot 'mountain' stood next to a small secluded beach, some distance from the tourist traps further along the coast.

To my dismay, however, as I pulled into the grassy field that constituted a car-park for the beach, I discovered it was almost full; my 'secluded beach' had been invaded by the very people I hoped to avoid. The last thing I wanted was an audience.

Sighing heavily, I hauled my backpack out of the car and looked skyward to the summit of what I had now christened 'Crucifixion Hill'. It was a long way up, and the climb to get to the top, a steep one at that. Struggling into the monster I'd created for my back, I took a deep breath, and began to climb, already aware of heads turning in my direction.

I finally reached the summit after several pauses to put my heart back into my chest and collapsed onto a nearby bench. Several minutes passed before I had the strength to begin my descent. Going back down the hill would be less challenging, I thought.

Like hell it was... By the time I'd slipped, slid, bounced and bounded back down to my car, I was ready to quit the whole idea of going on the trek.

As the doubts began to creep in, I pondered the alternatives...

What about a pleasant amble through the Chianti country of Italy? The promise of lodging at a vineyard every night sounded ideal. The reality, of course, was that such a trek would hardly qualify as 'scary'; besides, there was no way I was going to return to my Doctors to explain that with all that Chianti swilling around inside me, I'd done something 'scary' to my liver...

Resigned to my fate, I turned and made my way back up the hill, much to the amusement of the tourists who had just witnessed my first assault.

After descending 'Crucifixion Hill' for the fourth time, my legs finally gave way. Crashing to my knees, I rolled over onto my backpack and lay there, eyes closed.

Despite giving a good impression of being dead, or at least dying, nobody rushed to help me; the only sound I might have heard was the rustle of cash changing hands following a lost bet... I still had another twenty-five weeks to lose mine.

The next Sunday duly arrived and once more, I set off for another assault on Crucifixion Hill. That day, the sun had decided it would turn up the heat a little, and, as a result, the beach was even busier than it had been the previous week. There was something strangely familiar about some of the cars too. Thus, by the time I began my second ascent, I could see shaking heads out of the corner of my eye and hear mutterings of "What the hell is he up to... must be a nutter". Not wishing to invite questions, I ignored them, looked skyward, and set off once more.

After my third descent, I gave up and headed for the car. I'd had enough for one day. This wasn't going according to plan.

Yet my conviction was such that I returned once again the following weekend, and every weekend all that summer long.

Sometime around early December, in failing evening light, I finally counted out my twentieth ascent and descent of Crucifixion Hill. I'd done it. I'd conquered my mountain. Twenty times I'd climbed its five hundred feet, and twenty times I'd made my way back down it, and all in one single day. Now wishing for an audience, I stood Rocky Marciano like and shouted "yes!" at the top of my voice; my cries of joy met only by the gaze of Atlantic Grey Seals basking on the now-empty beach below.

There are, however, few more defining words than 'ignorance is bliss'. Had I examined the 'Detailed information pack' more closely, I would have realised the insignificance of my achievement, and instead made plans for a trek to the nearest pub...

BARRAS JARPA

The day finally arrived when I was to launch myself into doing 'something scary'. It was just forty-eight hours after I'd celebrated the New Year.

My mission that day was simple enough. I had to find and board a flight at London's Heathrow airport, bound for Madrid. When I arrived in Madrid, I was to find and board another flight bound for Buenos Aires, a city that lay somewhere a long way south of reason. Then, and assuming I made it, I was to meet the trek leader at the airport. There was just one problem... I didn't have a clue who this person was, or how I would identify them. That said, I'd also never been inside an airport terminal before...

(DAY ONE ~ FLIGHT TIME)

I woke early enough that morning for it to still be late enough to go to bed, and boarded the first train of the day bound for London. I'd given myself enough time to walk the sixty-five miles to the airport, let alone take the train. I guess with my calamitous travel record, the fear of cancellations, delays, or just simple failure of the train en-route, was, to me at least, genuine.

Much to my surprise, my connections all congealed to run so smoothly that by the time I walked onto the concourse at London's Heathrow Airport, it was still more than five hours before my flight was due to leave.

Having never done this sort of thing before, arriving at a 'check-in' was a new experience. I'd found the right terminal by using the clue on the booking form I'd received in the post; all I needed to do now was find the airline's desk. If I'd flown from a small regional airport, this would have been easy. In those places, you walk in the door, and typically, there's just one bored soul sat at the singular check-in desk waiting for someone to talk to. Not so at a major airport like London's Heathrow. There were desks as far as the eye could see and in both directions.

Having roamed up and down the desks twice, without finding the airline I was searching for, I sighed deeply as my shoulders sagged. I didn't think it was supposed to be like this. With backpack leaning in comforting support against my leg, I gazed mindlessly at the flight departure board.

Several minutes passed before I noticed that the flight at the bottom of the screen was the one I needed. When I blinked again, however, it was gone. Moments later, it re-appeared. For a moment, my naivety allowed me to think there had been a mistake, but no, there it was again and then gone again.

Noting that the two flights fighting for the same slot were both going to Madrid, I wandered off in search of the other airline's desk to ask about switching flights. To the seasoned professional who looked at my booking slip, I need not have mentioned I'd never flown before; it could not have been more apparent that I had no idea what a 'codeshare' was...

Thirty minutes later and having copied what everyone in front of me was doing at the security checkpoint, I was duly spat out into the waiting area of the departure lounge.

Apart from some snacks to munch, my mind was too busy pondering the flight to focus on sitting down and reading a book, or magazine like everyone else. In a vain attempt to pass the time, I tried to make a cup of processed coffee last an hour, but its lukewarm consistency had me wandering down empty corridors in search of nothing in particular, long before the Departure board declared a gate for my flight.

Bored, nervous, and in desperate need of something to occupy the mind, when I stumbled across a 'travellator', the temptation was too great to ignore. For the next five minutes, I alone, in a deserted corridor, stood on said travellator, as it chugged purposefully towards I knew not where. I'm rather glad nobody saw me.

When the travellator reached the end of the corridor, however, I stepped off to see a small huddle of airline staff, look up in surprise at my unannounced appearance. Hesitating, and feeling somewhat self-conscious, I turned to look questioningly at the Departure board, gave a rather animated expression of confusion, and hurried back to the Departure lounge; walking somewhat faster than the travellator had got me there...

Almost six hours after I arrived at Heathrow airport, I was still in Terminal One; this was a bit disconcerting. The plane had left thirty minutes ago according to my

Boarding Pass, but repeated looks out of the window assured me it was still there, sucked against the elephant's trunk of our gate.

A brief announcement confirmed we were subject to a delay because of a 'technical fault'. I noted the puddle beneath the plane, and a guy in overalls stood, hand on hips, looking at it... Innocently assuming everything would work out just fine, I continued to pass the time by following a bad habit of mine... people watching.

It wasn't long before I spied a small group toting backpacks. From the luggage tags, I noted they too were heading for Buenos Aires. The coincidence didn't really hit me at that point, but when they decided to head off to the airline's Help Desk, and enquire about alternative flights to Madrid, I felt an urgent need to follow them.

As it turned out, our flight was the only one with any hope of catching the connection to Buenos Aires. Thus, I returned to my seat by the gate and sat down to gaze once more at our aircraft, still apologetically sat outside the window.

At this point, I could do little more than smile inwardly as I considered the possibility that, after months of planning, getting fit, *(well sort of,)* and having spent a fortune on all the recommended kit *(at the not recommended prices,)* my adventure of a lifetime might only get as far as London's Heathrow airport before it was cancelled. I didn't even want to contemplate how my workmates would react if I walked back into the office the day I was supposed to be halfway up a mountain at the other end of the planet...

As these thoughts whirled through my head, my eyes finally got through to my brain. The message was a simple one; there was no longer a puddle beneath the aircraft. Looking up at the check-in desk for some sort of status report, I could see a flurry of activity taking place; our flight was back on.

After all the meticulous preparation of the last six months, the moment of truth had arrived. I took a deep breath and joined the queue to board the aircraft.

Hurrying down the walkway, I entered the plane, found my seat, stowed my backpack in the overhead locker, sat down, and closed my eyes. Breathing as slowly and deeply as my pounding heart would allow, I could sense every nerve ending in my body alive to the enormity of what I was about to do. There was no going back now.

I didn't perceive much from our flight; night had fallen by the time we boarded. I heard the engines roar as we started down the runway, the noise of the tarmac beneath us, the sudden feeling of weightlessness as we got airborne, the clunk of the wheels as they retracted, the gentle swaying of the aircraft as we weaved out of the crowded London skies, and, well, that was that. Despite looking out the window a few times in the hope of spotting something I recognised, I saw only rows of yellow lights defining roads, and a handful of multi-coloured blobs heralding the towns and cities of southern England; and then - nothing. We were above the clouds; and the moon, being on its twenty-eighth day, was fast asleep.

My first flight had turned out to be something I didn't expect... uneventful; perhaps that's how it's supposed to be.

When we landed at Madrid airport, instead of pulling up to the terminal building as I expected, we stopped somewhere out on the tarmac. It was so dark I wondered if we were still in the middle of the runway and our plane had suffered a relapse of its 'technical fault'.

Several anxious minutes later, the ground crew arrived with a set of steps. Following a brief announcement, those of us bound for Buenos Aires rose from our seats and headed for the doorway.

Stepping onto foreign soil for the first time in my life, I felt an overwhelming urge to do the Pope bit by kneeling to kiss the ground. I didn't get a chance. My first experience of a foreign land amounted to just four paces, the distance between the foot of the steps and a waiting bus. The driver of that bus had but one singular mission too, to find our connecting flight to Buenos Aires. I didn't even get to wander through Madrid's terminal buildings.

As our bus weaved to and fro across the runway, its driver squinting at tail-plane insignias, Spanish immigration officers wandered among us checking passports. If I'd hoped to get a Spanish entry stamp for mine, I was out of luck. Our time in Spain was going to be less than that necessary to make a request for asylum, let alone obtain some kudos for a passport.

Twenty minutes passed; the flight to Buenos Aires should have left by now. Things were not looking good. Then, as the lights of the airport faded into the distance, our driver finally stopped weaving and made straight for what appeared to be a forty-watt light bulb flickering in the distance.

He had done well. Our flight to Buenos Aires was hiding apologetically in the dark recesses of a gate too far from the terminal to have a number. And well it might, for even in the midnight gloom, the aircraft looked rusty from the outside.

Once onboard the dog-eared jet, my worst fears were realised. It had all the hallmarks of having rolled off the production line a few weeks after the Wright Brothers had got airborne.

While searching for my seat, the first thing I noticed was the luggage stacked in the aisles; the five-kilo hand luggage limit appeared to translate into Argentinean as fifty kilos. It didn't take much to recognise though that most of it comprised new years' sales bargains of things, as I would learn, unobtainable in Argentina.

When I finally sat down, the Emergency Exit next to me set off an alarm. This caused panic only for me, and the stewardess who raced up to re-affix the red tape that appeared to be holding the door in place...

Take-off was a protracted affair. When we finally charged down the runway, the black and white stripes at the end of it appeared beneath us... before we were airborne...

The twelve-hour flight to Buenos Aires proved to be a feat of endurance. The seats were narrow and uncomfortable, and it was just my luck that the giant Argentinean sat next to me was wearing a Boca Junior's T-Shirt. Our only conversation in those twelve hours boiled down to just two words:

Argentinian: "Maradonna"

Brit: "Cheat"

(For the uninformed, 'Maradonna' handled the ball into the back of the net during a World Cup soccer match, which, despite the entire world spotting, the referee didn't... presumably, because he had taken a bribe. As a result, England bowed out of the football (soccer) World Cup that year...)

With feral children crying, screaming, and generally running amok up and down the aisles, the snoring of my Argentinean giant, and the constant jabbering of the women on board, some of whom I don't think took a breath in the entire flight; any attempt I made to get some sleep, failed utterly.

The icing on the cake was the queue of people waiting for the toilet. To a one, they signalled their relief by banging the toilet door as loudly as possible in celebration of not having urinated all over the floor...

By the time we crossed the South American coastline, I was in a positively murderous frame of mind. Thankfully, Buenos Aires arrived soon enough. Ironically, the landing was so smooth I could have fallen asleep to it...

The ecstatic cheers and applause from the Argentinean onboard though suggested that landing in one piece was a rare and heroic feat.

As we lined up to disembark, the Captain and flight crew appeared from the cockpit and stood to attention by the exit. They were there to receive prayers and offerings of daughters' hands in marriage from the Argentinean passengers, grateful for their safe return.

I could not get off the plane fast enough. Looking back at the aircraft in the full light of day, it was worse than I thought; so much so, that I considered the prayers offered to the crew had some merit...

It was still early morning, but the temperature in Buenos Aires was an already stifling ninety degrees; sixty degrees warmer than London had been when I walked into Heathrow, little more than twenty-four hours earlier.

On reaching the immigration hall, I handed over my passport for inspection. The official proceeded to view it with some suspicion... there was not a single stamp in it. Resigned to the disbelief that he could find no reason to refuse my entry, he thudded 'Entrada Argentina' onto its first page.

Wandering onto the concourse, oblivious to my surroundings as I admired the passport stamp I'd just received, I didn't notice anything, or for that matter, anyone. A distinctly English voice brought me back from my fascination...

"Hello," it said.

It was coming from a tall, bespectacled twenty-something, who looked more like an Oxford student than a seasoned tour guide. Evidently, he had singled me out as someone way out of their depth... and perhaps easy prey for a drug lord...

Duly rescued, I offered a bewildered "Hi" to the rest of the group, many of whom I recognised from the backpacks at Heathrow; and followed our guide out of the terminal and onto a waiting coach for the journey to our hotel.

Hurrying our way through the suburbs, I spent the time gazing out of the window, still unconscious to the fact that I was now a very long way from home indeed.

We arrived at the grandly named Waldorf hotel and checked in. My room though confirmed the hotel was somewhat less grand or Waldorfian than its name suggested. On taking note of the mould in the shower, I switched on the air conditioning unit precariously mounted in the window frame, threw my backpack onto one of the single beds, and hastened back to the reception area, ready for the ubiquitous 'City Tour'.

Walking out of the hotel entrance to board the bus, the realisation that I was finally doing something scary began to take hold; the adrenalin had started to flow again.

Our first stop that morning was the paint commercial known as the Boca district. Traditionally, the houses here made use of paint left over from the day's shipbuilding in the nearby and now long-defunct docks. Thus, the houses were a lurid assortment of every colour imaginable. Which colour informed you a house was the home of the local drug lord I had no idea, but I noted the warnings advising tourists not to wander unaccompanied for fear of finding out.

Half an hour later and we had moved on to the Recoleta cemetery. We were there for one purpose, to find the burial place of Eva Peron... For such an iconic public figure, I was surprised to discover that her mausoleum was small and generally insignificant in comparison to others in the cemetery. However, it was difficult to miss - Abundant fresh flowers with messages of 'come back and save us' festooned the entire façade, while several pairs of praying hands could be witnessed pawing at its door...
Leaving the people to their hopes, we made our way to the city's cathedral.

Walking into its dimly lit, almost morbid interior, I noted the dark and private corners of it were full of people, mainly men, deep in prayer. I felt sure they should be working somewhere. Then it dawned on me that these men were probably unemployed and praying for the answer to the question of where the next peso was coming from. For a brief moment, I felt that a few dollars in the 'donations box' might find its way to some of them, but thought otherwise when I saw the glittering array of gold and silverware that made up the cathedral's Altar. Clearly, the cost of metal-polish was a far higher priority...

Heading outside to the comforting brilliance of the midday sun, I witnessed a demonstration taking place outside the lurid, pink-coloured presidential palace. Our trek leader casually informed us there was usually one every week...

Our tour continued with a visit to a small open-air market. It was the perfect opportunity to buy a memento, preferably something synonymous with the country. The reality that, whatever I purchased would have to survive the next two weeks undamaged in my backpack, as I trolled and toiled around Patagonia, was lost on me as I waved a vague amount of cash in the direction of a Maté bowl.

Maté is a sort of toe-curling tea made from a member of the holly family. I had already seen these bowls everywhere - perched on cash registers next to shop assistants, and even cradled in the cup holders of coach drivers. It was, therefore, the perfect souvenir.

When we regrouped, I showed it to our guide who seemed quite surprised that I had found one that was not only authentic but one he deduced, had been carved by an Araucana Indian, the original natives of Patagonia. I could not have been more pleased. I didn't feel the need to divulge what I'd paid for it, nor, perhaps out of a desire to rid my sense of guilt from the visit to the cathedral, the generous commission I'd given its maker...

Arriving back at our Hotel, our guide suggested we might like to find our own lunch. Being so new to foreign travel, this was a challenge I hadn't expected. Suddenly I felt nervous again. Nevertheless, I wandered out of the hotel, and ventured all of fifty yards up the street to discover a restaurant called 'El Establo'.

There was a menu in the window, of which I could not read a word. The drawn blinds gave no clue as to what it was like inside either. Feeling certain that Argentinian memories would still be sore over the losses they suffered during their war with Britain, I stopped to ponder my options. Did I go in and risk being knifed, mugged, held for ransom, and suffer an 'English pig-dog I spit on your grandmother's grave' response from some giant hairy grease-ball with a fifteen-inch knife, or should I pass it by and go find a Senor McDonalds? With that, 'Do something scary' command, coming back to haunt me; I gingerly opened the door, almost anticipating the greasy knife under the chin.

I didn't get past the threshold when a classically dressed waiter bounded up to me. He showed no sign of being a grease-ball, and he didn't appear to own a fifteen-inch knife...

Not sure what to say or do, I looked around for clues and with relief spotted a small group of my trekking companions. With an over-acted flourish of the hand, I signalled to the waiter that I was going to join them.

Pulling up a chair, I sat down and looked once more at the menu. Finally figuring out that one of the words on it was for 'coffee', I pointed to it and mumbled a vaguely Spanish sounding "por favor". This seemed to be enough to despatch the waiter to the bowels of the restaurant and return minutes later with a steaming hot jug of coffee in one hand, and a cup and saucer in the other. After pouring the coffee with a flourish, he placed it in front of me, bowed, and vanished back into the dark recess from whence he had first appeared.

I spent much of that lunchtime dipping in and out of the conversation; too busy ogling the polished wood walls, decorated floor to ceiling with shelves of pickles, wine bottles, jars of I knew not what, and kitchen utensils for every conceivable purpose. I was mesmerised too by the open-plan kitchen in the centre of the restaurant; its chefs, flame-grilling steaks I didn't think could be that big.

I was not the only one to lose track of the time that day... 'El Establo' was homely enough for our small group to become the subject of a search party led by our bespectacled tour leader. Time had marched long past our allotted lunch break. As we left, I hoped we would have an opportunity to visit 'El Establo' again.

We spent that night at one of the unavoidable Tango clubs that infest Buenos Aires.

Walking down the steps and through the front door, I expected to see something belonging to that classic, slightly seedy, smoky, round table image of film noir that was once the domain of overweight sixty-somethings, cavorting with roses between their teeth. But no; our venue for the night was a modern affair with thirty-foot dining tables, and professional musicians and dancers. The show also included a supporting cast from Peru...the inevitable, but beautifully played panpipes. I was particularly vociferous with my "Bravo's" however, for a band of musicians, who looked as though they had been playing those seedy round-tabled affairs since Humphrey Bogart had talked about his gin joint in Casablanca. If the owners' wife, conscious of an English presence, had not tried to sing 'Don't cry for me Argentina', and fail utterly on all the big notes, the night would have been perfect.

When the show was over, the artistes meandered among the audience for photographs and expected tips. I gave handsomely to the Bogart era musicians, and went to the restroom when the owners' wife moved towards our table...

I finally hit the mattress at one-thirty in the morning and fell asleep for the first time in forty-two hours...

(DAY TWO ~ EL CALAFATE)

Saying our farewells to the Waldorf that morning, we boarded the bus for the journey to Buenos Aires's domestic airport. There, we took a flight to el Calafate, a town three hours due south, and somewhere near the beginning of the trek, I had for so long prepared.

After thirty minutes in the air, the sky cleared to reveal a barren landscape, with no sign of human habitation. It stayed that way for the remainder of the flight...

We finally descended to land on the single black strip of tarmac that represented el Calafate's 'International' *(one flight a week to Uruguay)* airport, before coming to a halt outside the terminal.

For the second time in two days, the ground crew brought steps up to our plane. This time I did that thing famous people always do in these situations; I paused at the top of the steps to survey the surroundings. Resisting the urge to wave, and with a gentle push from behind, I walked down the steps and made my way towards the terminal building.

Crossing the tarmac, the first thing I noticed about Patagonia, was the wind. In this almost treeless wilderness, there is little to stop it from scouring the landscape into the dust that made up most of what I could see around me.

Once outside the terminal, we boarded a bus for the journey into town; this was a good thing, for el Calafate lies fifteen miles from its airport...

After a quick shower, I raced back to the reception area of our comfortable hostel to discover we had the rest of the day to ourselves.

Alone, I wandered into town making detailed notes of the way back to the hostel; the fear of getting lost was genuine, even if, as in the case of el Calafate, I could see the entire town from almost any vantage point.

Not being quite ready to test my poor Spanish at buying something, I followed a sign encouraging me to visit the local wildlife reserve. It was no more than four hundred yards down a small side street; this, and my being a nature lover, made it an easy lure. Paying my token entrance fee, I wandered in.

The reserve was a twee but unusual village pond affair, surrounded by reed-beds. Nevertheless, I could only wonder at how the wildlife observed me from little more than the distance of an outstretched hand. I was no threat to them of course, but clearly, their cousins further north hadn't told them yet about humanity's wholesale destruction of the planet. How much longer these magnificent creatures would act with such indifference, here at the frontier of package tours, I didn't know; but looking back at the advancing town, something told me it wouldn't be long...

An hour later and I was once more looking up and down the main street. With several new stores taking shape, el Calafate had the feeling of being on the brink of a gold rush. Those already trading even looked as though they had come straight from a Dodge City film set, the boarded 'sidewalks' completing the impression.

El Calafate's shops, like all shops in Argentina, open from late morning and trade until midnight. Thus, even though it was now seven o'clock in the evening, many were still busy with customers.

Finally plucking up courage, I entered one in search of the ubiquitous 'been there', *(got the)* T-Shirt.

It was not difficult to find, for it had a map of 'Terra Incognita' (Patagonia), across the front, and a Condor emblazoned over one corner. I needed no further encouragement; neither did the cashier when I rolled out an American twenty-dollar bill. A peculiar thing to do perhaps, but with the Argentinian Peso subject to raging inflation, and frequent devaluation, the American Dollar represented 'hard cash'. With a quick punch of an exchange rate on the calculator, I nodded to the resultant figure, collected my T-shirt, and an armful of Argentinian Pesos, and strode out of the shop.

Feeling rather pleased with my mini-adventure and cool looking T-shirt, I headed back to the hostel to learn that we were leaving shortly for another dining out experience.

We may have arrived well after nine o'clock that evening, but there was still a queue for a table at the restaurant.

Once inside, I could not help but stare at the novel cooking arrangements... In the middle of the restaurant floor, there was a 'teepee' of giant metal skewers, each with a sizeable amount of cow or sheep impaled upon them. In the centre beneath this teepee, was a large pit filled with a roaring fire. I drank wisely that night, as one had to circumnavigate the firepit to reach the restrooms...

The size of the food portions the restaurant served, only added to the experience. The smallest meal one could order, involved at least two pounds of steak or an entire rack of lamb; the only vegetable available, 'patatas espaniole' *(sautéed potatoes)*, arrived as little more than a condiment...

As we left the restaurant, I suffered a momentary crisis... For there, on the opposite side of the road, an Irish 'theme' bar beckoned. I sighed; surely not here, not already?

Thankfully no. It was closed; closed down in fact. I made a mental note that Argentineans were not as gullible as the rest of the world, and turned to follow our group back to the hostel.

(DAY THREE ~ PERITO MORENO)

I woke to a Patagonian sunrise and made my way to the reception area for the day's adventure... a trip to the Perito Moreno glacier. I had never seen a glacier before...

In the sparse plains of Patagonia, the roads are little more than gravel tracks. However, these tracks are laden with potholes, some large enough to require drivers to swerve violently to avoid breaking an axle on them.

Things tend to become a little more stressful when another vehicle appears heading towards you. Thankfully, the accompanying dust plume alerting you to its presence allows time to offer a few 'Hail Mary's', or provide more cultural expletives in the hope your driver returns to the right side of the road before it's too late... Fortunately for us, our driver appeared to be a seasoned professional at playing 'Chicken' with the other drivers.

More than two hours were to pass without incident before a barrier across the road finally convinced him to pause the game.

Next to the barrier stood a toll-booth, and from it, emerged a man dressed as a military commander. He wanted money. We paid up at the princely rate of three US dollars each. Sated by our bribe, he then raised the barrier and promptly saluted us as we drove under it.

From there on, the road narrowed and contained even larger bus swallowing holes in its surface. Clearly, we had advanced to Level Two in the game of chicken. Oncoming vehicles also tended to hide around corners...

Several miles later, and without warning or fanfare, we rounded a blind corner to witness the hills around us peel back to reveal the majesty of Perito Moreno.

The glacier lies between two mountains while the rest of the Andes line up chorus fashion behind it. Being too wide to fit between my ears, the view caused my brain to forget to control my mouth; at which point, I think a few of my colleagues began to realise just how much of a lifetime adventure I was truly on.

Relieved we had arrived in one piece; I jumped off the bus and hurried to the vantage point next to the face of the glacier. Until that moment in my life, these things had only ever existed in television documentaries; now I could almost touch one.

The eerie creaks and groans of the glacier on its endless journey across the lake echoed off the surrounding mountains, but despite the viewpoint being something of a melee, these were the only sounds anyone could hear.

Having now seen the glacier, I could not hide my delight on learning we were to walk upon it.

I was grateful for the seasoned help of the seventeen-year-old Argentinean student, who kitted me out with the necessary crampons though, for it's not your everyday footwear in temperate Britain...

I soon discovered too that it's a fine art to walk in these things. For the next few minutes, I practised walking like John Wayne after a hard day in the saddle. As I was to learn to my cost, the spikes and blades in crampons will make short work of your ankles if you try to walk any other way.

Thus, with everyone fitted out likewise and practising their own version of 'Bonanza', the sound of various infantile references to 'pardners', 'posses', and questions as to whether anyone had seen a horse, echoed across the glacier as we made our way, crocodile fashion, over the ice.

On reaching a narrow crevasse, our Argentinean student pointed to me, presumably as the largest in the group, and motioned that I stand astride it. Like an idiot, I followed his instruction, while everyone watched and waited for it to collapse beneath me. With my legs straddling the crevasse, he then instructed that I jump up and down; perhaps in revenge for the Falklands beating, I thought... Nevertheless, I followed his instructions once more, noting that every time I landed, I could hear a deep booming noise far below me.

As he continued his talk about the Perito Moreno glacier, and, to my relief, inform everyone that ice crevasses only gave way in Hollywood, my eyes drifted back to watch the meltwater running off the glacier, and down into the one between my legs. There was no 'splashing' sound as it disappeared below...

Having demonstrated my gullibility, the Argentinian student then directed me to walk over a nearby ridge, and wait for the rest of the group.

Clambering over the ridge, I looked down to see an incongruously placed table, upon which a large block of ice, was industriously being chipped away at by another of the Argentinian students. By his side, a collection of glass tumblers stood ready to receive one of the chunks of ice from the block. Beneath the table, I could see several bottles of alcohol. When I arrived at the table, he grabbed one of the bottles, and poured what I understood to be Argentinian Brandy, over the ice in the tumbler, and handed it to me. This was my reward; I had passed the initiation ceremony into the world of glacier trekking...

Later, after draining my glass, I repeated the John Wayne walk, but this time without the aid of crampons...

I didn't pay much attention to our driver's scorecard on the journey back to our accommodation that evening; my mind was still in download mode from the experience of Perito Moreno.

By the time I finally laid my head on the pillow that night though, there was something else occupying my thoughts; the start of the main trek, the one I had spent more than six months preparing for, was now only hours away...

(DAY FOUR ~ TO THE TORRES)

Today was another early start and another long bus ride... this time to the Torres del Paine National Park; a drive of six hours across the biggest nothingness outside the Australian outback.

After the first hour of playing the now anticipated game of 'chicken' with oncoming vehicles, I began to think our driver was some kind of world champion at it. Thus, I finally began to relax and take in the scenery. With nothing more than flat scrubland to look at, it wasn't long before I dozed off.

Sometime later, I woke to the sudden screech of brakes. Quite why my eyes wanted to see the end of my life coming towards me, I honestly don't know. However, as my brain caught up with my eyes, I realised that we had not lost the game of 'chicken' to another vehicle, but to a real-life chicken... a bloody big chicken at that; a Rhea to be precise.

A family of several females and twenty-plus youngsters were sitting in the middle of the road. Stood directly in front of our bus, and lording over his harem and kids was one single male, and he did not look happy.

While wondering what would happen next, our driver calmly informed us that Rheas sit in the middle of the road, because the ground is warmer there. He went on to reveal that once upon a time they were hunted by the local Gauchos who enjoyed turning them into dinner. Nowadays they are a protected species, and that was why he could not risk injuring, or worse, inadvertently killing one of them by driving through, or around, the flock.

Fortunately, just as he finished his narrative, the Rheas promptly decamped and scuttled into the surrounding scrubland.

Relieved, we began to drive off. However, the male Rhea, presumably upset that we had spoiled the family picnic, decided to give chase. With head down, he emphasised his superiority by passing unharmed in front of the bus; we were doing almost forty miles an hour at the time...

Another three hours passed before we stopped again, this time for fuel. I took it as an opportunity to stretch my legs and perhaps take a photo or two.

The first thing I noticed as I climbed out of the bus was the desolation; the accompanying silence broken only by the 'ting' of the pump counting out the fuel. Next, to the fuel station, a sign proclaimed that we had arrived in Tapi Aike.

A quick three hundred and sixty degree scan established that Tapi Aike was not a very large town. Apart from the fuel station and its kiosk, there was a small concrete toilet block, and, on the opposite side of the road, a tiny bungalow. That was it. There was no other human habitation visible, in any direction whatsoever.

With nothing better to do, I attempted to translate the sign on the Bungalow's front wall. This was not difficult; for somewhat perversely in such a desolate place, there was an English translation below the Spanish one. The sign proclaimed, rather astonishingly, that the bungalow was the administrative centre for the region. (*A couple of weeks later I finally got to look at a map of the Tapi Aike 'region'... it turned out to be the size of your average European country...*)

Walking out to the nearby crossroads, I tried to take a photograph of one of the roads fading into the distance, but the nothingness that surrounded it merely ran out of the camera lens. We could have been in the middle of an American road movie. I just wished Thelma and Louise, particularly Thelma, had stopped by...

Twenty minutes later, we departed... our bus; still the only vehicle we'd seen for the last hour.

The Argentinean Border arrived as another bungalow, also situated in the middle of nowhere. Its only companion, a small abattoir, hid behind it. I noted that we could have driven into Chile anywhere for several miles either side of the bungalow, for apart from the token barrier across the road, there was nothing to give you any clue where the border actually was.

The Border post was under the jurisdiction of someone with enough brass to have been at least a Commander-in-Chief; this, naturally, made him lord and master of all he surveyed. Thus, the process of leaving Argentina became a protracted one; clearly, we hadn't brought the right brand of cigarettes or whisky with us...

What I remember most about the Argentinian Border post, was paying a visit to the toilet. A strange thing to mention perhaps, but it was not the presence of urinals rather than a hole in the floor that made it memorable, but the maturing beef carcasses hanging from the ceiling... I suspect the nearby abattoir may have had something to do with their presence; I just hoped none of it would end up on my plate...

I re-joined the bus just as our guide handed back our passports. Opening mine revealed I had gained a 'Salidas Argentina' next to the 'Entrada Argentina' I had acquired four days ago. There were now two stamps in my otherwise entirely empty passport... and they were both from a country several thousand miles from home.

While driving towards Chile, through an apparent 'No man's land', our guide informed us that we were in an area where hostilities routinely broke out. It was not surprising then, to learn that the Chilean and Argentinian border posts were eight miles apart... Entirely what they were fighting over was beyond me though, as there was even less 'nothing' here than there was at Tapi Aike. I could have launched an Apollo moon rocket in the space between their borders, and neither Chile nor Argentina would have known who did it. I doubt either of them would have been brave enough to want to find out anyway...

Some fifteen minutes later, the Chilean Border Post hove into view. This time we had to present our passports in person. Stamp number three was only a few steps away.

As we queued for our turn with the Chilean inquisition, I noticed a poster on the wall. It appeared to contain a stern warning. Despite the lack of an English translation below the Spanish one this time, the graphic images accompanying the poster, soon made it clear that it was advising about the risk of 'Foot and Mouth Disease'. It warned, in bold capital letters, that bringing Foot and Mouth into Chile would result in a sentence carried out by a firing squad... or a jail sentence... or something. At that point, I stopped translating; it was my turn for interrogation...

Despite my cold sweat, the Immigration officer had no comprehension that I lived in the very heart of somewhere that had, only recently, been gripped by the very disease he was trying to keep out of his country. The potential for me to wipe out the entire national beef-herd seemed real enough to me, but to the officer looking at my passport, I was just another tourist. With indifference, he stamped it and handed it back.

I couldn't look him in the eye, as with head bowed suspiciously, I muttered a fumbled Spanish "gracias" and walked as dignified as I could towards the door, expecting at any moment to become the subject of a diplomatic incident.

Once outside and back in the relative safety of our bus, I looked at my passport. There it was - 'Entrada Chile'. It was though, not below the Argentinian stamps, for there was still plenty of room on that first page, but on the back page; eighteen blank pages away - a statement about their diplomatic relations if ever there was.

There was a shop hugging the dust by the Border post, and it was here that I got my first taste of the Chilean version of a ham and cheese roll... 'Barros Jarpa', something that was to become familiar and strangely addictive in the days ahead. To my delight and amazement though, the tiny shop also sold my favourite English chocolate, and in all three flavours. Unable to decide which one to get, I discretely bought all three...

Boarding our bus once more, we headed deeper into Chile.

At some point, we stopped to admire a herd of Guanaco's, a smaller relative of the llama, but one oh so much more photogenic. They were grazing by the roadside, close enough to touch, and not in the least bit concerned about our presence. Whoever owned them though, missed a golden opportunity to make a fortune in peso's, for the doe-eyed baby calf among them became an instant film star.

Not long afterwards, we stopped by a small lake. As some of us wandered down to the shoreline to take a closer look, our guide leaned out of the bus to inform us that the lake was the most southerly place on the planet where we could find scorpions. I promptly re-joined the bus...

Only twenty minutes were to pass before we stopped yet again, this time to take in the view. Looking ahead, I could see the three iconic peaks of Torres Del Paine. Drawing an imaginary circuit around them, I realised the enormity of the challenge that lay before me. Subconsciously, I didn't know whether the feeling inside was one of excitement or abject fear of what I was about to undertake.

We arrived at the park information centre, paid our dues, and signed the visitor's book. It was at this point I learned that the 'Paine' in 'Torres del Paine' was not pronounced as though something that hurt, but as 'pie-nay', a local Indian word for the colour 'blue'. Thus, the Torres were 'blue', and not named in honour of somebody called 'Paine'. I'd been pronouncing it wrong for the last six months...

Just to confuse things, I also learned that the 'Torres' had first been described and named by a travelling Scottish feminist, one 'Lady Florence Dixie', as 'Cleopatra's Needles'... I kind of preferred her description, but somehow 'Torres del Cleopatra's Needles' didn't have quite the same ring about it...

As we regrouped, our tour leader introduced our Park guide. It would be his job to lead us around the Torres. His name had too many 'r's in it for someone like me who can't roll theirs. Thus, as I shook hands with him, the vague attempt I made at pronouncing it, sounded more like an insult than a greeting. Suitably embarrassed, I shuffled quickly to the back of the group.

With little ceremony, our park guide led us out of the visitor centre and towards the first climb of the trek. Since it was already mid-afternoon, I had assumed our first night's camp was just over the hill. It wasn't. Nor was it over the next two, or three, or four hills... It was five hours away...

During that first afternoon of walking in the park, I became acutely aware that, while the mountains above us were magnificent in their snow-capped majesty, the flora and fauna that surrounded us, served well as their courtiers.

First among those courtiers, were the Orchids. Not expecting to see such exotic wonders this far south, I wanted to know more. Our park guide revealed they were 'Magellanic' orchids; adding that there were thousands of them in the park.

As the trek progressed over the coming days, I came to realise that almost everything in the park, was the antipodean version of what could be found in England, things just appeared to have the word 'Magellanic' added to their title. From then on, anything I saw that looked familiar; I, rather presumptuously, applied the word 'Magellanic' to their name... Sparrows, foxgloves, sweet-peas, even rabbits, all became 'Magellanic' in the catalogue of my mind...

We had been walking little more than an hour when somebody pointed skywards. Looking up, I caught sight of my first Condors, the icon of the Andes. This was a bird I had hoped to see, yet despite the panpipes playing in my head, I had to take our tour guide's word for it, that they were indeed Condors because, at ten thousand feet or more above our heads, they could have been crows; Magellanic crows at that...

We finally reached the last summit of the day and paused to look down at the snow in the valley below. This, however, was no ordinary snow, for as we got closer, it melted into a sea of ox-eye daisies... countless millions of them, a white, yellow spotted ocean that stretched to the horizon.

Following a vague path among their nodding heads, I tried desperately to avoid crushing them beneath my feet, but it was not easy; as my footprints would be in snow, so they were in those fields of Ox-eye daisies...

Eventually, and after several minutes of apologising, their chamomile scent retaliating by tickling my nose; the daisies dwindled away to reveal Campo Sernos, our home for the night. I had successfully completed the first day of my 'do something scary' trek.

Following a simple but hearty meal, I settled down to gaze back at those daisies, and meditate on the journey so far; it had been a surreal one...

Dusk fell quickly that night, and with it, the last of the adrenalin faded away. Offering a simple "Goodnight" to those around me, I headed for my tent.

My last memory of that first day in Torres Del Paine was the sweet but overpowering scent of Ox-eye daisies... and the stale and overpowering odour of my tent-mate's socks. Fortunately for me, he kindly left them to stand on their own two feet outside the tent that night ... much to the chagrin of the daisies...

(DAY FIVE ~ VAQUEROES)

I woke to a breakfast of Barros jarpa, porridge, marmalade - which looked and tasted suspiciously like apricot jam, and coffee; a quite surprising feast this far from anywhere in particular.

On finishing breakfast, cue much orchestrated 'yipping' and 'hollering' from our porters as they arrived with our kitbags.

Back at the Park entrance, I discovered, much to my relief, that for most of the trek, we needed only to carry the essentials for the day ahead. The local Vaqueros, a sort of lesser version of a Gaucho *(but one that still carried more than enough machoism for women to swoon over, and men to question their parentage,)* were to convey the rest of our kit to the various campsites along the route.

While making my way to join those gathering for the day's trek, I passed one of these Vaqueros feigning sleep amongst the daisies. He was doing that Clint Eastwood thing of having a tipped hat over his eyes. A white horse stood quietly by his side. I could hear panting, and it wasn't coming from the horse...

As several divorces loomed among our group, our park guide marched off in the opposite direction. Since he looked like one of the Vaqueroes but displayed a few extra muscles, it was not long before the females in the group turned to follow him; husbands and boyfriends sighing heavily as they trudged behind.

A couple of hours passed before we reached a sharp bluff that signalled a ninety-degree turn to our left. Here, our park guide stopped abruptly to pull on a windcheater. In no uncertain terms, he advised us to do the same.

It was a glorious sunny day, there was hardly a cloud in the sky, and the ox-eye daisies were still nodding merrily in the fields below us as I duly pulled on mine and nonchalantly followed him around the bluff.

I should have known... As I turned the corner, the hurricane-force wind hiding behind it caught me entirely by surprise. I promptly lost my balance and fell backwards. Grasping frantically at the jagged fragments of the rock-face to stop myself from falling off the path and down the side of the mountain, I hauled myself upright.

Breathing hard, I inspected the lacerations on my hands and looked down at the valley floor below. If I had fallen, it would not have required help from a drug lord to provide the separated limbs for the Condors...

Lesson learned, I regained my composure, and proceeded to move with greater respect for the mountains... and for our park guide...

We descended against the wind for over an hour, before the treeline finally gave shelter from it and our park guide signalled the removal of our windcheaters.

With the rustle of state-of-the-art fabrics now quelled, there was a moment's silence to absorb our surroundings. We were standing next to a broad, fast-flowing, grey-coloured river. Seeing my puzzled look, our tour guide revealed that the river's colour originated from the meltwater of a nearby glacier. This was news to me, as the only glacial water I'd seen, was crystal clear and pouring down the throat of some bikinied goddess in a television commercial...

By now, seven hours had passed since we left Campo Sernos. My legs had begun to ache, and my pace had slowed somewhat, but I was still keeping up with everyone. So far, so good; twelve hours walking in two days was already a new personal best... Little did I know at this point just what I would come to achieve in the days ahead.

We continued to follow the river for over an hour before climbing a small hill. On reaching the top, our park guide paused to point towards our home for the night.

Refugio Dickson nestled in a small, flower-strewn meadow, almost surrounded by Lago *(Lake)* Dickson. From the distant shores on either side of the lake, majestic snow-capped mountains rose to pierce the sky. In the centre, a glacier swept down from the Andes to bathe at the back of the lake. The painting was complete.

After a brief supper, I retired to an early night.

Lying on my bunk, I looked up at the ceiling, there wasn't one. I could see only the rafters of the roof above me. All the dormitories had the same view apparently, and it was not long before the consequence of this became clear...

Snoring is an art form. It is also the perfect weapon to ensure nobody within earshot will get any sleep. Regrettably, earplugs had not featured on the essential equipment list for the trek. Thus, as the explosions ricocheted off the rafters, I closed my eyes and began to search for the sheep I would have to count if I was going to get any sleep that night. I found them cowering beneath the ox-eye daisies...

(DAY SIX ~ REFUGIO DICKSON)

Today woke with an optional trek to take a closer look at the glacier at the back of the lake. I decided against it. Secretly, I knew that somewhere just ahead; lay the climb that would be my greatest challenge of the trek, and probably the greatest challenge of my life.

When I made my decision known to our tour leader, he responded by telling me that I had probably made the right choice. As if to cushion the blow, he assured me that I would see something better further up the trail. Some people just seemed to know that I was undertaking something so very far beyond anything I'd ever done before. Acknowledging his words, I moved to sit down at one of the tables outside the Refugio and watched the others leave.

Lost for ideas on how to kill the six hours until supper, I decided to explore the lake's shoreline. I'm glad I did. The host of wildflowers we'd seen on our trek during the last two days grew in profusion all around the Refugio; many of their cousins I hadn't seen before were also present.

For the next two hours, those flowers were kind enough to permit me some 'up close and personal' photographs. I never did find out their names though; flowers are private about things like that...

Returning to the Refugio, I took to washing some socks. As many seasoned trekkers will tell you, this sock-washing thing is something of a trekker's fetish, thus, despite the Refugio being almost devoid of people, it took a while to find an empty sink in which to commit this ritual. With socks washed, I headed back to the lounge in search of somewhere to dry them.

In the middle of the floor, the Vaquero's had raised a large oil-drum on two enormous concrete blocks. A fire simmered inside the drum. Suspended some distance above it, hung a washing line. But by the time I arrived, however, it was already full of socks. Nothing else you understand, just socks...

Disappointed, and with dripping socks in hand, I wasn't quite sure what to do next. Seeing my predicament, one of the Vaqueros beckoned me to follow him outside.

Standing near one of the picnic benches, he extended a hand and asked for one of my socks. Perhaps he had a different sort of sock fetish, I thought. Thankfully no. Taking one from me, he draped it over a nearby bush and stood back to wait for my response. I was a little slow on the uptake until he proceeded to demonstrate that it was difficult to remove the sock from the bush. On closer inspection, I discovered my sock had been impaled on the bush's long spines.

Now, as all sock-fetish people know, especially those who invest in sock technology... a sock with holes in it is not a lot of use. Dismayed but trying hard not to show it, I gingerly removed my sock and examined it. Remarkably, the bush's spines were so thin, they had found their way through the fabric without leaving a puncture mark. Mother Nature is, indeed, ingenious at times...

In the near-constant wind, I realised too that it would not take long to dry my socks, courtesy of this little shrub. Thus, with the secret of the 'Sock Bush' now mine; I set about artistically hurling my remaining socks onto its thorns... as though creating an action painting. With no million-dollar offer forthcoming for my attempt at modern art, I grabbed a cup of coffee and sat down at one of the picnic tables.

Casting my eyes on the scenery that curled over me like some giant blanket, I spotted a small wooden shed set a short distance from the Refugio. Its stable door arrangement and overhanging eaves would not have looked out of place in the Swiss Alps. For a moment, I thought it was an outdoor toilet, such was its diminutive size.... but then if that was the case, why was there such a large glass window in the door... for voyeurs perhaps? Puzzled, I rose from the table and wandered over to take a discrete look. There was a note taped to the inside of the window...

'SHOP. PLEASE ASK AT REFUGIO' it read.

Taken aback by this bizarre revelation, I re-read the note. On the basis that there was only one 'Refugio' within two day's hike; the one over my right shoulder; I turned and walked purposefully towards it.

I didn't get far. The same vaquero who'd solved my sock-drying crisis spotted my interest, and was already walking towards me... with a key in his hand. I quickly gained the impression it might have been HIS shop. If indeed it was, he'd made an inspired decision. With the nearest competition two days away, this had to be a goldmine, to say nothing of having the best view from any shop window anywhere in the world...

After unlocking the door, he stepped inside and sat down behind the world's smallest counter. I peered in. There was not an inch of bare wood anywhere. Racks of postcards, maps, guidebooks, tourist trappings, key fobs, fridge-magnets, snacks, and every conceivable life-saving essential trekking gadget, festooned the walls.

My sock guru then embellished the display still further by bringing out three boxes of my favourite chocolate from under the counter... Evidently, news of my love of it had travelled... Perhaps as expected, I bought one of each flavour and embellished my purchase with a guidebook, map, and several postcards.

It didn't matter to me that being so far from civilisation it would be several days before I could send the postcards; the kudos of being able to tell people I'd bought them from the world's smallest, and probably most remote shop was enough to outweigh any sense of practicality on my part. Handing over a generous amount of US dollars, I waved away any suggestion of change. It had been a unique experience.

That afternoon, some unexpected guests arrived in the form of uniformed border guards. We were only three miles, as the Condor flies, from Argentina, and they had already run into my colleagues on the glacier trail. Thus, alerted to the possibility of finding another tourist to scare the crap out of, not to mention obtain some free coffee, they had reason enough to visit the Refugio.

As they walked in, the Vaquero's advised everyone present to fetch their passports, just in case they wanted to check us out. They did. Satisfied I was just another English tourist whose US dollars were contributing to the Chilean economy... I was free to go. Clearly, these guys had no idea about my proximity to the English outbreak of Foot and Mouth disease either... Ordeal over, I controlled a quiet exhalation of breath and returned to perusing my newly acquired guidebook.

It was now mid-afternoon. What few visitors remained at the Refugio, had retired to their bunks for an afternoon siesta. Thus, in an inspired moment, I reasoned that since there was nobody else awake, there would be plenty of hot water for a shower. Grabbing my towel, I discovered I was indeed the only one to use the hot water, except it was still cold... Defeated, I headed back to the picnic benches just in time to see my intrepid colleagues return.

Walking up to the Refugio, one of the group spotted I was writing postcards. Puzzled, he raised his finger to point at them, and ask...

"Where did you get those?"

In a somewhat blasé manner, I replied:

"The shop."

Pausing long enough to get one of those 'asshole' looks from him, I smiled and nodded towards the tiny shed.

"Oh, I thought that was an outside toilet..."

Twenty minutes later, another of the group walked up to me with an armful of wet socks. The makeshift washing line over the fire was evidently still full. Understanding their pain, I suggested they used the 'sock bush', and pointed to the small shrub now cowering apologetically beneath a dozen lurid pairs of them... And yes, I also had to assure my colleague that the spines on the bush would not ruin the integrity of their socks...

That evening, a long way from Italy, we dined on a superb Spaghetti Bolognaise. We also discovered that even this far from civilisation, the Refugio had a good stock of beer and liberal quantities of wine; much of which, we did our best to consume during a mammoth game of Quoits. The pitch-black of our surroundings, or maybe our intoxicated state, finally ended the game sometime after midnight. It was a narrow victory for somebody, but I have no recollection who.

I don't think anyone heard snoring that night...

(DAY SEVEN ~ LOS PERROS)

Morning broke in witness to the beginnings of a steady, penetrating drizzle. Our park guide had left the start as late as possible in the hope the weather would improve. It didn't; it was time then for the waterproofs first outing.

We began the trek to the next campsite at a slow plod. The only way now was up; 'down' would not occur for the next thirty-two hours...

Before long, the path entered the most primaeval of forests. Our surroundings absorbed all sound as we continued our steady progress towards that night's campsite. Beneath my feet, the underworld of moss lay so thick it enveloped my boots with every step. Above, the motionless canopy did all it could to suffocate our breath and remove the light from around us; only the rain continued to percolate through.
The forest though was highly photogenic; perfect for trolls and fairies too; but I caught sight only of exquisite orchids, wood anemones, and countless other floral mysteries. Sadly, only pointing fingers paid homage to their existence, for with heads bowed against the rain, and voices silent, we trudged onward, and forever upward.

We left the troll lair abruptly to find ourselves standing on the edge of a desert of rocks of every shape and size, many large enough I couldn't see over them. This 'desert', I learned, is correctly referred to as 'moraine', the rocky deposit left behind by glaciers as they recede from the landscape.

Following a short scramble and a little guesswork as we made our way through the moraine, we finally reached a small bridge; on the other side of which, lay our campsite for the night.

Before crossing the bridge, I stopped to look up at the distant skyline. There, lying in wait for me tomorrow morning, was the object of my summer-long slogs up and down 'Crucifixion Hill'; the climb over the John Gardner Pass. There was no point in fretting about it, I told myself; I'm here now; tomorrow would either be a crowning achievement or a humiliation that would haunt me for the rest of my life...

Los Perros was an inhospitable place; cradled on one side by a raging torrent, and an icy lake on the other; beyond which, another glacier cast its white mantle down the side of a mountain that appeared close enough to touch.

The campsite bathed in a bitterly cold wind too; one that swept down off the surrounding mountains to challenge every fibre of my thermals, clothing I had bought very much as an afterthought, but something I was now so very grateful to for the warmth they provided.

We ate dinner that night beneath a wooden-framed tent, shaped somewhat like a giant wigwam. The oil-drum fire, the campsite's only source of heat, smoked continuously. Asphyxiated, I tried to choke down the most mediocre meal I'd had in years. Finally giving up trying to breathe, I retired to my tent for an early night; my only comforts, a dry kit, warm thermals, and a sleeping bag fit for the miserable night ahead.

That night was probably the wildest night I've ever spent under canvas. Lying there, I could hear cries for help as the wind tore tents from guy-ropes and scattered belongings across the campsite. As much as I wanted to respond, I was too busy clutching the canvas of the tent I shared with the same guy I'd spent the first night with at Campo Sernos. He also had no desire to leave the comfort of his sleeping bag. Thus, we chose to hunker down and hope it would not be our turn next... I wasn't even bothered about his socks that night; for they served a useful purpose as ballast for the groundsheet...

Sometime long after midnight, the guy-ropes finally gave out, and our tent caved in. Apart from a few choice words, neither of us moved though; we were of an accord to make do and hope the canvas would survive until morning; we were still dry, and that was all that mattered.

From that moment on, there was little chance of sleep, for my hands were gripping the tent with all the strength I could muster from the comfort of my sleeping bag. As my ears listened to the eerie groans and creaks of the nearby glacier, the raging torrent that was to feature in tomorrow's walk, sounded as though it was ready to burst through the tent walls at any moment...

(DAY EIGHT ~ THE JOHN GARDNER PASS)

I woke to a still windy but drier morning. It was not yet six o'clock. Today was the day I had almost been dreading since the moment we arrived at the Park. Today, I was to follow in the footsteps of John Gardner, a British Mountaineer who, with the aid of two local guides, first defined the route over the pass that bears his name and which I was now to attempt.

Morning ablutions were no more than necessary, but while making my way back to the remains of our tent, I spotted our park guide surrounded by a small huddle of tent orphans. He was pointing to something on the ground. I followed his gaze to make out a trail of paw prints. At some point during last night's mayhem, a Puma had walked through the campsite. It had not made a sound, and no one had seen it...

After the usual breakfast of Barros jarpa, coffee, and, thank god, some warming porridge, we were packed and walking long before seven o'clock.

We left the campsite by crossing the bridge over our first obstacle of the day, the raging torrent that had joined the constant wind in keeping us awake last night.

The bridge comprised two spindly tree trunks lashed together. Across which, at regular intervals, were pieces of wood, cut from an old pallet. The handrail, if you should lose your balance, was nothing more than a thin steel cable stretched between two insecure looking wooden posts that marked either end of the bridge. Naturally, we were to cross one at a time.

Being somewhat of the 'XL' size, I was keen, if a little selfish, to be among the first to do so; not just because I feared the bridge might collapse, but because I also have an atrocious sense of balance. The last thing I wanted was to be rescued from a raging ice-cold torrent and airlifted out of my dream holiday. I needed to get this moment over with as quickly as possible.

With a single-minded focus, I strode quickly across. As I reached the other side, I turned to watch several pieces of wood fall from the bridge... but I had completed Level One of the day's challenges without incident.

Once everyone was across, we turned to face our second challenge; another ridge of the moraine we had negotiated yesterday, and which lay between us and the path up the valley.

Perhaps thirty minutes elapsed before I was able to extricate myself from the maze of boulders; but when I did, it was only to survey the third of the day's obstacles... a swamp.

I could see the remains of rotting tree stumps and thorn-laden shrubs dotted among it. I sighed. Pausing to look back, I could see that we hadn't gotten far; the campsite was still in full view, a little less than two hundred yards away.

Turning my attention back to the swamp, I began to feel like a Mario Brother in need of a sizeable power-up; an 'extra life' would also have been useful...

As I started to pick my way through the swamp, my feet almost immediately began to slip on the rocks hidden beneath the slime-covered surface. Those rocks promptly served to destroy all that was left of my sense of balance.

Lowering my six-foot frame sufficient that I was almost walking on all fours, I slowly made my way forward. Nevertheless, within minutes, I stumbled headfirst towards the rocks beneath my feet.

In a desperate attempt to avoid splitting my head open, I instinctively reached out to grab something and plunged my hand straight into a thorn bush. I didn't hold back with the swearing. Raising my blood-stricken hand as though to justify my outburst, I apologised to the mountain and those around me, picked myself up, and continued on my way through the swamp. Having now lost a life, I moved more cautiously than ever.

In a blinding moment of inspiration, I took out one of my trekking poles, and began to use it as a probe, *(Mario brothers eat your heart out)*, and, thirty minutes later, cleared the swamp without further bodily sacrifice.

With everyone accounted for, there was a quick tally of points. Judging by the artistic damp patches we all displayed; one complete with strands of moss in the hair; we concluded that no-one had completed Level Three unscathed. Surprisingly, we were all still in good spirits, but now some considerable time behind our schedule. Nevertheless, we had no choice but to keep going.

Level Four of the day's challenges soon emerged as a large patch of snow that was not only knee-deep but had melt-water running beneath it. As each leg plummeted through the soft surface of it, my feet would punch into the ice-cold water below. Twice in twenty-four hours, I realised the importance of buying the best trekking gear; my boots were as waterproof and resilient as the store told me they would be.

We managed no more than a few yards across this snowfield before it gave way to reveal a hidden gully filled with an angry mountain stream. The excuse for a bridge across it lay in artistic fragments among the rocks over which the water now swirled. Undaunted, we tied a rope to our park guide and offered him to the river god. Naturally, he made it across the torrent with rather too much ease.
Having tied the rope around a tree on the opposite bank, he turned to face us and motioned for the first volunteer to cross... I didn't hesitate. I had already worked out that I was likely to need the most amount of time to dry myself after missing my footing in the challenge to hop, step, jump, and catch our guide's outstretched hand on the other side. Yet, somehow, I completed this bonus round with dry feet.
Grateful for this minor triumph, I offered to help form part of the catching team, but he of the too many 'r's had never dropped a catch in his life...

Regrouping once more, we spent the next three hours climbing through the snow against nature's wrath. As the wind tore hats and sunglasses from heads and threw them into the mountains, so it delighted still further by whipping the surface water off the ice; twirling it into small tornadoes of frozen droplets, and hurling them into our faces with all the force it could muster. It was enough to make my eyes water. Stood knee-deep in snow, there was nothing I could do to lessen the impact of those ice bullets, and there was nowhere to hide from them.

As I finally approached an island of rock among the snow, I looked up to see an outstretched hand. Grateful for the help it offered, I reached out only to have a sudden gust of wind snatch me from its grasp. Caught completely unawares by the strength of that gust, I fell on to my backpack, and then bounced airborne to complete a full reverse somersault before landing face down in the snow.
For a moment, I could do no more than lay there, silent while instinctively checking for injury as I caught my winded breath. Satisfied that nothing hurt except my pride, I offered a string of abuse at the mountain and punched the snow with all the frustration my fists could accommodate. With face still buried in the snow, I raised my hand to signal that perhaps, not a little miraculously, I was unharmed by my spectacular fall.

When I eventually looked up, I discovered I had fallen almost thirty feet back down the mountain. This was almost heartbreaking. I had felt so very close to the limit of my endurance long before the fall. With a deep breath and the loudest of groans, I hauled myself upright and started the arduous climb through the snow once more. With several pairs of hands patting my shoulders with a 'well done', I made it back to the rock and sat down in silence.

Sipping from the contents of my 'unbreakable' water bottle - another of those 'most expensive' kit options that had now proven to be worth every penny; I surveyed the valley we had just climbed. It looked almost benign, stretched out long into the distance below, but I knew better.

Swivelling my head around, I took in the view above us. The brooding mountain peaks appeared almost to be frowning upon our impertinence at being so close to them. I could also see that the terrain had flattened out considerably. The summit could not be far away now.

As the wind continued to roar, I rose to my feet and with head bowed against it, joined the rest of the group, arms stretched wide in an aerobatic formation as we raced for the top of the pass.

In the moments that followed, the agonies I'd gone through all summer long, evaporated in the view that lay before me. From our vantage point, I stared into the valley below and rested my eyes upon the mighty Grey Glacier, the third-largest glacier in the world.

From its birthplace among the distant Andes Mountains, and their mantle of snow-white clouds to my right, I followed the glacier's path down the valley until it faded from view. Somewhere down there, and still a very long way away was our home for the night; but as the sky above glowed that strange, dark blue intensity of high altitude, the journey still to come, no longer mattered. I had conquered the John Gardner Pass.

Motionless, I stared empty-minded, humbled, perhaps almost tearful as the realisation entered my head that I had achieved far more than I ever thought possible. For that, my reward was one of those views they say you should 'see before you die'. If I were never to set foot outside England again; if I never did anything 'scary' again, I could now go to my dotage, armed with a lifelong memory, and the knowledge that, 'I did that'.

Tearing my eyes from the glacier, I turned to see our park guide fill his water-bottle from the melt-water oozing from the base of a nearby sliver of ice. He encouraged me to do the same. For a moment, I hesitated, for the water was the same colour as the river we'd passed on the way to Refugio Dickson. Looking back at him for reassurance, he simply raised his bottle and drank thirstily. Filling mine, I raised it in salute and took a cautious sip.

To this day, I cannot adequately describe how clean and pure that water tasted. All I know is that it came from the remains of a glacier he of the too many 'r's assured me was probably more than ten thousand years old... I needed no champagne to celebrate my accomplishment that day, I was already drinking the best liquid in the world...

Our tour leader, conscious that it might be nightfall by the time we arrived at the Refugio, urged us to take our pictures quickly, before heading down the slope to the shelter of the stunted woodland we could see below. It was already mid-afternoon. We had been walking for almost nine hours...

After a short lunch, I rose to the protests of my body. Already pushed far beyond anything it had known previously, I had no desire to tell it we still had five hours walking ahead of us...

I don't remember much of those last hours except that I did not stop moving. I'd reached the point where the legs pump as though on autopilot, and the mind focuses only on keeping the body moving. Ploughing through streams, I ignored detours to bridges; and took all the short cuts through the mud; my eyes focused only on the path a few yards in front of me.

My focus was such that I didn't notice our Park guide standing in the middle of a fork in the path until I crashed headlong into him. Mumbling an apology, he merely smiled in reply and pointed to my right. Following his outstretched arm, I turned to see, just a few hundred yards away, our home for the night.

I had made it.

Reaching the clearing in front of the Refugio, I sunk to my knees. Melodramatic it may have been, but I was at the point of physical exhaustion, I didn't even have the strength to release my backpack; nor could I rise to my feet.

The Refugio staff, who had been forewarned of our fourteen hours on the trail, then moved into a well-rehearsed routine of doling out drinks laced with electrolytes, and helping those who needed it. I'm not afraid to admit, I was one of them.

When our tour leader finally arrived, I thanked him for getting me 'home' that night. His reply was simple and to the point:

"Destroyed a personal best, huh?"

I could only nod in reply.

As my strength slowly returned that evening, aided by a generous intake of beer, no amount of aches and pains could wipe the smile from my face.

(DAY NINE ~ LONE WALK TO PAHOE)

The morning dawned to a peaceful respite. We were not setting off for our next overnight stop until the afternoon. After yesterday's exploits, today's five-hour walk would be no more challenging than a stroll around the local park.

In celebration of this, I played my part in converting the Refugio into a Chinese laundry. Naturally, there was still not enough washing line on which to hang my socks to dry, so I wandered outside in search of a sock bush. To my delight, I found one hiding behind a small rocky outcrop. It need not have been frightened; however, for I was still a pioneer in the world of horticultural sock drying. I, therefore, had exclusive use of its services. With some degree of artistic merit, I placed my two pairs of socks gently on the bush, comforted it with a "there, there, little bush," and returned to the Refugio.

With still three hours to go before we set off, and becoming aware that my legs were beginning to suffer from cramp, I decided to take a short walk up to the snout of the glacier in the hope of easing the stiffness out of them.

In the stillness of the morning, I found a spot only yards in front of the glacier and sat down to listen to its creaks and groans.
Within minutes, a striking translucent blue iceberg appeared from beneath the face of the glacier; I could almost reach out and touch it.
I had no idea why the berg was blue and not a dirty white like the rest of the glacier, but sometimes answers are not necessary. Being the only person in the audience, I took a picture of it, thanked Mother Nature for the show, and headed back to the Refugio to check on my socks. To my amusement, the sock bush was now cowering under at least twenty other pairs...

We set off that afternoon with little sense of urgency. We didn't get far though before our park guide stopped to announce a departure from the usual arrangements.

To date, he had always taken the lead while our tour leader followed up behind with the tail-enders. Between them, they had used short-wave radios to ensure everybody was accounted for; today though would be different.

With a substantial lake to our right and almost sheer-sided mountains to our left, the path to the next Refugio could not have been easier to follow. Thus, our guides were to allow us the relative luxury of completing the remainder of the day's walk at our own pace. With the muscles in my legs still somewhat stiff, though, I was soon lagging behind.

As the path finally levelled out, however, my stride began to lengthen. I soon began to pass some of my colleagues. Eventually, I caught up with the leaders; something I'd never done since we had arrived in the park. When they stopped for a short break, I felt confident enough to strike out on my own. I was soon well into my stride, and before long, far enough ahead of the group, I could no longer hear them behind me.

I continued my sojourn for almost three hours before a hand-carved sign informed me the Refugio was just a mile away. With renewed enthusiasm, I picked up the pace still; further, half-expecting to hear the confident stride of those invariably first 'home' each day pounding up behind me; their supreme fitness, a constant reminder that I was still a novice in the art of long-distance trekking.

They never did...

I hadn't set out to prove anything that day, nor had I intended to be competitive; sometimes your body just surprises you. After yesterday's heroics, mine had done that for the second day in a row; its reward, a hot shower, the first it had enjoyed in four days...

Re-humanised, I headed out into the evening sun to claim a picnic bench, only too pleased to have the honour of buying the drinks that night...

(DAY TEN ~ VALLE FRANCES)

Another long day beckoned... There was an option to miss out a large part of it by not completing the point of today's walk, the Valle Frances. Buoyed by yesterday's success, though, I was not on the missing out list.

It was a beautiful morning too; the potential for adding to the copious number of photographs I'd already taken on the trek, would prove undoubted.

We started out with a leisurely stroll along the shores of 'Lago Skottsberg'. As the sun shone brightly in its clear blue sky, the air played a soft breeze on my face. I could not have been more content.

Soon, we reached the base of the Valle Frances at a place known as the 'Italian Camp'. Here, a group of Italians carried out an assault on some of the mountains that now closed in around us. Two of them died in the attempt to climb them; a sobering message I thought as we turned to head up the valley.

We had not been walking more than a few minutes when I heard what sounded like a crack of thunder. Puzzled, I looked to the cloudless sky for signs of a thunderstorm, and then at the surrounding mountains. There, on the opposite side of the valley, was the answer... an avalanche had begun its deadly descent... Within seconds, there was snow in the air.

Alerting our park guide, already some way ahead of me, he looked across the valley and with no sense of panic in his footsteps, calmly hastened our pace up a steep slope away from the valley floor. I needed no encouragement.

When we reached the top of the ridge, he stopped to look back. A light dusting of snow covered the track we had left only minutes before; while the bulk of the avalanche had come to an abrupt stop on the other side of the valley. He, of the too many 'r's in his name, had judged the situation perfectly. His knowledge of the Torres was consummate. I've never met anyone of his calibre since...

I had also learned a valuable lesson... if you hear the sound of thunder while walking in avalanche territory; it's probably already too late... unless your guide has too many 'r's in his name...

We continued to climb still further up the valley; at times, hauling ourselves up near-vertical rock faces, assisted only by ropes. The ropes had regularly spaced knots in them; an ingenious idea which enabled our hands to grip them without fear of slipping, and for people like me who never could climb them at school, to haul himself up by, without fear of having to ask for help...

Another hour passed before we reached the so-called 'British camp'. From here, British climbers, *(ahem)*, finally conquered the same peaks on which the Italians had so tragically died.

Thirty minutes above the British camp, the trail ended abruptly at a viewpoint. The sight that confronted us was rivalled only by the summit of the John Gardner Pass two days ago.

We were sitting in the middle of an amphitheatre of mountains that appeared touchable but aloof, as they pierced the sky. In the silence, even the Condors had left them centre stage. I turned to glance back down the valley and watched it melt into the distant Patagonian plain.

Little more than twenty minutes after we arrived, however, Valle Frances declared the show over, by hurling dark clouds over the shoulder of Cerro Aleta de Tiburon, *(the shark's fin)*, a giant monolith that stood sentinel-like to our left. The clouds were laden with snow, enough of a warning for our guide to curtail lunch and urge us to make a rapid descent.
We had not raced down the valley more than a few yards, before the sky, and everything in front of us turned white. We had overstayed our welcome.
For a few terrifying moments, I wondered if we were to experience a blizzard. Yet, as quick as the snow had started to fall, so it stopped, and the sun blazed from its azure sky once more; perhaps the mountains were only teasing...

We spent the last hour of the day's adventure walking along a beach of pure white quartzite rocks that glowed eerily in the evening's rain-laden skies.
On the far side of the lake, the wind was playing havoc with the water, causing several small waterspouts to develop one after another. I stopped to watch as one of the waterspouts headed towards us, only to dissipate long before reaching the shore. Mother Nature had made a profound statement of power today. Hankering for an encore, I was in no hurry to run for the shelter of the Refugio as the rain rolled steadily across the lake.

Tomorrow's walk would signal the completion of the grand circuit around the Torres Del Paine. A deepening sense of this reality hung over the subdued voices sat around the bar that night.

(DAY ELEVEN ~ FULL CIRCLE)

After a leisurely breakfast of Barros jarpa, porridge, toast and marmalade, which still looked and tasted suspiciously like apricot jam... or maybe it was plum; we were out the door and walking by ten o'clock.

I remember little of the day's walk, except the race to the finishing line. What I recall far more vividly, was our packed lunch...

Every morning the Refugio we departed from would make a packed lunch for us; this was always ham and cheese (*'Barros jarpa'*) rolls, an assortment of chocolate bars, half a litre of water, and a pack of *(usually out of date)* mixed fruit and nuts. Today, our packed lunch consisted of one bread roll filled with tinned tuna *(no butter)*... and one with nothing but green beans in it... canned green beans at that, the type that stain your fingers. When we sat down for lunch, I ate one of my rolls and encouraged the wildlife to enjoy the other. There were no takers.

Four hours after we had set out, we arrived at our last Refugio. It was still early enough to have all afternoon to soak up the hot water... but no one could find it...

That evening was our last meal in Torres Del Paine. I don't remember what we ate, but I do remember our group leader tempering the celebrations at a strategic eleven o'clock when he drew our attention to the fact that there was one more day's "optional" trekking to complete. This was the climb up the valley of the Rio Ascencio to take a closer look at the peaks which give Torres Del Paine its name. It would only take five hours to complete, he said, but it was still a significant climb at that.

Over the last eight days, we had circumnavigated those peaks; but tomorrow we would have the opportunity to get close enough to almost touch them. I had already touched them, metaphorically speaking at least... Six months previously, I had installed an image of them as the background picture on my laptop...

(DAY TWELVE ~ DEFEAT AND VICTORY)

Breakfast was at seven o'clock that morning; it arrived with a sure sign we were back in civilisation...

Every Refugio, no matter how remote, had met our requests for breakfast at whatever time we wanted it, yet this morning it was to be a Do-it-yourself affair because the Refugio wouldn't serve breakfast before eight o'clock. Thus, on discovering the kitchen door unlocked, we set about ransacking the place for something to eat, and something to make packed lunches with.

To our delight, somebody found a large slab of beefsteak. This we set about converting into sandwiches while others brewed up enough coffee to cause a surge in the gross domestic output of Brazil.

While all this was going on, I opened a large pantry door to reveal a Valhalla of tuck-shop goodies, that prompted sixteen starving Neanderthals to do their best to empty.

With a modest sense of guilt, we left a thoughtful 'Sorry but thanks' note in Spanish, added a few pesos, barely enough to cover the cost of the beef, let alone everything else, and hurriedly left the Refugio.

We never did return to find out what happened at eight o'clock when the kitchen opened; but our tour leader, oblivious to the attack of the Neanderthals, later commented that he needed to thank the Refugio manager for the steak sandwiches...

It was hard going that morning; my legs had finally started to refuse uphill slogs. The longer we climbed, the more I struggled... Several had opted out of today, but I hadn't planned to be one of them. As we trudged ever upwards though, I began to lag ever further behind. For the first time on the trek, our tour leader joined me to offer some encouraging words; I feared there was more to it than that...

In his company, I finally made it to the small bluff we were aiming for and stopped to look down into a hidden valley. The scene was one of dense beech forest, raging torrent, and yet another Refugio with a view rivalled only by that of the one at Lago Dickson.

In my mind, I pictured the trail going past the Refugio and up through the trees towards the pinnacles of the Torres Del Paine standing at the head of the valley. Those peaks stood resolute, beckoning all who could make that last mile through the forest, and up the almost sheer ascent that stood as one last defiant challenge to reach the lookout point below them.

When we reached the Refugio, however, our tour leader spoke the words I had feared for most of the previous hour... that I was probably too weak to tackle the final climb. The reality was simple; he could not afford to take the risk that I might slip and fall in the attempt to reach the lookout point. I let his words sink in slowly. There was no point debating the issue with him; he had my absolute respect.

Despite comforting words from others in our group, I sat heartbroken as I watched those I had spent the last twelve days with, vanish into the forest.

I don't mind admitting that for some time afterwards, I had an overwhelming desire to ignore our tour leader and make my own way along the path to the Torres. Instead, I reluctantly chose to listen to the small voice inside that bade me otherwise, and consoled myself with a mug of coffee, and a wander along the riverbank in search of a small pebble to take home as a memento.

With token pebble in hand, I returned to the Refugio, just in time to see a mule-train and its accompanying Vaqueros, do the John Wayne thing of charging through the river as they made their way up to the Refugio.

In what was a highly fortuitous moment, I captured the moment on film. Of the thousands of photographs I have taken over the years, that image remains my all-time favourite. Ironically, had I ignored our tour leader's advice and made my way that last mile to the Torres, I would never have witnessed the event. Fate can play strange games at times...

A little more than two hours later, the conquering heroes returned. Perhaps to lift my spirits, they informed me that the views we had enjoyed of the Torres during the trek had been far better. By the time they arrived at the lookout, clouds had shrouded the peaks; peaks I could, in fact, see more clearly from my vantage point back at the Refugio. Perhaps that voice within had been doubly right...

Whether from exuberance or mere fitness, the return journey down the grassy mountainside took on the appearance of a fell runner's race as we spontaneously began to bound from one grassy foothold to another. By the time I reached the bottom, my earlier disappointment had dissipated completely.

In a perhaps prudent move, we didn't return to the Refugio of the Steak sandwiches though but headed towards the nearby hotel.

Despite depositing the dust of our trek all over their lovely clean floor, and traipsing across a carpet with boots caked in the mud of more than a hundred gruelling miles of Andes Mountains, there was nothing but a welcome smile from the hotel staff; perhaps the two dozen cans of beer we bought, helped...

With an hour's wait before our minibus was due to arrive, we took to sprawling out across the hotel lawn. I contemplated the scene... Smelly socks, mud, kit bags, dust, backpacks, abandoned shoes, bandaged limbs, and even more dust; we could not have looked more seasoned if we had tried.

Looking across the lawn to lock eyes with my tent-mate, now minus his socks. I could feel a broad grin spread across my face. As he raised his beer in salute, so I did likewise. I may not have climbed that last mile, but I had made it around every other inch of the circuit. It had been far harder than I ever imagined it would be, but I'd done it. There was now a confident voice growing inside me that no longer considered drug lords as a reason to avoid a country... I had been very firmly bitten by the adventure bug.

It was a silent coach that took us the three hours to the Chilean town of Puerto Natales and our hostel for the night. We arrived to find every room had all the hot water we could possibly want... Thus, it would be impolite to describe the cries of relief that rung out through the walls as our group washed two weeks of grime down the plughole; suffice to say we headed out for our meal at a local restaurant that night, refreshed, and looking in the rudest of health.

We had just begun to eat when the restaurant's door opened to reveal a group of strolling minstrels. They walked in and proceeded to wander among the tables, serenading all who could tolerate them.

For the next ten minutes, they fumbled more chords than I care to remember; and their singing was even worse. They were so bad, in fact, they didn't receive a single peso. Perhaps seasoned in their tactics, they continued to play and sing badly until someone paid them to leave. Moments later, another group of strolling minstrels wandered in, and proceeded to play and sing just as poorly as the first group...

Regardless, it was a good night of celebration, tinged only with the sadness of our first farewell, that of our park guide; he of the too many 'r's in his name. His job done it was time for him to go home. He had gotten me safely through the most extraordinary adventure of my life, for which, he richly deserved every dollar I gave him.

It had been a long day, but a triumphant one at that. By eleven-thirty, I was comatose, deep in the warmth only winter quality duvets, duck feather pillows, large quantities of alcohol... and copious amounts of hot water can induce.

(DAY THIRTEEN ~ THE PACIFIC OCEAN)

I woke early. It was still some time before breakfast. Thus, with nothing better to do, I headed down to the seafront, a short distance from our hostel. When I arrived, it took a moment to realise I was looking at the Pacific Ocean. I wondered if this, the first time I'd seen it, would also be the last.

Standing in silent wonder, the emotions welled up inside once more. I found it almost impossible to comprehend what I was looking at. From my home back in England, the Pacific Ocean was halfway around the world, but there it was... I dipped my hand into its cold waters. Yes, it felt like the seawater back home and smelled like the seawater I knew, but it was different, it was the Pacific Ocean...

Scanning the horizon, I didn't find it any easier to comprehend the fact that I was also just seventeen hundred miles from the South Pole.

Looking over my right shoulder, I witnessed the last of the Andean mountains tearing their moody clouds and dressing the scene with a couple of rainbows. In this place, one rainbow would not have been enough...

After breakfast, I headed into town to shop for some Chilean souvenirs and find the town's post office, where I finally got to despatch the postcards I'd bought several days ago at Refugio Dickson. Amazingly, and despite being so very far from England, they arrived there just forty-eight hours later... the same day I did...

All too soon, we boarded our bus and headed back to the Chilean border. The time had come for our own farewells.

I spent my last Chilean pesos on more Barros jarpa in the little shop by the border post and pondered the 'Salidas Chile' in my passport.

We drove across no man's land and on through Argentinean customs like long lost friends. We were almost back in el Calafate when our driver stopped at a viewpoint to allow us one last look at Patagonia.

As we stood on the ridge looking across the barren wasteland, and towards the distant mountains, a male Condor chose that moment to glide past at eye level, no more than a thirty feet in front of us; his effortless display defining of why Condors are the icon of the Andes. I could not have wished for a more fitting sign-off to what had been a unique experience...

From el Calafate airport we took a flight back to Buenos Aires and checked back into the Waldorf hotel for one last night. The last two weeks in Patagonia now seemed like a dream.

(DAY FOURTEEN ~ ADIOS AMIGOS)

The morning arrived to discover we had ten hours to kill before our flight home that night. Not having any particular plans, I shared a taxi down to the Puerto Mujer Bridge, a not insignificant icon in the heart of the city's old harbour.

On giving our destination to the taxi driver, though, he merely gave us a blank look. I smiled. Having travelled all this way, I would have to be the one who found the only taxi-driver in town who didn't know his way around where he lived. Despite having visited the bridge only once, I duly obliged with directions. Ironically, by the time we arrived there, I realised it would have been quicker to walk...

For the next three hours, I did little but soak up the street café scene along the quayside and conduct some window shopping. In truth, there was simply nothing I needed or wanted to see. My trekking gear packed, I was ready to go home.

To my delight, we returned to the 'El Establo' restaurant that lunchtime to enjoy a farewell dinner. When we trouped in, the waiters led us upstairs to what I can only describe as a Banqueting table and proceeded to wait on us with a masterclass in attention to detail.

Having witnessed the cooking of steaks during my first visit, my menu choice could not have been easier... 'Bifes de Lomo', Sirloin of Beef. What arrived on my plate that day has never been equalled since for flavour, or ability to dissolve in the mouth. I could have picked it up and sucked it like an Ice-pop...

If my steak needed any entertainment, then the accompanying selection of condiments provided for it. Dipping teaspoons revealed a sweet chilli sauce, a cinnamon flavoured cream concoction, and a strange caramel sauce called 'Dulce con leche'. The latter, I understood, was something Argentineans are addicted to almost as much as they are to drinking Maté. Whether that 'Dulce con leche' was meant to be on my steak or not, I don't know, but I did understand the addiction...

After wading through nearly a pound of steak, there wasn't much room for anything else... Nevertheless, I ordered what I thought would be a 'light' dessert... a glass of lemon sorbet. It was not until I had consumed most of it that I realised it had been laced with Limoncello liqueur... about four or five measures of it...

Thus, as the meal concluded with thanks to our excellent tour leader, I rose unsteadily to reveal through the haze of Limoncello, that Torres del Paine represented the first time I'd ever left England.

If I'd thought crossing the John Gardner Pass had been the pinnacle of personal achievement, I was wrong. A few comments and one or two gasps of amazement, assured me that it was the act of taking a first-ever flight lasting eleven hours, travelling not to France as many would; but halfway around the globe, only to then undertake one of the world's toughest treks, with no previous experience at that level whatsoever. I could do no more than utter an "oh" before sitting down to allow their compliments to sink in...

As we made our way to leave the restaurant, I gave generously to the waiter's tip. In return, he pressed a calling-card for the restaurant into my hand; another moment of wondering if I would ever return, and another memento for the scrapbook.

Having staggered back to the hotel and collected my backpack, the journey to the airport was all too short. There, I said farewell to our Tour Leader. Shaking hands, he grinned. I grinned back. I think we both knew how extraordinary my journey had been.

The blues finally set in as I boarded the flight home. With the adrenalin of the last sixteen days thoroughly exhausted, I dozed off within minutes of being airborne; my mind filled with visions of Condors, majestic mountains and glaciers; and my ears with the sound of panpipes.

I woke just as we landed at Madrid airport. We had only an hour layover there before boarding our 'puddle-jumper' back to London, and home. I had set foot in Spain twice now, but could still only credit the country with a total of seventy minutes exploration, and all of it in Madrid's airport.

Rather than sit and stare out of the featureless window while waiting for our flight, I wandered off in search of a bottle of Chile's classic 'Pisco' spirit; *(no that's not a spelling mistake)*. Sadly, this far from Chile, where it serves as something of a national drink, my requests to the countless bars and shops selling alcohol at the airport were met only with deep suspicion. The desire to reminisce with a glassful was thus, lost...

The flight home from Madrid was uneventful. The crew, a sullen bunch, could hardly be bothered to throw the plastic snacks into my lap, let alone offer a cup of tea.
Bored, I began to re-live the last two weeks. So remote, so surreal had they been, that, for all I knew, England could have become a republic in my absence... Newspapers? Television? The interminable Net? Torres del Paine had taught me life was better without them.

It was cold, wet, and miserable when we landed back in England, but I didn't care. I'd travelled more than eighteen thousand miles and completed a life-changing adventure.

Strolling through customs, I made my way back to the world of fast food, traffic pollution, and social media. Something inside me just wanted to turn around and go back to Patagonia...

(EPILOGUE)

A few days later, I returned to my Doctor's office, not out of illness, but because I knew I had to see him; I had to thank him for the wake-up call.

When I walked into his surgery, he rocked back in his chair, and exclaimed:

"Good God!"

I didn't exactly look 'Olympian', but I was, no doubt, in the best of health, and not a little fitter than when he had last seen me.

I smiled and replied that Torres Del Paine had shown me that adventure was out there. The trouble was, now I'd found it, I wanted more of it.

Opening a drawer in his desk, he fished out a pamphlet detailing the vaccinations required for travel to half the world's nations and handed it to me.

Looking at the number of needles required to visit some of the countries in it, I wasn't so sure about this thing called 'adventure'... Nevertheless, when I arrived home, I fired up the laptop and started browsing...

CLIPBOARD MAN

Reeling from the euphoria of my first overseas trek, it was not long before I had booked my second, well, attempted to anyway, for the travel company cancelled both my first and second choices. Perhaps feeling a little guilty of upsetting my plans, they offered a place on a 'new' trek, one they'd never done before... and it came with a generous fifty per cent discount if I accepted.

The trek was to take place in the Languedoc region of southern France. On the face of it, and despite being in a country, I'd already defined as severely lacking in the scary stakes, this had some attraction. The area produced some of my favourite French wines and was heavily associated with the mysterious Cathars people. Among other things, these guys believed Jesus and Mary arrived on their shores with daughter Sarah, and something called the 'Holy Grail'. Unfortunately, the Roman Catholic Church didn't like the idea that someone might have a different version of the Bible from the one they preached, and so, decided the act of genocide was the best way of dealing with the Cathars. Thus, quite where Jesus and Mary might have lived, or where they were buried, seems to have been lost, along with the 'Holy Grail'... If only the Cathars had known about the potential for book and film rights... Nevertheless, with the trek offering a good dose of history and mystery, not to mention the possibility of sampling some good wine, I was hooked... OK, so the fifty per cent discount helped...

France would be a bit of a comedown from Patagonia, I thought, but at least it would serve as a 'warming up' exercise for something more challenging. If I'd known that I was going to be boiled alive rather than warmed up, I would have elected to sit on some package tour holiday beach and used the sun to pick up a tan, rather than the collection of blisters and griddle marks I ended up with...

(DAY ONE ~ DEPARTURES AND ARRIVALS)

Studying the trek's 'Detailed information pack', I noted the 'Pack for hot climate ... but be aware that it can be changeable, so bring waterproofs and warm clothing' instruction. It also suggested I 'bring a change of clothing for evening wear'...

Thus, I arrived at London's Gatwick Airport with all the swagger of a seasoned traveller. Swagger though, due entirely to the excessive amount of kit I was toting. Evidently, my swagger also profiled me as an overloaded drug smuggler, for airport security searched my kit, twice...

Once freed from the Security team's clutches, I spent the next three hours wandering aimlessly amongst the detritus that is an airport departure lounge.

I could have bought a draw ticket to win a Bentley Continental... on my wages clearly a wonderfully stupid idea; or I could have had my bum massaged by a vibrating 'stress relief' massage chair. Five Pounds for five minutes the sign declared; but as I watched one hapless soul arise from it, he appeared to be only de-stressed of Five Pounds more than he was five minutes earlier. I gave that a miss too.

Amongst the waiting flotsam, I noted the inevitable package holiday crowd; in this case, a group of young women bound for Zante, a far too popular holiday island off the coast of Greece. I could tell they were bound for Zante because that's what all their T-shirts said. I could also understand what they were going there for too, as most of the T-shirts declared various permutations of 'Little Miss Naughty'. Judging by what was highly visible beneath those too tight T-Shirts, their constant swearing, and less than dulcet tones, I considered it a wise man who ensured they returned as 'Little Miss Untouched'...

A further two hours passed before the electronic departure board proudly announced that my flight was boarding at Gate 10496... Well, at least that's what I think it said, for some of the critical numbers kept phasing in and out. What did not phase out though was that departure was in forty minutes... an intriguing fact because the board offering directions to Gate 10496 calculated that I should allow at least an hour to get there. Cue panic as two hundred people lurched simultaneously from the waiting area and stampede in its direction...

I found the gate and without further ado, boarded the flight and sat down; first checking there was no puddle beneath the aircraft. Thankfully there was also no sign of the Zante crowd either. If there had been, either they or I, were on the wrong plane...

A short while after take-off, I looked out of the window to see Paris for the first time in my life; the view from thirty thousand feet perhaps better than the one from the ground.

We landed a mere thirty minutes later in Montpelier; a town that lay deep in that non-descript part of southern France that is neither in Provence, Saint Tropez or anywhere particularly 'Nice'... *(Yes, I thought that was a clever play on words too.)*

After wandering through the can't-be-bothered immigration hall, I strolled into the Arrivals lounge. It was entirely empty save for a twenty-something individual half displaying his purpose in life with an occasional flash of a clipboard; the trekking company's name writ large upon the underside of it. I wasn't sure if he felt the clipboard was an embarrassment or whether on seeing me walk towards him, hoped I wasn't on his trek... If it were the latter, he was too late, I'd read the sign. I walked straight up to him and introduced myself.

'Clipboard Man' as I shall now christen him, shook my hand and chaperoned me towards a small group of women he had corralled near the lost property office.

I dropped my backpack to the floor and offered them a breezy:

"Hi."

Their response suggested I'd contracted leprosy during the flight. Things had got off to a great start...

Once satisfied everyone on his list had checked in, Clipboard Man insisted on conducting another roll-call. I was beginning to think Zante might have been more fun.

Satisfied for the second time in twenty minutes that everyone was present, he led us out into the evening sun to join a small minibus adorned with an unusually large trailer... the driver had evidently read the 'pack for hot climate' instructions too.

Clipboard Man took yet another headcount on the bus and satisfied he hadn't lost anyone during the hundred-yard walk from the terminal, nodded to the driver, and we set off down the French AutoRoute to Carcassonne; our 'unusually large' trailer swinging gaily behind us.

We arrived in Carcassonne and drove through the streets towards the citadel. I thought for a moment our hotel was actually inside it but soon came to my senses; no trekking grade hotel could ever hope to prosper by being inside the walls of a tourist trap.

With a sharp turn right, just before the citadel gates, our minibus finally abandoned us at a hotel more typical of the standard I had become accustomed to.

Opening the door to my room, I conducted the usual survey, and, after noting the lethal-looking shower and dubious marks on the bathroom walls, hurled my backpack onto one of the bunks and headed back to the lounge. I was hungry.

Thankfully, Clipboard Man, in one of his more coordinated moments, had planned for this, and so, instructed us to follow him out of the hotel and towards the town square.

We arrived at the town square to find hundreds of people enjoying a local festival. I noted the stage show, and the numerous vendors plying everyone with delicious smelling food and copious amounts of wine.

Clearly taken unawares by all this, Clipboard Man checked his notes for details of the festival. For a minute, he appeared to know what it was all about and launched into the melee with all the enthusiasm of someone who was an old hand at these things...

After some exciting detours behind the food tents and past string-tied rabid dogs, we emerged back where we started. Our guide's failings could not have been more embarrassing. I sighed, and wondered how Clipboard Man would fare, leading a trek around the Torres del Paine circuit... At least the festivalgoers were too busy watching the stage show to concern themselves with a bunch of blundering Brits.

It was at this point I realised Clipboard Man was actually looking for his approved restaurant. He finally discovered it on the opposite side of the street, thirty feet from our hotel...

The restaurant was almost empty when we walked in, a sure sign the food at the festival across the road was better. Nevertheless, in keeping with my new approach of doing something scary, I chose Ostrich from the menu. I'd never eaten Ostrich before. I guess by some peculiar logic, I'd figured it had probably started life in the restaurant's freezer and was therefore unlikely to have attracted the sort of bugs that tend to serve up the 'Holiday tummy' so popular of most 'hot climate' destinations.

When I ate the first tentative mouthful, ostrich reminded me of braised beef... perhaps that's what it was; you can never tell with French food.

When we returned to the hotel, I discovered I had a roommate, who, despite my reservations, decided we would sleep with the window open that night; unfortunately, most of Carcassonne decided we wouldn't sleep at all. Listening to the sound of rural French nightlife gave me a deep and overwhelming understanding of why we Brits hate the French so much...

ADVENTURES OF A MIDDLE-AGED FART

(DAY TWO ~ A GOOD BURNING)

I woke to the violent clamour of church bells and cursed them loudly. It was only seven o'clock. I had forgotten we were in a staunchly Roman Catholic area. They, more than anyone, appear to relish in the opportunity to clang away at almost any time of the day, but much to my annoyance, especially in the early morning.

As the week passed, I noticed that each village we stayed in, no matter how small, seemed to have its own distinguishing peal. The complexity of the carillons never failed to astound me either. This led me to wonder if the entire population of these villages crammed into their bell-tower each morning, or whether the Vatican had supplied them all with a ghetto blaster and hot-wired it to a massive switch back in Rome. I had a mental image of a deranged cardinal gleefully pacing up and down as he waited for his seven o'clock call of duty; a duty aimed exclusively at frightening the crap out of every non-Roman Catholic among us as he threw the switch and thousands of churches blasted out their own version of the Hallelujah chorus...

Clipboard man was already well through his breakfast when my roommate and I walked into the dining area. Not wishing to disturb him at his table for one... we looked around the room and, spying an empty table for four, sat down to wait for service.

Despite several attempts to attract the attention of the waiter, he ignored us. Ten minutes passed; then, two women arrived and sat down at the table next to us. We smiled inanely in their direction. Much to our surprise, they invited us to join them. It was a bit early for hanky-panky, but we were game...

Once lured to their table, we discovered they really did want us for our bodies... With the table's four seats now occupied, the waiter walked straight over to take our order...

The women were gracious enough to let us down gently with the knowledge that the hotel dining room only served full tables. Now understanding why we were ignored for so long, I looked across the room to see a lone individual sat at a table for four, but couldn't be bothered to let him in on the secret... He looked French anyway.

Our two female companions were on a cycling holiday they told us... these good-looking, sporty types usually are. Just as the conversation started to get interesting, however, two disgustingly handsome guys walked into the room. When the women rose to drape themselves over them, my fellow room-mate and I looked at each other. Feeling suddenly ignored, we shrugged our shoulders, made our excuses, and headed back to our room to make ready for the day's adventure.

By ten o'clock that morning, we were on our way to visit the walled citadel of Carcassonne. Clipboard Man, or more correctly, his itinerary, had given us a few hours to enjoy looking like all the other tourists...

Roaming its streets, I quickly discovered that everything was three times more expensive inside the Citadel than it was outside it. Thus, I took only photographs; splashed out on just a single bottle of water, and spent the remaining time sitting in a shady courtyard, people watching.

Realising that I was English, some of the French people around me smiled knowingly. The joke, which Clipboard Man had at least had the decency to warn us about, was that when Hollywood couldn't find a suitable castle in Nottingham for Kevin Costner's version of Robin Hood... they came to Carcassonne... Well, they would, wouldn't they? After all, there are only about seven hundred other castles to choose from in England, and that's before Hollywood might have to consider rebuilding one of the three thousand or so ruined ones we also have...

By two o'clock, we were back on board our minibus and heading off for the day's adventure. We were not to return to Carcassonne. I, for one, was not particularly upset about that...

A short while later, while driving through the non-descript town of Lavelanet, we passed a chemist with a digital temperature gauge glued to its front wall. It read thirty-four Centigrade *(that's ninety-four Fahrenheit for those who need this sort of thing)*. I thought it was hot, I could tell by the burning smell emanating from the hairs on my arm as the sun-baked them to a crisp.

Leaving Lavelanet, we started to climb a typical continental mountain road. This one measured about ten hairpins to the mile and came with the bonus of several blind corners. It also offered an impressive array of oncoming lunatics doing seventy miles per hour down the middle of it, causing our driver to provide a useful lesson in French profanities... Nevertheless, we eventually pulled off the road and disembarked into the sauna of the midday sun. We had reached our second objective of the day, Chateau Montsegur.

The Chateau - it's more of a ruined castle really - sits like a cherry on a Bakewell tart, on top of a limestone monolith several hundred feet above the surrounding countryside.

Now, fascinated by all things historical I may be, but trolling up a near-vertical goat-track in the sort of heat that would fry an egg, is not my idea of fun. Nevertheless, in the spirit of that thing the French call 'entente cordiale' I kept my discomfort to myself and joined the rest of the group for the climb up the monolith to take a closer look.

Arriving at the top, we discovered the Chateau was little more than a shell comprised of four ruined walls with a token gesture of a tower at one end. An information board stood in the centre of the courtyard.

I wandered over to read that Simon de Montfort; *(no, not the one that built England's first Houses of Parliament, another one – there were a lot of Simon de Montfort's about in those days;)* had decided to burn two hundred and fifty Cathars people to death here because they didn't believe the Roman Catholic version of the Bible. A bit rich perhaps but since the Cathars considered the human body to be a sin and that the good times came after you were dead; a good burning was had by all...

Noting the less than authentic burnt patch at one end of the ruin, I discovered that the entire building was not quite so authentic either... The locals had reconstructed it from the remains of the original version that used to sit a few yards closer to the - truly authentic - edge of the monolith we had just climbed.

Having escaped unburned, we descended to the village of Montsegur and checked in to our Auberge for the night.

There was still time that afternoon to buy a postcard or two and get fleeced for a book about the Cathars before making my way to the local Museum. With everything in the museum written in French, I must have recorded the fastest visit to a museum on record... something around five minutes...

Back at the Auberge that evening, the owner's wife produced a meal she described as being a local speciality... 'Cassoulet' – a sort of savoury pork and bean casserole, or stew. Helped down with copious amounts of the local wine, it was soon to become a favoured dish of mine... which was no bad thing as you will find out.

That night, I mentally recounted the day's events. Despite the warning signs of a dysfunctional group, and our leader being something of a novice; it had been a promising start to the week. All I really needed was a drop in temperature by around twenty degrees, and I would be content.

It didn't, and so I wasn't...

(DAY THREE~ BECOMING A CATHAR)

Awake long before anyone else, and with breakfast still more than an hour away, I decided to take a look around the village.

Montsegur is typical of the south of France – sleepy, of shuttered windows, and home to a mix of locals, holiday homes, and ruins advertising themselves as bijou residences for gullible Brits to buy. The morning light gave the village a timeless quality. Thus, I could understand why so many people dreamed of living in places like this; Montsegur had made me one of them...

Breakfast is something the French do incredibly well. Our morning spread of freshly baked croissants, sweet spreads, eggs served with almost anything, coffee, and of course, fruit du jour, was practically a feast. Things were looking up on the seating arrangements too. We didn't need to fill all the seats on a table to attract the waiter's attention... this was no bad thing as there was only one table... and it seated sixteen.

We set off for the day's trek as the sun passed eighty degrees and steamed towards ninety-something.

Set off we might have, but within minutes, Clipboard Man's steps faltered. He was looking for a path that led away from the road we had followed out of the village. Unable to find it, he resorted to his collection of maps for clues. Peering over his shoulder, I noted the first one didn't appear to have France on it... this was not going well.

For the next twenty minutes, we retraced our steps, twice, before Clipboard Man finally plumped for a well-trodden path suggesting it would lead us away from the road and up into the tree line. Unfortunately, the path lasted no more than a hundred yards before returning us to the road we had just left.

Fifty yards further on, and another path; maybe this was the one he was looking for? Not quite, we managed about two hundred yards this time before it too led us back to the road. At this point, Clipboard Man gave up and decided it would be far less embarrassing if we just traipsed down the road we had been trying so hard to avoid for the last hour...

We had not walked more than a mile when I spotted some randomly placed picnic benches among the trees and flowers of a roadside verge. With the temperature now soaring past ninety and rapidly making its way towards infinity, the shade offered by those trees was all the invitation I needed; I made straight for them. Much to Clipboard Man's annoyance, everyone else promptly joined me. The myriad butterflies also apparently trying to avoid the sun were not too impressed by our arrival though, and rose in a shower of protest before realising we were a potential food source. ... Isn't it amazing how something so delicate can paralyse a human being, just by landing on the back of your hand...?

Regrettably, Clipboard Man ended my date with a Painted Lady by rising to once more have us traipse down the tarmac; the heat now reflecting off it only adding to the sensation of being slowly roasted alive. I began to think our trek was fast becoming a feat of endurance rather than the 'moderate' grade, the 'Detailed information pack' declared it to be. Nevertheless, onward we walked; our only respite - having to leap into the shade of the roadside trees to avoid the occasional passing car.

Eventually, we rounded a sharp bend in the road to see the tarmac end abruptly against a limestone cliff. Having now found a mystery of almost equal stature to that of the Cathars, I wandered up to the cliff and in a desperate attempt to provide some humour, began pushing various bits of it as though trying to find a lever that would reveal a secret tunnel from whence the cars had come...

I never did find it before Clipboard Man asked us to gather around him so he could make a few announcements. Purposefully folding my arms, I made an exaggerated effort to hone in on what he had to say; half-hoping he was going to explain where the cars had come from... Not for the first time, he disappointed me.

With the car mystery unsolved, and whatever he said, forgotten, we turned away from the road to head down a well-trodden path into the 'Gorges de la Frau' and towards the village of Comus.

Much to my dismay, the path soon began to climb at an alarming rate. Thus, in the now unbearable heat, I began to lag further and further behind, finally stumbling to the ground, panting.

With sweat pouring down my face and soaking my clothes, I looked up to see Clipboard Man staring down at me, not quite sure what to do or say.

Cursing, I rose to my feet and launched into a tirade about why we had to walk in the blazing heat and not the cool of the early morning. I could see Clipboard Man pondering this as he turned to follow me. If it were not for my preoccupation, I should have thanked him for making sure I was OK...

We arrived at the summit of the path several minutes behind the remainder of the group. Finding a token patch of shade, I sat down, forearms resting on my knees, as I struggled for breath. With my mouth already too dry to chew food, I drank the last of my water ration; we were still some way short of the halfway point of the day's trek.

In desperate need of finding water, I set off ahead of the group. I was soon so far out in front, I couldn't hear their voices. Nevertheless, I continued to press on.

For the next three miles, the continuous flight of butterflies and springing of crickets and grasshoppers provided all the company I needed. It was a bug collector's paradise; the local Praying Mantises, however, were the only ones doing the collecting.

Eventually, the shade of a tree invited me to sit beneath it. Taking off my boots and rubbing my feet into the cooling grass, I closed my eyes and settled down to wait for the rest of the group.

At this point, the idea of leaving the trek for somewhere more tolerable first crossed my mind. Thoughts of jumping on a train and heading for the French Alps and all that lovely cold snow suddenly became an attractive proposition.

I guess the truth is that one reaches a certain age where responsibility overtakes recklessness. Right now, my responsibility was to Clipboard Man. As much as he exasperated me, I would rather he didn't lose his job over the disappearance of a middle-aged fart with a heat problem.

I enjoyed all of twenty minutes bliss beneath that tree before the rest of the group strode into view. They didn't stop to join me this time but merely stared in my direction as they tramped past.

Waiting until they had all but disappeared from sight, I struggled to put my boots back on and rose to follow them at a discreet distance.

To my surprise, Clipboard Man dropped back to join me. It was perhaps time to apologise and plead that I had raced ahead only to find some shade. He generously accepted my apology, although I was sure he knew what I had been contemplating.

An hour later, we reached the hamlet of Comus where I gratefully refilled my water bottle and sat down to watch an ageless couple; their bodies bent from a life of hard work and wrapped as though winter was upon us, amble past. They were holding hands. A tattered wicker-basket swung from the woman's free hand; while the man rested his on the shaft of the adze slung over his shoulder. I continued to watch as they made their way down to a vegetable patch incongruously set along the edge of the village football pitch, and there, oblivious to the world around them, set about digging up that evening's vegetables.

I wanted a photograph of the moment, but the clock had ticked seconds past our scheduled stop. With Clipboard Man hustling everyone to rise, the opportunity to frame the old couple's place in history was lost.

Another three miles of blistering tarmac beckoned. I was soon out in front once more and searching for shade.

When I arrived at Camurac, another of those ancient and long-forgotten places so desirable of holiday homes, I noted the trees on the village green and made straight for them. Propping my backpack against one of them, I sat down and placed my feet once more into the soothing grass.

I could have stayed under those trees until the sun set, but when Clipboard Man finally arrived with the promise that our destination was little more than two miles away, I rose reluctantly and followed him and the rest of our group down the track towards the town of Belcaire and our hotel for the night.

Following a very average version of yesterday's 'Cassoulet'; I headed upstairs to my room and spent most of the evening repairing my now blistered and somewhat bloodied feet; everything everywhere just hurt.

With feet suitably bathed and bandaged, I shuffled across to my backpack and tipped its contents over the floor. I don't think there was a sweat-free item in it. After rinsing a couple of essentials in the room's washbasin, I hung them over the shower rail to dry.

It was barely nine o'clock when I crawled into bed, but the coolness of the cotton sheets brought such a sense of relief that I fell asleep almost immediately.

(DAY FOUR ~ TWO GROUPS ARE BETTER THAN ONE)

I was awake before most, and hobbling towards breakfast by seven o'clock. Seeing Clipboard Man already tucking into his, I joined him. It was clear he felt awkward by my presence. Nevertheless, he said not a word, and I didn't offer any.

Now, I have a confession to make... I am one of those people who possess the strange if annoying, ability to read upside down, in my case, almost as well as I can when the text is the right way up. Thus, seeing Clipboard Man's notes lying on the table, I began to surreptitiously read them. Realising he was following what appeared to be an itinerary planned to the point of military precision, I had to ask the obvious question... I asked him...

"How many of these tours have you led?"

I didn't exactly get a straight answer, more of an assurance that he had received all the necessary training... I left him to his breakfast and headed back to my room to make ready for the day's walk.

Boarding our minibus; *(yes, it was the same one that left us at Chateau Montsegur; presumably, it had been sunning itself on a beach, or something;)* Clipboard Man made the announcement that we were going to visit another Cathars Chateau before an afternoon trek would take us to that night's accommodation. Chateau Puivert he continued; was the home of the "fabled" Troubadours - the original travelling minstrels if you like.

Little more than an hour later, we alighted from the minibus and made our way up the short but gruelling slog to the Chateau. There, we were greeted by a young boy. He could not have been more than ten or twelve years old.

Clipboard Man promptly stepped forward to confirm our group booking. Without a word, the boy merely pointed to a hand-written notice on the wall informing everyone that the entrance fee was the princely sum of three euros each; there was no mention of group discounts or any other discretionary terms. If Clipboard Man's itinerary told him there should have been one, it was too late to argue about it; I'd already deposited my euros into the boy's hand and pushed through the turnstile.

I walked into the courtyard to be greeted by a shell of broken stone walls and towers. On one side, there was a lean-to stable sporting a child's rocking horse. In a nearby corner, lay a large pile of old vines... evidently, I thought, in readiness for a re-enactment of Cathar burning. At the back of the courtyard sat the Keep, a modest three-storey square building, which also appeared to be the only item of potential interest. I headed straight for it.

On reaching the first floor, I peered into the only room to discover it had been heavily and unsympathetically restored. It was also unsympathetically empty. The second-floor room was also empty.

On the third floor, I stopped to read the information board. The room on this floor, it declared, was the fabled music room of the Troubadours. Peering inside, I noted the empty glass cabinets, solitary 'Made in China' lute, and a small harp with nearly all its strings missing. Evidently, the musicians were on tour... Either that or they had left centuries ago...

I spent the next few minutes taking photographs of the view from the roof of the Keep, and then made my way back to the Chateau's entrance. Twenty minutes into our allotted one hour visit, I, like everyone else, was ready to leave.

ADVENTURES OF A MIDDLE-AGED FART

As Clipboard Man counted down the minutes to our planned departure time, I witnessed an elderly man in a wheelchair emerge from the door of one of the ruined towers, and slowly make his way across the courtyard. As he approached, the young boy walked over to him, spoke softly, and positioned his wheelchair by the entrance.

The old man looked as though the world was on his shoulders, his age-weary face rested in a shaking and weathered hand. He said nothing and looked at no-one. It did not take much to deduce that he lived in the ruined tower; that the old vines were his winter firewood, and the young boy, his grandson, was the heir to the ruins I had just mercilessly ridiculed...

Feeling a little guilty, I offered a respectful "Merci" and turned to join the others on the trek to our lodgings for the night.

The first few miles were almost pleasant amongst the dappled shade of the trees. However, they soon faded away, and once more, the sun, whose temperature had long passed insufferable and was now well on its way to impossible, began to burn everything it could touch; the parched fields and sun-baked track only adding to the searing temperatures by reflecting the heat back towards us. The day had now become a feat of endurance.

As we reached the village of Nebias and passed the only sign of life, a tiny but ever hopeful-for-a-customer shop, I nipped inside to buy a large bottle of cola. I needed energy and lots of it.

A few minutes later, on finding the only shade in the village, I sat down to take out the sandwiches last night's accommodation had provided. Pronouncing them dead on arrival, I quietly tucked them back into my pack for a discrete burial later and made do with a half-melted bar of chocolate, and most of the bottle of cola I'd just bought.

As I drifted into a thoughtful mode, my eyes focused on a battered-looking stone fountain on the other side of the village square. There was an inscription on it. Curious, I wandered over to read it, half expecting to discover the fountain dedicated to something mundane like a village elder or a defeat by the British. To my surprise, the inscription declared that it marked the site of the parting of the biblical waves. This was news to me; perhaps I'd got my geography wrong; maybe the Red Sea once flowed through this part of France, despite being two thousand feet above sea level...

Although my translation had been accurate, the fountain's real purpose was to demonstrate that water flowing from one side of it ended up in the Atlantic, while the water flowing from the other side emptied into the Mediterranean. I was hoping for a demonstration but, like all the rivers we saw that week, the fountain was bone dry.

Prescribed lunchbreak over, we wandered out of the village and back into the dusty fields and scrubland that surrounded it.

We had been walking for barely thirty minutes when Clipboard Man called us to a halt and signalled another rest break. With the morning's visit to Chateau Puivert over much quicker than planned, we were some way ahead of his schedule... I just wished he hadn't chosen the middle of a field for us to resync with it. There was no shade whatsoever.

Noting that our group appeared to be missing a few people, I looked up to see those I presumed to be unaffected by the heat, sat some distance away from the rest of us. Clipboard Man did not seem to approve of this and strode over to remonstrate with them. From the fragments of raised syllables that wafted back to the rest of us, it became evident he was unhappy about the way they had gone yomping off. With his patience clearly at an end, something I felt sure I'd helped him reach, Clipboard Man continued to range on them for several minutes. Lecture over, he returned to sit with us. I waited tensely for him to say something to me about my performance, but he said not a word. In the silence that followed, I came to realise I didn't envy his job.

Minutes later, we set off once more and almost immediately, watched those he had just chastised, break away again. They were soon far enough ahead to suggest they were on an entirely different trek. Clipboard Man, his life now complete hell; could do little more than run back and forth between the groups as we slowly made our way towards our home for the night.

His consternation must have reached crisis point when those of us lagging behind, sneaked off the track to record a photogenic field of sunflowers and, to our delight, discover a water trough filled with 'potable' *(drinking quality)* water.

In a scene reminiscent of those found after ten days in a desert without water, we quenched our thirsts greedily and poured ever more of the precious liquid over our heads. Sated, and with an air of satisfaction, we sat down to enjoy the shade of a field boundary wall, and marvel at the sunflowers that had first attracted us.

When Clipboard Man discovered our delinquency, there was no complaint on his part though; he just smiled and with some encouragement announced we were only ten minutes from that night's accommodation. This time, thank god, he was right.

The Auberge turned out to be a wonderfully rustic French farmhouse, one that would not have been out of place in a remake of 'Les Miserable'.

For the evening meal, our hosts served Spaghetti Bolognaise. It made a welcome change from my waning enthusiasm for Cassoulet...

By ten-thirty that evening, I was the only one still awake. Sitting on the patio in the cool of the night air, I laid my head back to explore a billion stars in the unpolluted sky above, and promptly fell asleep...

(DAY FIVE ~ RENNES-LES-CHATEAUX)

At breakfast, Clipboard Man finally yielded to reason. In an attempt to beat the sun, we were to set off at eight o'clock. This was the news everyone had been waiting for. Now on a winning streak, he added that we would stop for a lunchtime siesta while the midday heat passed us by.

I didn't join in the jubilation though... my feet were so blistered I could hardly walk ten yards, let alone the ten miles ahead of us. Thus, as the others set off that morning, I took a long sojourn in the swimming pool at our benevolent farmhouse, and then carefully patched up my feet once more. My journey today would be by taxi. I had agreed to meet the rest of the group in the village of Rennes-Les-Chateaux, some twenty minutes ride for me, but three hours of toil and sweat for them.

Despite my now basic grasp of the French language, I struggled to converse with the friendly taxi driver that morning, his thick brogue made it extremely difficult to pick out the gist of his conversation. The reference to "Petit jour" was about as close as we got to communicating and that only after he motioned his hands to define how narrow the road was. When we reached our destination, I thanked him as best I could and consolidated that with a generous tip.

Rennes-Les-Chateaux is a village famous for a legend about a monk who began writing strange books and followed this up with a mysterious source of wealth. Many believe he had found the fabled treasure of the Cathars. If he did, it would seem he spent a considerable amount of it extravagantly remodelling his church, and providing for his housekeeper, who was also his mistress.

When the monk died, his housekeeper continued to live in some comfort, presumably because he had left the source of his wealth to her. If she was in on the secret, though, she too took it with her to the grave.

With a penchant for the curious things in life, it was a given that I would have to do the tourist thing and pay to see the Monk's church. Once inside, it was indeed as gaudy as had been described, albeit that those responsible for its upkeep, needed to do some significant 'up-keeping' judging by the sizable cracks I could see in some of the walls and ceiling. Visit complete, I pondered the purchase of the ubiquitous 'been there, *(got the)* T-shirt', yet ponder was all I did. At twice the price I expected to pay, it dawned on me that perhaps the Monk's mysterious wealth was really in T-shirts...

Disappointed and with little else to do, I wandered up to the viewpoint in the village, and was slightly taken aback to see four members of our group sat admiring the view; they too it seemed, had deserted today's slog.

Having made it as far as the town of Esperanza; barely two hours into the day's folly, they had decided enough was enough and grabbed a taxi for the remainder of the journey. I began to think the Monk also ran a taxi company...

From our vantage point, the five of us watched with some inward delight, as the hard-core few, notably those who had yomped off into the distance yesterday, toil for more than an hour up the long hill from Esperanza; the sun, merciless in doing its best to melt them into the surrounding dust.

We did not start walking again until late afternoon. It was still blisteringly hot, but with the promise from Clipboard Man that it would take only an hour to reach our lodgings for the night, we set off with some purpose.

TWO hours later, we arrived in Granes, a village filled with stabling for horses and all things equine. The overpowering smell of manure, though, did little to attract the army of flies away from trying to eat our third serving of Cassoulet in five days, before we did. That night's version of this regional 'speciality', however, didn't contain anything quite as recognisable as pork; those who knew about these things voted for horsemeat...

The Auberge was also home to a group of English women on an equestrian holiday. They were about as 'Tally-Ho' as gentrified women can get. Thus, it was not long before the men in our group began enjoying copious amounts of wine in their raucous company, much to the disgust of the females in ours, who, despite the invitation, declined to join us. Ah well...

Frivolities over, and long after everyone had retired for the night, the men's dormitory continued to resound to a boisterous discussion about abandoning our trek, and joining the equestrian women on their adventure instead. As the noise increased to an adolescent schoolboy level, I began to smile for the first time that week. There was, at last, a suggestion of group bonding taking place; maybe it was just the wine...

(DAY SIX ~ RENNES LES FOOT SPA)

Morning set out with promise, so I followed her...

Today's trek began through softer woodland, and smaller patches of sun-tortured heath. Perhaps still buoyed by last night's high-jinks, and the easy day I'd had yesterday, I found the heat more tolerable; it may even have been half a degree or so cooler - maybe the sun was losing its grip...

France it seems, has its fair share of landmark rocks and monoliths, and naturally, each has its own legend. Thus, it came as no surprise to arrive at one called the 'Trembling Stone', which, when struck, would... well... tremble, or so the sign claimed. Despite our best efforts to hit it hard enough to send it into Spain several miles away, however, the rock refused to tremble. Perhaps I should have expected to be disappointed, It was a French rock after all.

The next rock we set out to find was called the 'Devil's Armchair'. According to Clipboard Man, it was just a few yards further down the track. It took a while to find. It was only when we lowered our expectations, and our eyes, that we eventually found it, cowering beneath a small shrub. Judging by its less than impressive size, the Devil must have been a pixie when he last sat on it...

Monolith hunting over, we descended into the Roman spa town of Rennes-Les-Bains. There was no sign of any Romans, and the spas had all gone private by the time we arrived. Nevertheless, Clipboard Man decreed we would siesta here.

After a short soirée around the tree-shaded town square, I discovered there were just two cafés. Seeing the elite among us sat at the first one, I headed for the one on the opposite side of the square and ordered a true French classic... pizza. As it was, the hand-made pepperoni version I received, along with its accompanying aioli dressing, still ranks as the third-best pizza I've ever eaten...

With pizza suitably despatched, boredom set in. Since Clipboard Man didn't have any free spa treatment vouchers, I decided to go exploring. My roommate from the first night in Carcassonne tagged along.

It didn't take us long to discover something far more exotic than the claustrophobic town square we had just left. A well-worn flight of steps led us down to a river, one, the town gave no sign of possessing when we first arrived. I could see why; the river's setting, hemmed in between banks steeped with honey-toned houses, could not have been more perfect, or more secret. The broad, but shallow waters, cascaded gently over an array of large stone slabs that invited the child to use as stepping stones, and the adult to sit upon and dangle their feet from.

In the heat of the midday sun, I could not help but dip my sore feet into the river; the intense relief it provided, was almost intoxicating. I watched with some trepidation though as dinner-plate-sized trout swam around them admiring the blisters...

A little further upstream from us, a group of young rakes were also making the most of the cooling waters. Periodically, one or more of them would climb out of the river and run between two large rocks that formed part of the riverbank beneath the houses. Moments later, they would re-emerge and return to the river, shrieking as they jumped back in. Curious, we had to investigate.

Peering into the gap between the rocks, we could see an ancient and presumably little-used, natural thermal spa. It looked heaven, and look at heaven is what we did; both of us being several rakes too fat to fit through the gap... There was no disappointment in returning our feet to the trout-laden water though; even the realisation that we were going to be several seconds late in getting back to the rendezvous point, did nothing to hurry our return.

We were still sat dangling our feet in the river when Clipboard Man homed in on us. Our delinquency had evidently ruined his schedule. Thus, to reclaim the lost seconds, it became evident that the afternoon trek was to be something akin to the route march I'd been trying to avoid all week. Being long past having my brain boiled by the fierce sun, and my feet blistered by tarmac, I once more begged for a taxi.

Sougraigne lies only a few miles as the taxi flies from Rennes-Les-Bains. Thus, I arrived at our Auberge three hours before the rest of the group. This didn't bother me in the least, for the village was arguably the most enchanting of the week.

That afternoon I photographed my way through an entire roll of film while wandering around its tiny streets, delighting in seeing grapevines hanging over doorways, dogs hanging over steps... and French surnames like 'Smith' and 'Jones' scrawled over post-boxes...

The Auberge that night featured another swimming pool and another Cassoulet. The bean bit I enjoyed every time, but the lottery of insidious gristle and dubious zoology of the remaining contents, made Cassoulet something of a gamble each time we lifted the lid from the pot. The pork and chicken versions were easy to spot, but tonight's meat content defied description... Pushing the mysterious lumps around the plate, I tried to remember if I'd seen a doorstep missing a dog...

Later that evening, I set eyes on an iconographic hint of cloud, one illuminated by a gloriously pink sunset. At last! Perhaps we might enjoy some cooling rain tomorrow... or so I hoped.

I lay awake that night, rueful that morning would herald our last full day of trekking. I regretted the weather. Had it been a little kinder and the tarmac a little less prevalent, the week would have been a delight. I just hoped and prayed that the rain from those wisps of cloud I had seen earlier, would bring the temperature down twenty degrees or so by morning. Judging by the size of them, it was a big ask...

(DAY SEVEN ~ ALL PASTIS AND LAVENDER)

I woke to call last night's clouds "traitors" as brilliant sunshine once more carved its way through the curtains. Despite this, I set about my morning ablutions, vowing to make this a good day for a walk... come sun, come blisters.

To do so, however, meant I would have to break a cardinal rule of trekking. Boots... these things are, of all one's trekking gear, the most essential item; try walking anywhere without a good pair, and you won't get very far. Despite knowing this, I elected to abandon mine and instead donned my trusty pair of canvas shoes. They were lighter and softer than my walking boots, and thus, I knew they would probably be ruined after the day's walk. Nevertheless, I also knew my feet would be grateful for their sacrifice...

To get to the start of the walk today, we re-joined our minibus; now reunited with its unusually large trailer, for an exhilarating ride up the narrowest of lanes towards the village of Bugarach.

The village sits astride a steep gorge straddled by an ancient yet spectacular single-arch bridge. If that didn't provide enough interest for the visitor, the nearby mountain is a mecca for those seeking everything from fascinating geology and ancient human history, to sightings of UFOs... It was also one of the less than exclusive claimants, to be the only place on the planet where human beings would survive the apocalyptic ending of the Mayan calendar.

Sadly, we flashed past all this and continued towards the 'Gorge de Galamus', which, despite its impressive title, proved considerably less so when we arrived at its crowded car-park.

Looking over the retaining wall, I could see a river far enough below us for it to be silent where the white horses tumbled over the rapids. The challenge of descending the gorge and making our way downstream could not have been more inviting. However inviting it was, though, Clipboard Man tore us away from the invitation, and led us towards another adventure of tarmac and asphyxiating car exhaust.

The road through the gorge turned out to be the main route between two sizeable towns; as a result, it was significantly busier than those we had experienced to date. To my delight, a large part of it was also a single carriageway. Sanctuary for those pedestrians stupid enough to walk down this road amounted only to the handful of passing places otherwise intended for vehicles. I thanked the spirits for the decision to wear my canvas shoes that day, because, if I'd worn my boots, I doubt I'd have been agile enough to avoid becoming a British trophy for a French driver...

On reaching the car-park at the end of the gorge, Clipboard Man decided to take our group photograph. In this vain group, everyone wanted the picture too, and so handed him their camera. I found it difficult to smile as Clipboard Man set about corralling us into the frame, until the moment a German tourist elected to take a spontaneous photo of him battling with more than a dozen camera straps around his neck... When he finally extricated himself from those straps, he directed us to cross the road and head up the track we could see on the opposite side.

Some distance up the track, and long after the noise of the road below had faded away, I stumbled upon a group of men hiding in the bushes. Around them lay an assortment of shotguns, several rabid-looking dogs, and more than a few bottles of savage tasting Pastis liqueur... a sort of brain-rotting alcohol made from anise and liquorice root. The men were hunting wild boar they said- I now understood the Pastis...

Despite their rustic accent, Clipboard Man deduced that they had got three that day. I wasn't entirely sure if that meant Frenchmen killed by wild boars, wild boars killed by Frenchmen... or Frenchmen killed by Pastis ...

We left the hunters with the knowledge that we were now in the realms of wild boars. Regardless that these creatures are not known for asking questions before taking a chunk out of your leg, especially if they've already had a few shotgun pellets up their arse, I struck out ahead of the group.

With the rest now following me at a safe distance, I continued to plough my way ever closer towards the sky. Naturally, we heard and saw nothing of the wild boars.

Sometime later, we arrived at a plateau. In the centre of it, a tiny patch of alpine meadow had once been home to a field of Lavender. Now abandoned to its fate, the remaining plants provided a meditating scent, strong enough to induce a feeling of peace. There was nothing else for it, I promptly sat down for lunch.

Unwrapping my sandwiches, I began the familiar ritual of feeding the local population of omnivores with them, while stuffing the contents of a large bag of crisps into my mouth. Almost an entire litre of cola also disappeared down my throat. Sated by this, I belched loud enough that if there had been any wild boar planning on taking a chunk out of a leg, I felt sure the noise would have frightened them off...

Two hours passed before Clipboard Man was able to encourage us to get back on the trail again. I suspect most of the group had finally also been worn down by the heat.

Rising with a groan, I headed down the long and monotonous track that led into the baked cauldron of the valley below. Somewhere at the end of that valley lay the village of Duilhac-sous-Peyrepertuse, and our last night's accommodation.

A little while later, we spotted our target for the day, the formidable Chateau Peyrepertuse. It looked impregnable on its lofty perch high above the valley. It almost was; holding out against our Cathar burning lunatic from Montsegur, for more than three years before its residents finally succumbed to his genocidal intent.

Eventually, we reached the track that wound up to the Chateau. Having got this far, I was not to be denied the view from the top. Several denied themselves and chose to wait under the only sheltering tree they could find.

The commanding views from the top were achingly beautiful and worth the grief of getting there. The Chateau sat high enough above the valley that the free-wheeling Para-gliders swooping below me, appeared indistinct when framed by the camera...

By the time we reached the Auberge, I was exhausted beyond measure but satisfied that I had completed the challenge I'd set myself that morning, every sun-baked yard of it. That, to me at least, was all that mattered.

An orgasmic shower; one complete with snazzy lights that switched on automatically as you walked into the cubicles, and switched off as you walked out; was enough to set up a glorious evening in the semi-tropical garden of the Auberge.

When our hosts announced the meal as Cassoulet, *(for the fifth time that week,)* I smiled and said not a word; it seemed France had to have one last joke at my expense.

Perhaps the joke this time though, was on me. For as I poked around the bean-feast to investigate the meat content, I discovered that we had been given a king's ransom... a wild boar and venison ransom to be precise... I wondered if the owners of the Auberge knew anyone with a fondness for pastis...

Much later, and after everyone else had retired to bed, I enjoyed a glass of wine in the company of Clipboard Man. I hadn't planned to, and I suspect neither had he, but it seemed the right moment to apologise to him once more, for being such a pain in the arse during the last seven days.

Perhaps because I apologised, or, perhaps because the trek was almost over and he no longer felt the need to remain diplomatic, he revealed that for all the grief I'd given him about the heat, I'd played only a small part in what he had had to deal with that week.

He also admitted that the itinerary had been a shambles. *(Really?)*. Nevertheless, it was quite a confession to hear him say that, he thought whoever had written it had probably never been to Languedoc, let alone surveyed the actual trek...

I pondered his words. If I'd had his job, I would have left half our group at the airport, but then, I'd also have been up and walking at seven in the morning, and not boiling my brains out in the midday sun, now begrudgingly setting itself behind the village church.

Despite my frustration, I gave generously to his gratuity fund that night and wondered if he would return the following week with another group as dysfunctional as ours. Somehow, I doubted it... on both counts.

(DAY EIGHT ~ C'EST LA VIE)

Our final day began with a visit to Chateau Queribus. We approached it and then, in some confusion, drove straight past it towards our second visit of the day... a vineyard.... except that it was not the 'sample some wine at a local vineyard' of the trip dossier, but a shop in the small town of Maury, several miles below Chateau Queribus.

After a quick disillusioned look around the touristy and overpriced wine shop, I wandered down the town's main street in search of something, anything, of interest. There was nothing.

I finally settled in the shade of some trees under which, a local café had enterprisingly set out its tables. Not feeling particularly hungry, though, I ordered lemonade and spent most of the next hour poking at the lemon in the glass with the fiddlestick, and knocking back the resulting crush. There was not a word of conversation from anyone.

After my second lemonade, I rose from the table and sauntered back down the street towards the minibus. I still had an hour to spend in Maury, but could no longer find anywhere to spend it.

For reasons unknown, perhaps looking for an escape route by which to avoid the minibus, I stopped to peer down a narrow alleyway. Much to my surprise, there was a tiny shop half-hidden among its dark recesses... and it appeared to be selling wine... In the hope that it would not be just another brash, over-priced affair offering tourist grade plonk, I turned down the alleyway to investigate.

I was not expecting much as I walked through the door, but soon spotted bottles of a considerably better pedigree than those I'd seen earlier. Picking up one of them proved to be the signal to the owner to place two glasses on the counter, and motion me across to join him.

Almost immediately, we both knew that conversation would be virtually impossible... he knew as much English as I did French... What followed though was proof that language need never be a barrier to understanding and respect...

As I entertained his first offering and muttered: "lavender" and "poivre" (pepper), his smile broadened. Before long, he was blowing the dust off cherished bottles, produced, I might add, from beneath the counter.

With exaggerated facial expressions, hand gestures, and occasional words and noises of pleasure, we proceeded to work our way through several bottles, while offering 'salut's' on every Anglo-French subject we could think of, that didn't involve Rugby, Agincourt, the European Union, or Napoleon Bonaparte...

I finally bade the owner "adieu mon ami," and left with not a coin in my pocket; the bag I was carrying, however, was priceless.

Much to the chagrin of Clipboard Man, I arrived back at the minibus ten minutes late. Much to the chagrin of the rest of the group, I was smiling, and not a little intoxicated... Clearly, I had enjoyed the better field trip to Maury.

In keeping with the farce of the last week, we proceeded to drive back up the road to Chateau Queribus, where we spent the next two hours wandering around its battlements and stuffing our faces with our packed lunch.

Visit over, we then proceeded to drive back to Maury for the second time, where we finally took the road for Montpelier and our flights home.

At the airport, I gave a respectful farewell to 'Clipboard Man', and witnessed his smile for the first time that week. I felt sure he was glad to be rid of me, but I think ultimately, he was delighted to be rid of all of us...

While waiting for my flight in the Departure lounge, I enjoyed a solitary beer with my roommate and fellow paddler from Rennes-les-Bains, there were few goodbyes from anyone else.

London's Gatwick Airport and English soil arrived soon enough, though almost too soon... The sudden and dramatic aborted landing, while avoiding another plane on the runway, turned out to be the highlight of the week...

When we landed at the second time of asking, I raced up the walkway, barged through immigration, collected my luggage, exited the Terminal, and walked straight into a torrential downpour...

NIGHT ON A BARE-ARSED MOUNTAIN

Lightning can strike twice in the same place. I know this, for despite the cancellation of my preferred trek last time out, and the subsequent flambéing my body got in France as a result; I still chose to ignore the warning signs from the spirits as I booked my next trek.

My original choice, a trek around the Five Lakes of Poland's Tatra National Park, was cancelled only a day after I'd clicked 'submit' for the online payment. Naturally, I waited in high expectation of a discount on another trek, and looked forward to a gentle ramble around the Austrian Alps, or walk across the wild landscape of Iceland. No such luck. What they came up with was a walk on the Great Wall of China, something that would have still cost a second mortgage even after the discount, or Base camp Everest. Torres Del Paine may have been a personal triumph, but climbing Mount Everest was in a different league.

Reluctantly, I finally gave up and asked for my money back. It was time to find another company with a penchant for trekking holidays.

After a long search, I finally opted for one claiming to have won several awards for their treks. Duly suckered in, I registered for two weeks in the High Atlas Mountains of Morocco.

I've no idea why I decided to go to Africa. The continent was never on my wishlist. All those nasty diseases that live there had me believing I'd be the one to contract the Ebola virus, bring it back to England, and proceed to wipe out half the population with it. It also concerned me that much of Africa appeared to be subjected to almost daily coups. Given my opinionated self, I felt sure I would either end up getting shot the moment I stepped off the plane or held hostage by some obscure organisation demanding five billion Matabele gumbo beads for my release...

Nevertheless, a quick check on Morocco confirmed that it had a reasonable track record of stability; that it had just one nasty disease - which didn't occur where I was heading; and above all, it was one of those African countries with a strong European influence, albeit a French one. Theoretically, this meant if I needed medical attention, I would be able to obtain it, rather than have the local Witchdoctor prescribe something made from cow dung, snake venom, or something I'd rather not guess. Applying the same logic, I also assumed, wrongly as it turned out, that I would enjoy a reasonable standard of accommodation and some decent food. Oh alright... there was also the cost to consider... it was a little less than a package tour to Zante...

(DAY ONE ~ HYPERSPACE)

Those spirits I'd ignored when booking for Morocco, tried to get their dire warning through to me yet again when I arrived at London Victoria underground station...

With complete oblivion, I walked onto the Northbound Platform and stepped purposefully onto the service for Green Park. That's when I should have been listening to them, for when I arrived at Green Park, someone had placed a large 'Closed for Engineering Works' sign across the entrance to the platforms for the Piccadilly line, my direct route to Heathrow Airport. With no other option available, I returned to Victoria in the hope of finding an alternative.

Standing on the concourse, I finally listened to those spirits - their ethereal voices were broadcasting over the loudspeakers with the information that, "passengers for Heathrow should take the..." ...and that was that... The critical information about which line this passenger for Heathrow should take was drowned out by a booming:

"Are you lost, honey?"

I spun round to face, well, look down at, a five-foot-tall, buxom, hands-on-hips West-Indian woman who had sidled up on my blind side. Her enquiring face meant business. Taken aback by her sudden appearance, I blurted out:

"Err yes. How do I get to Heathrow, err please?"

In a well-rehearsed monologue, she told me that I didn't want to listen to the rubbish "they" (the train spirits presumably,) were telling everyone else to do. What I needed to do was to boogie on the right, then shuffle to the left along the angle of the hypotenuse, (but only if I wanted a sandwich,) and take the purple line to the point where it joined the red-brown coloured line at the apex of the Isosceles triangle. I would then need to jump through hyperspace - because there was a white bit on the map, and complete a short hop on a green bit. If I made it that far, I would find myself back on the Piccadilly line to Heathrow, somewhere the other side of the Engineering works that had so abruptly curtailed my Green Park plans... *(phew!)*

Despite protestations that her plan would take the rest of my life to complete, she was confident that I "should" arrive at Heathrow with plenty of time to spare.

The subtle use of the word 'should', stayed with me as I tried to recall my high school Maths while deciphering the faded, smudged, and critically torn in the wrong place, map on the carriage wall as we hurtled through parts of London meaningless and unexplored even by those of us who'd lived there.

For a long time, I didn't appear to be travelling in the right direction. My hopes of arriving at Heathrow much before my plane landed in Morocco thus began to fade.

Thankfully, I remembered to take the purple line - I didn't want a sandwich - and finally arrived at hyperspace, where I discovered several other forms of human life, all apparently with the same instructions.

As I tried to recall what came next, one of 'honey's' henchmen cajoled us into joining a deserted train sat quietly at the far end of a platform some distance from where we had arrived. Like sheep, we all followed his instruction without question. I had barely sat down when the train fired into life and raced out of the station.

As my instincts reached the critical point of telling me we had been kidnapped by an alien race, we arrived at another almost deserted station. Almost, because sat there, quietly pondering whether it would have any passengers that day, was a train going to Heathrow airport. The only people to board it in fact, were those who had followed 'honey's' advice. Feeling guilty about my lack of faith in her, I hoped somebody would one day go back to Victoria Station and buy her a bunch of flowers...

After almost three hours travelling on London's underground railways, I finally arrived at Heathrow and headed for Terminal Two.

By the time I reached the Departure gate, there were less than twenty minutes to spare before boarding time, but I had made it.

Strapping myself in, I looked around to witness that the plane was half-empty. I began to wonder how many people still lost on London's underground system, should have been filling those seats...

The stewardess ended the mystery by informing me that another flight for Marrakech had left only twenty minutes earlier. This one, however, allowed me the luxury of flying via Casablanca and wait there plane-bound for an eternity, before enduring another circuitous flight to Marrakech. Now I knew the real reason why my flight was half-empty...

It was ten o'clock in the evening by the time I arrived in Marrakech, but several minutes after walking through Immigration, I was still in the Arrivals lounge looking for the guide who was to lead our trek.

Noting that a tall, lean, nonchalant looking individual I'd walked past at least twice, was eyeing me intently, I walked over to him. In the most rudimentary French; *(the second language of Morocco,)* I asked if he was the guide for my intended trek. He was... and he replied in English...

With little or no emotion, 'Youssef' methodically ticked my name off his list, and pointed towards a monetary exchange bureau, where I learned that it was illegal to use US Dollars, Euros, Sterling, or for that matter any other currency except Moroccan 'Dirhams', to buy things in Morocco. Having no idea how much Sterling to exchange, I took the advice offered. I left the airport a Dirham millionaire...

That night I shared a room with one of those no-nonsense retired teacher types. As we sized each other up. I concluded he would not be out of place on a Scout Jamboree, but as I was to discover later, he turned out to be as tough as nails.

(DAY TWO ~ MULES AND MOBILE SHOPS)

I woke to find 'Tough as Nails' long gone, no doubt off to circumnavigate Morocco before breakfast, I thought.

It was still a little early to head down to the restaurant, so, with nothing better to do, I peered out of the window at the traffic below. This may be a mundane thing to record I grant you, but in the space of just twenty minutes, I witnessed two accidents with not a policeman, or paramedic, in sight. The most spectacular of which involved a large truck and a bicycle. *(Look away now if you're squeamish while I describe the scene...)*

Having been knocked off his bicycle by the truck, the cyclist lay prostrate under the front bumper; the remains of his bicycle, with front-wheel neatly folded in half, lay by his side. Moments later, Truck-man jumped out of his cab, grabbed the bicycle, and in a quick no-one's looking manner, flung it into the back of his truck; having first stepped over Bicycle man to do so.

Truck-man then returned to haul his victim out from under the bumper, whether his legs were still attached or not, and bundle him into the passenger seat. Seconds later, and with the play far too short for an audience, he drove off, no doubt to dispose of the body, and repair the bicycle for sale later on eBay. All this occurred as traffic hurtled by several lanes abreast; which was interesting, as there were only three lanes marked on the road...

The traffic that morning not only consisted of Lorries and bicycles, though but every manner of transport in between, including mules, one of which finally drew the camera.

I watched patiently as the mule struggled by with a cart loaded with fruit stacked high enough I could almost smell it on the second floor. Despite the urging of his driver to the contrary, the mule decided to stop a nose short of the same roundabout where I'd just seen Truck-man act out his crime. For several minutes, the mule stared implacably at the challenge before him; before, and with total indifference to the traffic, and his driver's frantic persuasions, he visibly strained forward to haul his fruit mountain through the melee, and across the roundabout without a scratch. He'd done it a thousand times before...

Following breakfast, it was time for the official announcements of what's permissible to do or say in a Muslim country, and what's not; and that we were leaving Marrakech in ten minutes...

After frantically cramming the waiting minibus with two weeks' worth of backpacks and twelve bodies, we headed for the mountains, already in plain sight, yet still some distance away. Despite it being mid-May, I noted that some of the peaks were snow-capped...

Two hours later, we arrived at a rest stop. Extricating myself from the bus, I was immediately confronted by a mobile shop... He and several other mobile shops were offering "real silver" bangles made from 'real silver' fizzy drink cans and ring-pulls. They were all reasonably priced at one hundred dirhams' a ring pull, which became buy one for one Dirham and get two free by the time we left...

An hour later the road finally ran out at a village called Imlil. I climbed out of the minibus and learned to breathe again.

As I walked past our driver, he held out his hand, I presumed in the expectation of receiving a tip. I ignored him. It was not as though he had unloaded my backpack nor provided any particular service. He had just driven us to Imlil, something I felt sure the trekking company would have paid him for.

This didn't go down too well. When Youssef accosted me with the suggestion that it was customary to give tips for service rendered, *(whether they had been or not)*; I begrudgingly peeled off a ten dirham note, guessing that this would be adequate, and handed it to the driver, who promptly spat on it. Things had got off to a great start.

The walk to our Gite at Aremd, some distance further up the mountain though, was idyllic.

Pacing ourselves in the already high altitude, we followed an aqueduct through shady Walnut groves and Olive trees, and wandered past small terraced fields of wheat, maize, pear, and apple trees; each served by a complex arrangement of sluices that ensured they remained green, and fertile oases among the stony wastelands of the surrounding mountains. I could not help but admire the ingenuity of the local Berber people whose home this was.

Our Gite had all the amenities; including hot showers, cold *(non-alcoholic)* drinks, and modern toilets. It also had a ringside view of our ultimate destination, the summit of Mount Toubkal.

That night's meal though was high on vegetables and low on meat. I nibbled the sparrow's leg of questionable chicken and promptly turned vegetarian.

Despite my disappointment with the main course, the dessert, large slices of Melon, was delicious. Much to the chagrin of those who regretted stuffing the sparrow's legs, I took an extra slice...

The dormitory at the Gite was an unusual arrangement. An array of padded benches positioned around the edge of the room served as places to sleep... head to foot fashion with your neighbour; while the abundant cushions served as pillows on which to rest our heads. The only privacy afforded us by this arrangement were our sleeping bags.

(DAY THREE ~ THE MARTIANS HAVE LANDED)

I woke to discover that today would be an acclimatisation walk and descended for breakfast.

The porridge that morning was tasty, if runny. There was some locally made bread too... so local in fact they were making it in the kitchen. In the middle of the table, stood a small bowl containing an assortment of those little pots of jam found in every hotel, and second-rate restaurant in the world. Fishing around for one marked 'marmalade', I opened it to reveal something that looked and tasted suspiciously like Apricot jam, or maybe it was pink grapefruit. Nevertheless, I was hungry enough to take a second slice of bread, ...and a second pot of 'marmalade'.

The grand finale for breakfast was the much-anticipated Moroccan version of Mint tea...

The Berbers make it with rolled gunpowder tea-leaves, and add a local form of mint which smelled nothing like the mint I was familiar with back in England. 'Nana' mint as the Berbers called it, had a much softer, almost aromatic quality about it. It was not until much later in the trek, however, that I privately witnessed the mysterious art of making this Mint tea, and learned enough about its ingredients to take home one of the world's best-kept secrets.

After taking note of the forest of leaf-mould in the bottom of the glass cup they served it in, I closed my eyes and took a large sip. Much to the horror of my palate, I discovered that Moroccans prefer their mint tea sweet, very sweet. From the toothless smiles that confronted me over the coming days, I got a regular reminder that drinking sweetened Mint tea here, was a lifelong passion.

Youssef had us hurtling through the village, and out into the mountain shadows, long before the porridge had been tongued from the teeth. He was a mountain guide he told us, and could patch up a broken leg or two if required; the last comment delivered with a smile revealing that he had a surprisingly full set of teeth... I discovered later he was also adept at finding poisonous scorpions...

A few minutes into the acclimatisation walk, we reached a path that appeared to zigzag its way to eternity, perhaps three thousand feet above us. For the second, and last time on the trek, Youssef grinned before turning to begin the steady climb towards the summit.

It didn't take long to establish there were two types of people on our trek... those that puffed and wheezed up mountains, and those that could leap over them in a single bound... well, perhaps not quite, but you get the picture...

Every so often, Youssef and these mountain goat types would make a token stop to allow the rest of us to catch up. Sure enough, each time we reached their position, they would march off again. I'd been here before...

After the third stop, the mountain goats didn't stop any more. I looked up to watch them disappear over the summit, several hundred feet above me.

When the rest of us finally reached the summit and stopped to gather our breath, I looked around for Youssef. There was no trace of him, or for that matter, of the mountain goats. Either the Martians had landed and abducted our fellow travellers, for the landscape told me they might well have; or our erstwhile colleagues had vanished over an unseen precipice. I began to hope for the latter...

After spending several fruitless minutes searching for signs of a path, a mountain goat, or a Youssef, we spotted a vague sandy track meandering its way down towards the valley floor. We made to follow it.

We had descended perhaps two hundred feet when something made me stop and look up behind us. There, just to the right of where we had crested the summit, the mountain goats were stood waving at us. Muttering words of contempt, we scrambled back up to join them.

In the middle of our silent lunch beneath the cypress trees, Youssef suddenly upped and ran off into the distance, eventually disappearing behind a rock. I wondered if he had abandoned us to the Martians. Twenty minutes later, he returned. We asked nothing and presumed everything. The reality was that Youssef, native Berber or not, was a Muslim, and it was his time to pray.

As we set off for the return journey, ever downwards and back to Aremd, I began to relax and enjoy the walk. We had climbed to an altitude of almost eleven thousand feet, test enough to discover our tolerance levels for altitude sickness.

For my part, I learned that the short-lived prickly sensation I'd felt behind my eyes as we passed nine thousand feet, and which dissipated only a couple of hundred feet higher, was all the altitude sickness I would suffer. Others had not been so lucky; one of our group had been forced to return to the base of the hill and wait for us. We never saw them again...

Having been lucky with altitude sickness, I became unlucky with altitude falling. Slipping on the scree-covered path, I slammed my right knee against a rock, and promptly dislocated it...

In agony, I clasped my knee with both hands. Miraculously, by doing just that, my kneecap popped back into place. With the damage done, the few who'd witnessed the incident offered a 'bad luck' and promptly hurried past, fearful I suspect, that they might be called upon to carry all six foot and two hundred pounds of me, back down the mountain to the Gite.

After everyone had passed, I slowly hauled myself up and hobbled down towards a waiting Youssef. Sizing up the situation, he sprung into medical mode; I sincerely hoped he didn't think my leg was broken and needed resetting...

A few minutes later and with my knee now heavily bandaged, I rose to my feet and very carefully applied weight to my leg. So long as I didn't try to bend it, the pain was bearable.

In the odd moment that followed, Youssef halted the Mountain goats and ushered me past them; apparently, I was to lead the group back to the Gite. I never really understood why he did this. I can only conclude that perhaps he thought my trek was over, and this was something symbolic.

That evening, I nudged the couscous on my plate, ate some token vegetables, and thankfully avoided the lamb gristle that no-one considered putting on my plate anyhow... The melon hadn't lost its flavour though, and nobody disputed my second slice. It felt like the last supper.

As night fell, I rued my failure to pack a first-aid kit, something I'd never forgotten before. With no painkillers available, it was a long and sleepless night. I began to think those spirits I'd been ignoring, had, by dislocating my knee, made one last desperate attempt to force me to abandon the trek... I wish I had listened to them.

(DAY FOUR ~ "YAH-LAH")

Six o'clock woke to a bright warm day, but I decided to join her more sociable friend, thirty minutes later.

Rising from my cushioned bench, I realised I couldn't bend my leg. In agony, I hopped down the steps from the dormitory and staggered into the breakfast room. Nobody asked me how I felt; I guess it must have been obvious.

Picking slowly at my porridge, I had a decision to make. Did I go home, or did I grin and bear the pain, and see if it would ease off over the next day or two?

I had assumed we would return to the Gite that night. This, at least, would have given me time to see how my knee faired from a day's walk. However, Youssef put an end to that by announcing we would not return to Aremd for another ten days. With this information playing heavily on my mind, I crawled back up to the dormitory and packed my kit, still unsure of what to do.

A few minutes later, we gathered at the foot of the steps leading from our Gite, to hear Youssef issue a "Yah lah" command, a local expression for 'wagons roll' if you like, and with that, we set off back down the track towards Imlil.

Not thirty minutes into the walk, we stopped to witness several local women toiling up the track. Strapped across their backs were enormous bundles of rough-cut meadow hay.

Youssef informed us that working the fields was women's work; the men were out maintaining the aqueducts and, presumably, making money from tourists. He would not allow us to take a photograph of the women and their burden; that, apparently, was a decision only their husbands could make... Instead, he arranged for one of the women in our group to act as a stooge.

Some days later, I learned that Berber men permit the photographing of Berber women, just so long as they *(the men)* received the negotiated fee... In some places, it's still very much a man's world...

Shortly after passing through the familiar walnut groves, we arrived at a fork in the path. To my left, the track led back to Imlil and the road home; to my right, lay infinity and beyond... well, to places I had no clue about at least...

As the group turned towards infinity, I had a decision to make. With no knowledge as to what lay ahead, and Youssef already some distance up the track, I hesitated. With some foreboding, I finally decided to take a chance that my knee would hold up and turned to follow.

Two hours up the trail, we stopped for a break beneath the shade of a cedar tree. Here, Youssef surprised us all by producing a giant sack of assorted nuts. Grateful for the energy they contained, I took a handful, only to discover, as I should have perhaps expected, that they had been sweetened.

Munching on nuts can bring observation though... in this case, observation, that the two large rocks in full view of us, were marked 'Men' & 'Women' respectively...

A little while later, we passed our first Europeans. They were German. Thus, in the spirit of all that is European, I offered the traditional German greeting of "Salaam alaikum!" *(Peace be with you,)* to which one of them responded with the conventional English reply of "Wa Alaikum Salaam" *(and also with you)*...

We arrived at the summit of the trail to discover a ramshackle tin hut, sat squarely in the middle of several converging tracks. This was prime real estate, and the owner knew it; cases of cola and boxes of chocolate and crisps; all the desires of western civilisation, lay everywhere. It was also home to a shiny new four-wheel-drive pick-up truck, at least two other trekking parties, and a hard-core of mountain biking enthusiasts. Based on the amount of money that changed hands during our short stay, I figured the truck belonged to the owner of the shack...

As we made ready to move off, I viewed the four-wheel-drive truck longingly, sighed heavily, and rose to follow our group down the other side of the mountain.

Much to my chagrin, I discovered that my knee worked better, going uphill than downhill. Thus, my pace slowed dramatically, and I was soon a long way behind the others. I was also beginning to regret my decision to follow them.

Five hours after leaving Aremd, we arrived at Amsoukrou. Our campsite for the night, nestled in the shade of some Walnut trees at the far end of the village. By the time I arrived, most of the mountain goats were already unpacked and sitting around their tents.

I didn't expect to have to put up a tent on this trek, but that's what I found myself doing at Amsoukrou. It was one of those carbon fibre types with the super-strong, *(and super-springy,)* rods that enable piles of shapeless nylon to take on the appearance of something paying homage to the space-age. Naturally, there were no instructions, and since the last tent I'd erected was that typical of camping thirty years ago, I soon began to make a hash of putting it up.

It was just my luck that 'Tough-as-Nails' had set up camp opposite. He watched intently as I launched into the tangle of rods and canvas that lay around me.

After placing the end of one of the rods into an eyelet, I proceeded to force the other end into an eyelet on the opposite corner of the canvas. As the rod bent ever further under the force I was applying to it; I had visions that if I let go, there was a good chance my tent would reach the summit of Mount Toubkal, several days before I did...

Having provided a demonstration of how not to erect a tent, 'Tough-as-Nails' rose to offer some help. With a flick of a finger, he demolished my efforts and resurrected it likewise, only this time, according to the non-existent manual. I mumbled my thanks and sheepishly crawled inside.

That evening, as was to be the practice every night, we filled our water bottles from a common source... an iodine stained plastic drum, filled with what we were told was treated water. It didn't smell that way...

Sometime later, I visited the standing room only, broken zipped, ominously stained latrine tent we all had to share. As I paid homage to the toilet gods, I couldn't help but make the lurid observation, that all could not be well with some of our group. Thus, on returning to my tent, I spent a long time washing my hands with the army of wet-wipes and dry soaps my washbag contained. I had a genuine fear that my prissy stomach, notorious for getting upset at the tiniest of morsels or microbes it didn't like, would be next to fall ill.

The evening meal turned out to be yet another feast of vegetables, and things I didn't know could be vegetables. Perversely though, the nearest thing to real meat I tasted during our time in the mountains, was also present... a plate of tinned sardines. The Melon though was still as good as ever, and thus I pushed my luck once again for a second slice.

That night, Youssef offered an alternative tea to our usual fayre. It was made with Vervain *(Verbena)*. Apparently, it would help us sleep, he said. He was not wrong.

(DAY FIVE ~ DISCONTENT)

Breakfast was the usual feast of gloopy porridge, with apricot, strawberry, or possibly banana-flavoured marmalade; the mint tea, however, remained the saving grace.

By eight o'clock, we were backpacking our way on the ascent to the town of Oukaimeden.

My damaged knee had gone through a minor transformation from yesterday... Painfully stiff when I woke up, it had gradually eased off as I moved around. While still swollen, and capable of giving out on me if I put too much weight on it, the gamble to persevere with the trek, appeared to be paying off.

The day's walk began with a gentle but steady climb, and continued as a gentle but steady climb for the first hour, before turning into a gravity-defying haul for the next two. As the track steepened, I began to plod ever more slowly, and soon lost sight of the mountain goat party.

I was not alone that morning, though. As I paused to catch my breath, I noted a few of my colleagues sitting by the path a few yards ahead of me. Some of them looked ill. A brief conversation revealed they were struggling with violent stomach cramps and suspected either food poisoning or contaminated drinking water had caused it. This was not good, for we had all eaten the same food served by the Berber crew, and drunk the same water they had prepared.

There was not a lot I could do for my colleagues of course; there's not a lot anyone can do in these circumstances; thus I continued my way up the mountain, leaving them with the knowledge that I would alert Youssef to their plight the moment I caught up with him.

With the adrenalin doing its best to numb the pain in my injured knee, I pushed on and eventually reached a small ridge. Pausing to look up towards the crest of the mountain, perhaps still some two hours hard slog above me, there was no sign of Youssef or the mountain goats. Behind and below me, there was no sign of those I'd left behind either. If there'd been a taxi service from that ridge... or a four-wheel-drive pick-up truck... I'd have jumped in and gone home, leaving behind only a tirade of abuse towards what was rapidly becoming a farce.

I sighed. However dysfunctional my French trek had been, Clipboard Man had always ensured no one got left behind. I could not say the same of Youssef in Morocco.

Now somewhat demoralised, I thought back to how I'd ignored the omens... The protracted jaunt on London's Underground railways; the half-empty flight from Heathrow, the embarrassing farce at Imlil, dislocating my knee during the acclimatisation walk, and now, here, several thousand feet up a mountain, dealing with the prospect that I had probably been poisoned. I wondered how long it would be before I too fell ill...

Eventually, I reached the summit to see Youssef sitting in the shade of a tree. He rose to greet me. I took his hand half-heartedly and reported my concern for those still back down the mountain.

Message delivered, I sat down, presuming Youssef would head off to rescue our colleagues with his first-aid kit. Showing no sign of concern whatsoever, he simply sat back down. Exasperated, I picked up a stick and began to poke idly amongst the rocks beneath my feet. Youssef picked up a stick and began poking idly at his own rocks and revealed a poisonous scorpion hiding under one of them. I stopped poking my rocks...

After an anxious wait, those I had left behind finally appeared. Youssef greeted them with indifference and turned to point towards the town of Oukaimeden, lying barely half a mile down the other side of the mountain. He hadn't mentioned it before, and I hadn't noticed it.

On tired legs, I stumbled down the path towards the town, longing for a decent shower and a cold beer; I hoped Oukaimeden could provide both.

As we approached the town, several of us took the road towards the nearest hotel in expectation of enjoying some comfort after two tough days of walking. Youssef didn't follow us; and turned instead towards a campsite on the opposite side of the valley. With heavy hearts, we doubled back to join him.

While I enjoy a night or two under canvas when in sight of civilisation, I will always plump for something more comfortable. That night, I could only stare at comfort... and it was less than five minutes' walk away.

Dumping my backpack in one of the tents, I made for the latrine. What I saw there defies description. I was not alone in this opinion. After a brief conversation, a few of us decided to head back into town in the hope of finding some hot showers, and a restroom fit for use. We discovered both showers and restroom, and, with some delight, a bar serving cold beer.

As afternoon faded towards evening, I headed outside the bar to contemplate the meadow that separated our campsite from the town. It was ablaze with thousands of orchids and other species of flower I knew not what. Being the only place of colour in the sterile scenery around us, it had drawn a large gathering of butterflies and insects of every shape, size, and colour. It was about to draw my camera.

Focusing on my first target, I became aware that in the distance, I could see an assortment of Moroccan army helicopters, resting incongruously among the pristine mountain scenery. Noting that they appeared to be guarded by a solitary, dishevelled looking individual, I wondered if his post was the Moroccan equivalent of the 'Russian Front'. From that point on, I could not have made a more exaggerated effort to avoid pointing my camera in any direction vaguely towards him. I felt quite sure he would love to win a reprieve; shooting a tourist for spying seemed a sure way to do it...

I returned to the campsite just in time for the evening meal, and a surprise dessert... 'Berber' pancakes.

The cook produced them with not a little ceremony, and with Youssef translating, proceeded to describe how to make them using semolina flour. They were sweet enough that I wondered if honey, rather than water, had been the binding agent. Nevertheless, I enjoyed my allocation and polished them off with the now customary 'Berber' Melon.

I was not so keen to take a second slice that night though, the mind had become preoccupied with a small voice in my stomach, and it was complaining about not feeling well...

As dusk crept over the town, I could hear tales of sickness creeping over the campsite, a sickness that was now also creeping over me...

(DAY SIX ~ INCONTINENT)

Morning arrived with a token respite of humour. I thanked her for putting in an appearance; we hadn't seen much of her.

As usual, we broke camp and made ready for what the day had in store; our mules, though, had their own ideas about that.

Somehow, they had gotten loose from the corral and had unanimously decided to go for a romp through Oukaimeden. With our support team giving chase, the mules turned to head up the Berber equivalent of a high street. We could just make out the contents of their saddlebags heading skyward, as they did their best to kick and buck everything they could from their backs.

Laughing, I turned to see Youssef staring impassively as he watched his authority being rebuked by these lowly four-legged creatures. The look on his face made me feel as though I needed to apologise for our western sense of humour. I didn't get that far. Pre-empting my words, he declared that it was our "right" to laugh... I stopped laughing... This was fast becoming the strangest of treks.

With mules finally secured, Youssef held court to inform us that the trek was to split into two groups. The Mountain goat party would join him for the trek to the nearby summit of Mount Oukaimeden, while the rapidly growing number of sick would form an invalid party, and take the low road around its base; the intention, to meet on the other side of the mountain where the paths converged.

I didn't ask if I could be a mountain goat today; something inside me was fast becoming too delicate to attempt the climb.

Glancing at the departing mountain goats, I turned to survey the remainder of our group. A quick head-count revealed we were already one short before we'd even set off. Alerted to this fact, our new guide; the former cook's assistant, motioned the rest of us to head off along the path around the mountain, while he returned to Oukaimeden to find our missing colleague.

We hadn't gone far when two more of our group disappeared into the surrounding undergrowth. The rest of us stopped a discrete distance further up the path and waited for them to reappear. They didn't. Calling out that they would wait for our guide to return, we set off once more towards the rendezvous point.

Thirty minutes later, our guide caught up with us. Resplendent on the back of his mule, was our missing trekking companion from Oukaimeden; his hands tied to the saddle horn to prevent him from falling off. He looked almost unconscious.

At this point, our guide elected to go on ahead with his patient; making it clear that he planned to leave him at the rendezvous point, before returning to fetch the two that were still in the undergrowth, now some way behind us.

Once again, I had a strong desire to abandon the trek. Yet, perhaps out of a sense of duty towards my ailing companions, I chose to persevere.

An hour later, we arrived at the rendezvous point to see our delinquent colleague from Oukaimeden, propped up against a rock, his eyes closed. There was no sign of the mountain goats. At this point, we had no idea whether they had deserted us, or were still somewhere on the mountain above our heads. Thus, we sat down and waited for someone to arrive.

It wasn't Youssef and the mountain goats who arrived, but our guide. I looked up to see one of those he'd rescued, sitting on the back of his mule, with his hands tied to the saddle horn...

With the situation deteriorating rapidly, it became clear we needed to get help. With no sign of Youssef and the mountain goats, the solution was simple... With only three of us still able to walk, one would remain with the guide to help with the sick, while the other two would find the campsite, and raise the alarm. The decision as to who should go for help seemed obvious... only two of us had grey hair; we might have been considered expendable at this point...

To reach the campsite, our guide pointed to the track we had been following, and demonstrated with his hands, that we should always take the path that stayed highest on the mountainside until we reached the head of the valley. There we would find the village of Tachedirt and our campsite. We bade our sick colleagues farewell and set off.

Perhaps an hour passed before a village appeared below us. Reasoning that we were not at the head of the valley yet, we ignored it and continued to stay high on the mountainside as instructed. A little while later, and another village, and another decision to ignore it.

I don't recall exactly how long we walked through the insanity of the heat that day; all I remember is that we finally reached the head of the valley, and the village of Tachedirt, just as the sun finally began to sulk behind the mountains.

Making our way down into the village and towards the stream in the valley just below it, I was stunned to see our guide, the cook's assistant, stood in the middle of the stream, beckoning us to follow him.

On reaching our campsite a few minutes up the other side of the valley, I stormed into the communal tent, only to find the mountain goat party enjoying a glass of mint tea. I was too exhausted to question why they hadn't waited for us, but I think my face must have said it all...

Moments later, our erstwhile guide peered into the tent, presumably to report to Youssef. I had no idea how the hell he had gotten ahead of us, nor did I ask what had happened to those we'd left behind on the mountainside. For all our apparent heroics, it seemed my colleague and I had been sent on a fool's errand; at what personal cost I was about to find out.

Removing my boots, I became aware that I had begun to shiver. Taking a deep breath, I lay down foetal fashion and closed my eyes.

I don't know how long I lay there before one of the mountain goat party raised the alarm. Apparently, they thought I'd passed out.

Youssef finally arrived with something from my second visit to his first-aid kit. Whatever he poured down my throat though, came straight back up. I could do no more than lie back down and close my eyes again.

It was dark when I woke up. The campsite was silent. I was lying in my tent but had no recollection of how I'd got there.

Conscious my stomach felt like it was about to explode, I fumbled around for that western miracle that is toilet paper, and, thank god, found the roll I'd packed as a last-minute thought. Whatever those spirits were trying to tell me, one of them must have gotten through with a recommendation to take some with me. I promise I will never ignore them again.

In bare feet, I stumbled across the sharp rocks towards the hideous cesspit of our latrine tent. I didn't get halfway before collapsing in a violent, uncontrollable, convulsion.

In the process of trying to pick myself up, my body completed the misery by vomiting the remaining contents of my stomach all over the hillside.

Enough was enough, I crawled back across the rocks to the relative sanctuary of my tent, lay down, and closed my eyes.

I don't recall any more of that night.

(DAY SEVEN ~ BRING OUT YOUR DEAD)

By early morning, I woke to discover that I had been passing blood, rather too much blood. My stomach had also retched to the point where I could vomit blood.

I must have passed out again, for the next thing I remember, was someone trying to rouse me. It was Youssef. Despite his impassioned pleas, I had no desire to move. I couldn't feel my legs anyway. What followed was nothing less than humiliating.

In front of an unwilling audience, Youssef dragged me from my tent, only to watch as I crumpled to the ground when he released me from his grip. On all fours, I looked up to hear him declare, in a calm, almost disinterested voice, that I was to join the invalid party and return to the Gite at Aremd. My trek finally appeared to be over...

Resigned to my fate, I watched as the remains of our trekking group headed up the valley towards the next campsite. They had not gone a hundred yards before two of their number made their way into the bushes by the side of the track...

In the belief that medical help would be waiting for us at Aremd, I crawled back to my tent, and with some sense of relief, packed my gear, donned my walking boots, and made my way to join the rest of our invalided group.

The Berber crewman Youssef had charged with ensuring our safe return to Aremd, motioned me towards one of the mules. Somehow, I climbed onto its back. Seated, I looked around to see someone else on the back of another mule. There being no more mules, the rest of the invalid party, whether they were fit enough or not, had to walk.

Perhaps two hours later, we reached the cola shack we had first stumbled upon three days ago.
As we stopped nearby, the owner of the shack ran outside to urge everyone to stay away from us. Whatever he told his customers, it had the required effect. No-one ventured to ask about our condition, or whether there was anything we needed. We must have looked thoroughly contagious. Leaving abruptly, we began our descent towards Aremd.

When we reached the impromptu 'men' and 'women' rocks we'd passed on our way up from Aremd, I turned to look once again at our bedraggled party. Something was amiss. Convinced that we had lost somebody, I tried to make our guide check our numbers. Despite my urgent mumblings, he ignored me and continued our descent. Perhaps he thought I was delirious. If I were, I would not have remembered what happened next...

When we arrived at the Gite, I slid off the mule and collapsed to the floor. Looking back up at our guide in the hope he would help me to my feet, I saw his extended hand, not with any desire to help me you understand, but in expectation of his tip. I could do no more than utter something not exactly sympathetic to his request and crawled towards the stairs.

I don't recall much more of that day other than entering a cool darkened room, collapsing onto one of the cushioned benches, and drawing my sleeping bag over me like a veil.

(DAY EIGHT ~ THE LOST DAY)

I woke to find it was dusk. Heaving myself upright, I stumbled down the stairs to the restroom. It was a relief to be back in civilisation again.

As I made my way back towards the stairs, I became vaguely aware of whispered voices and several pairs of eyes following me across the courtyard. Turning to see my colleague from the fool's errand at Tachedirt, I paused. Our eyes met knowingly. Perversely, my first thought was to ask him the time. He told me it was eight at night, but there was something more... I was not witnessing the setting sun of the same day we had arrived back, but the setting sun of a whole day later...

He continued by revealing that efforts to rouse me the previous night had failed. Attempts to wake me that morning had also failed. My timely appearance that evening had prevented the Gite owners calling a medical emergency; which, I deduced, also meant that we had not received the medical attention we so desperately needed.

I felt no emotion as I thanked him for telling me this, and crawled back up the stairs. I did not wake again until mid-afternoon the following day.

Apart from my brief foray to the toilet, and subsequent conversation, I had slept, or perhaps been in a coma, for forty-eight hours...

(DAY NINE ~ 'THE RESCUE')

That afternoon, I had enough strength to want to take in some sunshine. I was also in bad need of rehydration and a copious amount of electrolytes. I had to make do with bottled water...

Now more compos-mentis, I learned that the two colleagues we had left in the bushes near Oukaimeden, were still bedridden; one of whom was now thought to be critically ill. It had also not been my imagination, that we were indeed missing one of our fellow-sufferers; the one the cook had returned to find in Oukaimeden; his whereabouts, unknown. The last member of our group had left the Gite the previous morning, bound for Marrakech, but had no idea how he was going to get there...

Help finally arrived that evening in the form of another trekking party. Their leader, another Youssef, listened as we related the events of the last few days.

With our story told, we waited to see what would happen next. Perhaps not surprisingly, Youssef informed us that he had no way of contacting the rest of our group. What he could do was decisive.

Following a brief visit to our bedridden colleagues, he put in a call for a medical emergency. Returning to face us, he offered to make the necessary arrangements to get us back to Marrakech for medical assessment, or a flight home too if we wished.

I came close to accepting his offer, but out of perhaps foolish concern for the rest of our group, including the one we had lost, I elected to stay at the Gite.

Little more than thirty minutes later, our two bedridden colleagues departed for Marrakech, with the support of two medics, and half the village children, as they crossed the valley in front of the Gite, and boarded the helicopter waiting patiently on the other side.

In the middle of this drama, our missing colleague strolled unnoticed into the Gite. This was his story:

He had fallen so far adrift of our group during the evacuation from Tachedirt, that by the time he reached the cola shack, he had lost sight of us. With no idea which direction to take, he had blindly followed the path down the mountain, and in the process, completely missed the turning for Aremd. He finally arrived at another village he recognised as the place where we had alighted from the minibus on the first day. There, he had approached the first Gite he could find. Fortunately, the owners, recognising his distress, promptly invited him in and called a Doctor.

For the next two days, he had been confined to bed under Doctor's orders. Meanwhile, the owners set about contacting more than a dozen Gites in an attempt to find out where he should have been. It was only when someone in the village mentioned the disaster our trek had become, that they knew where to send him. They had, in fact, offered to drive him to Marrakech if he wanted to get a flight home. However, he, like the rest of us, viewed the Gite at Aremd as the place where any coordinated rescue would be based, an assumption he'd thought proven right when he spotted the helicopter.

After narrating his story, he wanted to know ours. As the disbelief spread across his face when told how long I had been comatose, that there was no medical support nor coordinated rescue taking place; he decided he'd had enough. We watched him leave that afternoon. I should have gone with him.

Our horror story had now also become common knowledge among the groups coming and going from the Gite. It was not one I wanted to revel in or narrate in any detail; suffice to state that one group heard about us shortly after joining their tour in Marrakech; a little over seventy miles away...

By late evening, only two of us remained from the invalided group that left the trek at Tachedirt. Summing up our situation, we realised that without communication, we had no idea where the rest of our group was. For all we knew, they could still be out on the trail somewhere, or on their way home too. If they had abandoned the trek, the thought crossed our minds that we might have been left stranded...

(DAY TEN ~ TWO-MAN SOJOURN)

The morning broke to the dilemma of what to do. Did we abandon the trek, or did we sit tight and hope Youssef, and the remainder of our group, would arrive according to plan two days from now? There was a third option, however, - We could attempt to meet them somewhere on the trail.

We discussed this with Youssef – he of the decisive action. He told us that our group would be aiming to reach the Neltner Refuge at the foot of Mount Toubkal. The Refuge, Youssef continued, lay some five thousand feet above us. It was not an easy trek, even for someone in good health, let alone those in our condition. Yet, if we were prepared to give it a go, he would organise a support team to get us there... and bring us back if we didn't. Perhaps it was the suggestion we could take some medical supplies with us that did it. Feeling as though we now had a purpose in life, we agreed to make an attempt to reach the Refuge.

Within the hour, Youssef had arranged for a muleteer to carry our backpacks and supplies.

As we prepared for our journey, I watched Youssef gather his group together, and set off ahead of us. I couldn't help but think we'd gotten the wrong Youssef to lead ours...

The urge to declare we were going outside and may be some time, *(Lawrence Oates ~ see 'Scott of the Antarctic')*, was overwhelming as we set off from the Gite. I sensed the Berber families and children who gathered to see us off probably thought we are either mad, wasting our time, or perhaps just British...

We made slow but steady progress along the river valley and up into the foothills of Mount. Toubkal; our muleteer all the while continually checking to see if we wished to stop.

After little more than an hour, we caught up with Youssef of the decisive action, and his group; something I did not expect to happen. As we beckoned to pass, I began to feel a fraud, despite what my stomach was telling me. Youssef came to our rescue with an explanation to his group that despite our crippled state, we had already spent more than a week living at high altitude. Thus, we had acclimatised to the conditions his group had only just begun to encounter. For a moment, I felt like 'Tough as Nails'; and wondered how he was getting on.

A little while later, we turned a corner to reveal a waterfall and a large white painted rock; we had reached Sidi Chamharouch, a Muslim sacred site, and one out of bounds to those of us, not of the Islamic faith. Out of bounds, it may have been, but not so, the less than sacred shops that surrounded it. Ignoring the sales pitches, we continued on the path towards the Neltner Refuge.

A few minutes later, we reached a small isolated shack. Suspended over the entrance was a large awning. The welcome shade it offered was enough to tempt us to stop.

Our muleteer, seeing this, invited us to sit on the traditional Berber white plastic chairs; as available from any DIY store or garden centre; while he went inside to summon the owner.

Duly summoned, the owner's first offer was a glass of Mint Tea. This, we gratefully accepted. Smiling, he disappeared into the shack, and moments later returned with a small tin teapot, which he waved in our direction. He then walked over to a lone standpipe, turned on the tap, and took a mouthful of water from it. Filling the teapot, he returned to the shack. It dawned on me that he was demonstrating that the water from the standpipe was fit to drink.

A few minutes passed before he reappeared and proceeded to empty the now boiling water from the teapot onto the ground in front of us. He had sterilised the teapot... On refilling it from the standpipe, he returned to the shack once more, all the while making sure we witnessed what took place.

He then returned with two glasses and placed them ceremoniously on the table in front of us. Nodding our thanks, he upped the ante by producing a large rock crystal from one of the shelves that adorned the shack. We both looked at it in respectful appreciation but declined to barter. Undeterred, he disappeared into the shack only to return with another rock. This, he held as close to my face as I think he dared, and with a flourish, deftly parted its two halves. The effect was stunning... so was the quality of the crystal inside the geode. I had to have it.

This was my first attempt at bartering Moroccan style, but following sound advice from my colleague, I halved the Berber's asking price and then worked towards somewhere in the middle.

With the deal completed somewhat nearer his middle than mine, he ran back into the shack, retrieved the now boiling teapot, and poured its contents from an extravagant height into our glasses.

It was the best mint tea I'd tasted since arriving in Morocco. What was more, with a little help from our guide, I obtained details of the ingredients from our host. The secret to making Moroccan mint tea was now mine, a secret far more valuable to me than the most priceless of geodes...

A few minutes later, Youssef of the decisive action appeared once more with his group. As they passed by, we raised our glasses in salute and received looks suggesting homage from the breathless individuals, now panting hard behind him. For the first time since Marrakech, a feeling of being content settled in my soul; even my stomach had finally stopped cramping.

Rested, we thanked our host for the tea, and said our farewells, noting he appeared to be packing for a Tax Haven; and pressed onward and upward towards the Neltner Refuge.

We eventually spotted the Refuge just after passing the snowline. Its appearance among the patchwork snow and mountain scree gave it a mirage-like quality in the desolation that surrounded us.

As we neared the Refuge, I noted a campsite on the other side of the valley. Fearing the worst, I crossed over to inquire. Alas, it was our campsite; and perched far enough away from the comfort of the Refuge, to suggest we had all contracted the Black Death. What was worse, if we were hoping for a welcome, we didn't get it. The place was empty save for a few Berbers, who did no more than stare at us.

I walked back across the valley to reluctantly confirm the camp was ours. On taking my backpack from our benevolent guide, I offered him a sizeable tip, the first I'd given with genuine appreciation on the trek. He refused. From what we could understand, Youssef (of the decisive action), had already arranged a handsome payment if he delivered us safely. We thanked him as best we could, and crossed back over to our campsite.

Dumping my kit in one of the tents, I made my way up to the Refuge. For the first time in four days, I was hungry. I also had no intention whatsoever of using the latrine tent at our campsite.

To my relief, the Refuge had clean toilets, and, even better, a room doubling as a small shop. Armed with a bag of crisps, several bottles of cola and bars of chocolate, I returned to the campsite to take up a Buddhist position outside my tent, and break open one of the bottles of cola. Whatever the sugar content of this stuff, it is good for settling the stomach; mine was only too happy to receive it.

What remained of the mountain goat party duly arrived a couple of hours later. Yet, despite our warm greeting, the medical supplies, and words expressing concern for their wellbeing, there was little or no response from any of them.

I cannot define the almost uncontrollable rage that welled up inside me at that moment. It may have been aimed at nobody in particular, or perhaps it was aimed at everybody in particular, I don't know. Regrettably, I knew that I could not afford to make my feelings known, for even if I had left the trek at that very moment, I would never have reach Aremd, or preferably, Imlil, before night set in. Thus, I would have to sit out the consequences of my words. I bit my lip and stormed back to my tent.

Over the meal of gristle and dubious vegetables that evening, I related the story of the invalid party to 'Tough as Nails'. In reply, I learned of filthy Gites, dangerous climbs, and the same rampant dysentery we had experienced. At least two of their party had also been tied to the back of mules at some point... I felt sure that 'Tough as Nails' must have been suffering too, but somehow suspected he had lived through worse... if that was at all possible...

Taking my second slice of melon, I turned my attention to Youssef, *(he NOT of the decisive action,)* to hear the announcement that tomorrow, the group would climb the last three thousand feet to the top of Mount Toubkal... However, there was a twist... After reaching the summit, our return route would involve a steep descent down the other side of the mountain. This, he continued, would be too technical for some, and that, apparently, included me...

Incensed, I challenged him as to why I could not return from the summit, via the same well-marked route up which we would reach it. Youssef looked at me impassively; the same impassive stare I had seen several times before. His answer was still "No". I could have punched him. I may have been here before, but last time our guide had earned my respect; Youssef, on the other hand, had not earned a grain of it ...

With the announcement made, the chosen few retired to their tents for the night. I returned to sit outside my tent and watch the light fade from the mountains as the Milky Way carved the sky in two above them.

After thanking Mother Earth for her consolation prize, I crawled into my Sleeping Bag and fell fast asleep.

(DAY ELEVEN ~ BREAKING THE RULES)

I woke to an early breakfast and wished those bound for the summit a gracious "good luck" as they left. They said nothing in reply.

For a while, I didn't really know what to do with myself. Ahead of me lay the choice of making my own way back down the mountain, or spending a miserable day waiting for the others to return. However, just as there had been at Aremd, there was a third option, an almost daring one at that...

Waiting until Youssef had led his group over the ridge behind our campsite, I grabbed my backpack and made for the Refuge where the main path to the summit began. Sure enough, other groups were also heading for the summit too that day. Thus, as the first of them set off, I followed at a discreet distance, all the while doing my best to suggest I was making my own way there.

In the end, it was not a particularly challenging climb. The well-trodden path was clearly visible among the barren landscape, and with almost two weeks of living at high altitude, I ploughed my lonely furrow with relative ease. In fact, I had to make frequent stops for fear of overtaking those I was following. In this barren landscape, that would have risked exposing me to the very group I needed to avoid, and who I could still see some way ahead of us.

When those I'd followed reached the summit, I stopped a respectable distance away while they took their photographs. Then, as they left, I made my own way to the summit.

For reasons unknown, the photograph I took of the summit never came out. For that, I blame the rusty pyramid that sits atop Mount Toubkal... either that or the mountain had frowned upon my perhaps foolhardy lone venture.
Nevertheless, after a quick three-sixty degree scan of the surrounding mountains, and a respectful 'Thank you' to the spirits, I hurried back down, returning to the campsite with time to spare before the mountain goats returned.
When they arrived, I said nothing of my day and asked nothing of theirs. The illusion was complete, even if I felt 'Tough as Nails' knew better...

I retired to my tent that night in the knowledge that tomorrow we were heading back to Aremd, Marrakech, and finally, home. With my stomach now deteriorating once more, my desire to get the trek over and done with, could not have been more apparent.

(DAY TWELVE ~ EVER DOWNWARD)

I could not wait to break camp that morning, and had long packed everything ready for the descent before anyone else was awake.

Following our last camp breakfast, there was to be a group photo. Considering my general alienation, I was deeply reluctant to join in but did so at Youssef's insistent request. Standing half-hidden on the edge of the shot; I had no desire to infer to Youssef's paymasters that the trek had been anything but a complete disaster. The evil cynic within me also suspected Youssef had to send the photo to prove we were still alive at some point...

Saying goodbye to the Berbers, we crossed the stream to join the main path back to Aremd. Stopping to take one last look back at the summit of Mount Toubkal, and our campsite beneath it, I then turned to make my way down the mountain, some distance behind the others.

At Sidi Chamharouch, Youssef invited us to stop and spend as much cash as possible.

Wandering among the melee of fleecing shops, looking for something unique to take home proved hopeless. Almost everything I saw was fit only for gullible tourists; a title I had long since shed...

I continued to gaze around with little interest until my eyes rested on an unassuming shop, sandwiched between two stores akin to the Berber equivalent of supermarkets. I wandered over to take a closer look. Nobody else was in the shop. I walked in.

Half-hidden at the back of it was a range of jewellery suggesting there were people in Morocco, capable of producing something requiring skills beyond that of welding Ring-pulls. My interest rose.

It is an experience to watch a Moroccan shop-owner react to the presence of someone intent on spending good money in his shop. In this case, the money belonged to an incontinent Englishman who had asked to see something "special".

The word 'special' is not a Moroccan or even Berber word either, but it is one they fully understand. As the shop-owners' smile broadened to reveal teeth subjected to a lifetime of heavily sweetened mint tea consumption, he gestured me to sit down. Mystified, I looked around to see which seat he was referring to. I almost didn't see it, for it was low enough that when I finally sat on it, I was in danger of losing as many teeth as he had; not through mint tea abuse, but by knocking them out with my knees...

Seated next to a table of equal stature, the owner shuffled around it to sit opposite me, and from beneath a nearby piece of cloth, produce an ornate chest far larger than was fit for a tiny shop in a village too small to appear on any map. Placing the chest on the table, and with a flex of the fingers as though about to conjure a rabbit from a hat, he opened it. The chest contained treasures that would not have been out of place in Tortuga.

Almost immediately, I spotted a bright silver necklace of lapis lazuli and turquoise. On pointing to it, he handed it to me for closer inspection. Noting the hallmark, and being satisfied with its authenticity, I pitched at half his opening price.

He was quick to learn that I'd been in Morocco long enough to have mastered the complex rules of bartering with a Berber. Thus, I rapidly pinned him to the usual seventy-five per cent nearer what he asked for than what I wanted to pay...

Transaction complete, he presented the necklace in a beautifully carved, circular-shaped, Burr-walnut box. It was probably included in the price, even if my delusion hoped it was in gratitude for the down payment on a Lear jet I'd just given him.

From here on down to Aremd, I cared for nowt and continued to trudge along at my own pace, lost in my own thoughts. I lagged far enough behind that it forced Youssef to stop the rest of the group and wait for me. This, I relished in, even though it meant that when I eventually caught up, there would be no point sitting down, because the moment my arse touched the ground, I knew they would get up and wander off again. Nevertheless, ten minutes after we arrived at the Gite, I was back in the restroom suffering from a relapse.

Avoiding everyone, I crawled upstairs once more to die quietly in one of the Gite's darkened rooms; my body no longer had any desire to retain organs, no matter how vital they were to my survival.

A few hours later, Youssef demonstrated the existence of a heart by making a personal visit to my tomb; either that, or he was genuinely concerned about the tip he expected to receive at the end of the trek...

Ignoring his urging that I needed to eat something, I continued to lay there, eyes closed. However valid his words were, I could no longer face anything, anything at all. Undaunted, he disappeared only to return minutes later with something he said would help cure my stomach.

He was carrying two small bowls. One contained boiled rice water, the other, a blend of rice, a substantial amount of cumin powder, and something else I knew not what. Reluctantly, I worked my way through perhaps a couple of mouthfuls of the rice and then sipped a little of the rice water.

What I remember most about that meal, was the latent fire in my stomach and witnessing my fingertips sweat...

Whatever was in that rice, worked, at least temporarily; for two hours later, I felt well enough to make my way downstairs, and join the others for our last meal in the mountains.

Walking into the dining room almost unnoticed, I saw the remaining member of our Tachedirt leper colony, sat quietly, some distance away from the rest of the group. Fittingly, I walked over to join him with my four tablespoons of rice and glass of mint tea.

I spent our last evening at Aremd sitting on the balcony of the Gite, watching the sun set over Mount Toubkal. By the time I headed upstairs for my last night in the mountain air, the stars had also begun to fall asleep...

(DAY THIRTEEN ~ FALLING OFF THE MARRAKECH EXPRESS)

At breakfast, Youssef informed me that he had arranged for a jeep to take me to Imlil, where I would meet the rest of the group for the bus ride back to Marrakesh. It was, perhaps a nice gesture, but something less than an hour's walk would not have been beyond me that morning, especially after all that I had been through.

When I arrived at Imlil, I didn't bother to go looking for our group; I figured in this small village we would bump into each other soon enough. I can't say I really cared much whether I found them or not anyhow; thus, I walked into the nearest shop with little concern...

Mohammed was a smiling, youthful, and highly seasoned haggler. In an enterprising move, he convinced me that if I bought something from his shop, he would let me into a big secret. Euphoria at going home left me vulnerable to his tactic, and I fell for it. In truth, it didn't take long to find what I was looking for anyhow; a small but exquisite rug, one that had been hand-made by a local Berber family, rather than some anonymous sweatshop in China.

If you are unfamiliar with Morocco, let me tell you that it is as impossible to leave Morocco without buying a rug or carpet, as it is to visit England and not try 'Fish n' Chips'... thus, I had to buy it.

As I parted with most of my remaining Dirhams, Mohammed revealed the big secret... England had won a game in the World Cup... a global event I had completely forgotten about for the last two weeks.

Perhaps in celebration of our victory, but more likely in salute of Mohammed's dazzling salesmanship, I added a pair of Babouches, *(Moroccan slippers,)* to my rug.

The journey to Marrakesh was an uneventful one, and soon enough, we arrived at our hotel, where Youssef gave me a key to my own room.

That afternoon I proceeded to do to the bathroom what most guests, confident of never returning to a hotel, always do. Satisfied with the carnage, I trolled down to the reception area to join the rest of the group for the official 'end of trek' meal.

When we arrived at the restaurant, I was hungry enough to choose a lamb tagine from the menu, a dish I didn't expect to have to wait almost two weeks before trying. Naturally, it was the best food, perhaps the only real food, I ate all week...

As the waiters cleared the table, Youssef surprised us all by producing a handful of crystals from his pocket. With some ceremony, he began to pass them out, meticulous in who each piece was for. I received a small piece of quartz from the Sahara desert. It was for my son, he said.

I have never been quite sure what this act of Youssef's was all about; I can only assume, it, like the invitation to lead the group home after dislocating my knee, had a symbolic meaning. Nevertheless, once everyone had received his or her gift,

Youssef stood up to announce that we would see him only one more time; at the airport. It was his job to ensure our safe departure. That was it. Tonight then, was his official farewell. Reluctantly, I contributed the going rate to his tip; a decision I still regret. Moments later, he slipped into the night and was gone.

(DAY FOURTEEN ~ MY BLUE HEAVEN)

Day Fourteen woke with no Youssef; a Mohammed had replaced him. It was his job to lead us on a guided tour of Marrakech.

For the next two hours, we were led into every shop he had an arranged commission with. These included somewhere I tried on a traditional Djellaba, and a shop selling cannabis - in several flavours and forms. I came dangerously close to buying the candles...

Mohammed also took us to visit a traditional Moroccan apothecary, one, where, on having been given a thorough examination, they suggested I needed a massage to ease my aches and pains. I'm a sucker for a good massage, but rather wished they'd spotted that most of my organs had fallen out of my arse...

Just as we were about to leave, the thought crossed my mind to ask if they had something for my son's eczema, a condition that had plagued him since birth. Sure enough, they handed me a tiny, almost insignificant pot of cream. So small was this pot that for a moment I thought it was a sample. For the price, it should have contained gold...

(As an aside, it did contain gold... After using it sparingly on my son' eczema for two weeks as instructed, he woke up one morning with not a patch of eczema on him. It had only taken sixteen years to find something that worked. His eczema never returned... I only wish I'd made a note of the name of the apothecary, for I owe them the sincerest thanks of a grateful parent.)

Mohammed ended the tour with the culture shock of Djemma el Fna Square. Wandering among the melee of people, I stopped to watch one of three snake charmers in action. Curious as to why this one, in particular, had drawn such a large crowd, I asked Mohammed for an explanation. He casually replied that in the middle of yesterday's show, the snake had bitten the charmer...

Being somewhat sceptical, I suggested the snake's venom sacks had been removed; either that or this was a different snake. Mohammed, however, assured me this was not the case. He claimed that the snake charmer was from the poor part of the city, and would not have been able to pay someone to remove the venom sacs.

Apparently, Cobras are also rather expensive to replace... With the snake charmer's performance now taking on a whole new air of authenticity, I watched, fascinated, if with a slightly ghoulish desire for a repeat performance...

As the show finished, I wanted to put a few Dirham's in the charmer's bowl, but on calculating the distance between the Cobra's basket, and the bowl, regrettably decided against it...

After fending off a mob of Henna ladies intent on turning me completely brown, I went on to witness a 'live' public, tooth extraction, one acted out with no anaesthetic whatsoever...

Now completely fazed, I ventured to turn my attention to something more mundane... a display of Belly-dancing... Noting the similarity of movement between the woman and the cobra I had just witnessed, I wondered if the woman would bite me if I moved to place some Dirhams in her begging bowl too...

After a long and lazy meal with the rest of the group, I made my way through the square and back to the hotel.

That afternoon brought solitude without the need for my fellow trekkers to provide it. Thus, I decided to head for something I'd read about before signing up for the trip; Jardin Majorelle.

The garden, hidden deep among the sprawling run-down tower block, and rubble-infested suburb that lay behind our hotel, had no signpost by which to find it. When I eventually did find it, I understood why. This was a place of peace and tranquillity; one I suspect the locals would prefer to have kept private, despite the tourist leaflets recommending otherwise.

Paying the pittance of an entrance fee, I walked through the unassuming gate, and into a haven of exotic greenery and brilliant blues.

Jardin Majorelle was created by French painter, Jacques Majorelle. It took him fifty years to develop the two-acre garden, apparently. Unfortunately, after divorcing his wife, the house and garden were sold off and subsequently fell into ruin. Cue the arrival of one Yves Saint-Laurent...

Thus, what the visitor sees today is a meticulous restoration of Majorelle's garden; the cubist designed house though is original and open to the public. Majorelle's legacy is not his paintings, however, nor perhaps is it his garden. It is the exquisite blue paint colour he created and later patented, and which had been liberally applied to everything inanimate in the garden, including the house.

Attracted by the stunning richness of the colour, I had to find out if one could buy it. I rather fancied painting the window frames of my miserable home back in England with it. Much to my chagrin, I discovered it would also be cheaper to build a new home than paint it with 'Majorelle blue'...

For all the stunning scenery of the Atlas mountains, 'Jardin Majorelle' was all I really needed to see of Morocco, and it was something I could have seen without risking the complete destruction of my intestines. Sighing, I rose to make my exit, pausing only to read that Yves Saint-Laurent's last wish, was to have his ashes scattered in the garden. I could understand why...

That night, the reality of this miserable tour came sharply back into focus. Sitting alone in the featureless, people-less, void that sufficed as the hotel's restaurant, the food I ordered arrived as something reheated from the previous night. It wasn't even hot.

With my anger and frustration fully ignited, I exploded with such a tirade of abuse towards the waiter, that it left him trembling. Having narrated the complete unexpurgated version of the hell I had endured during the last ten days, I closed my eyes, sighed, and with a feeble wave of my hand, bade the waiter to remove the plate from under my nose. He stooped to pick it up in a manner fearful that I was going to behead him, and hurried back to the kitchen.

For perhaps five minutes, I sat there not knowing quite what to do next. To my surprise, the waiter returned with an alternative dish... one freshly produced from the freezer. After barely a mouthful of something that tasted like cardboard, I threw down the knife and fork, rose from the table, and stormed back to my room. The waiter had perhaps been trying to appease me, but, in my book at least, Morocco had already done far too much damage to warrant clemency...

In desperation, I fired up the television to discover the two channels available, were filled only with unintelligible foreign nonsense. Switching it off, I hurled the remote control across the room and opened the window to listen to the vitality coming from Djemma el Fna square. For a moment, I was tempted to make the two hundred yard journey across the road to take another look, but the reality was that I could no longer bring myself to venture out; I had simply become too tired of Morocco.

Sighing, I closed the window, packed and re-packed my kit, showered one last time, and, feeling guilty for those who have to clean hotel rooms, made an effort to tidy up the carnage I had created in mine, before retiring to an early night.

(DAY FIFTEEN ~ FREEDOM)

After dumping my backpack in the lobby, I took breakfast in isolation, and less than an hour later, with our minibus now groaning from the weight of bargain-burdened luggage, spent my time staring out of the window as we hurtled towards the airport. If this was how it felt to be released from prison, I understood the emotion entirely.

After an interminable wait to check in, I said my courteous goodbyes to the apparition of Youssef and headed through security for the flight home.

I don't recall anything of the time I spent in the Departure lounge. I don't think I spoke a word to anyone from our group; I don't even remember anything of the flight home for that matter. What I do remember though, is approaching the Customs checkpoint at Heathrow airport, and reading signs informing everybody what he or she could and could not bring into England from Morocco. There were also some equally large signs defining the penalties for doing so.

Without stopping to consider that what I'd brought home might bend or possibly break some of those limits, I made for the exit... Marrakech 'express' or not, I no longer cared for the consequences.

To my surprise, as I scuffed my way past the sniffer dogs, and customs officers... all the while toting the world's most obvious roll of carpet over my shoulder, which, as everybody knows, contained things it perhaps should not have... nobody stopped me.

I guess I must have looked like I'd contracted the Ebola virus after all...

(EPILOGUE)

The human brain has a fantastic ability to blank out horror, and the human body an extraordinary ability to recover from trauma; yet the scars both physically and mentally from this trek will remain with me for the rest of my life.

These were the words of my Doctor after he saw the results of a catalogue of tests he'd ordered, following my return from Morocco. I also discovered I'd lost twenty-eight pounds in just two weeks...

So, I close this adventure by saying this...

While some people claim 'time heals', it indeed does not. My right knee still twinges occasionally to remind me of that fall on the acclimatisation walk, and I remain incredibly wary of any food or drink, served that I have not prepared myself.

When all said and done then, I still have no desire whatsoever to set foot on Moroccan soil ever again, even if I am addicted to their mint tea...

… ADVENTURES OF A MIDDLE-AGED FART

REELING IN THE BILGES

Adventure, I had now learned, was not always something you can plan; sometimes, the most innocuous comment can provide the fait accompli that propels you into one. Being on a ship though is a fait accompli I will do everything to avoid, for despite being born on an island, I cannot swim. I can also get seasick rowing a canoe across a village duck pond. Thus, the thought of being on a ferry crossing the open sea strikes such terror that I will do anything I can to avoid it, even if that means parting with twice as much money to fly across instead. Knowing this, it might come as a surprise to learn, and believe me when I say it was a hell of a shock to me, that I once volunteered to join the crew of a wooden schooner, on a voyage across one of the world's most treacherous stretches of water... the Bay of Biscay. When I think back, that adventure bug must have bitten me pretty badly to agree to do it... I might have been delirious at the time...

(FOOLISH THOUGHTS)

For some years before volunteering, I had watched the slow but meticulous restoration of a beautiful old schooner on the quayside of my adopted hometown. When the day finally arrived for the Schooner's re-dedication, I had to be there for the event. When she finally set sail on her maiden voyage, I had to witness that too. Thus, it's perhaps understandable that I would harbour a wish to spend just a little time on board; not enough time to get seasick mind you... just a little trip down the estuary, or maybe a short cruise along the coast would suffice. I would pay for the privilege, of course, or perhaps work my passage as a deckhand... Bear this last remark in mind as you read on...

As luck would have it, the owner of the schooner was a lifelong friend of my employer, a connection that brought me into regular contact with him. Thus, there were frequent opportunities to make my plea to go on that voyage. The reply was always a non-committal, "maybe"... It wasn't a 'No', but it wasn't exactly a 'yes' either. On reflection, if I'd known the consequence of making those pleas, I would never have opened my mouth...

(THE CALL)

More than two years had passed since the ship's re-dedication. I had almost forgotten my blithe request to sail on her when the phone rang, and a voice reminded me...

"Do you still want to sail on the ship?" it inquired.

"Errr Yes" I hesitated, as my brain brought 'the ship' sharply back into focus.

"Good! Can you get some time off?"

"Errr I think so."

"Good. Pack your bags and report to the Captain when you arrive."

" Errr when do I arrive?"

" As soon as you can."

'As soon as you can' turned out to mean I had to be wherever the ship was, in just four days. Naturally, I assumed the ship was somewhere up the coast, perhaps the city of Bristol, just a day or so sailing away, but it seemed prudent to check...

"Errr; one question... Where is she?"

"Bilbao. Good luck."

After which, the familiar 'click' told me he'd hung up.

My mouth fell open as the news sunk in. 'Bilbao'? Where the hell was Bilbao? It sounded foreign. My boss had an answer.

"Spain. It's on the north coast. Good luck."

Being on the north coast of Spain meant that the city of Bilbao faced out onto the notorious Bay of Biscay, graveyard of many a ship, and home of some famously violent storms, something I had no wish to encounter.

As the nerves set in, I tried to kid myself that the ship would not take the direct route across the Bay on her way back to her home port, or even put to sea if there was a threat of bad weather. Perhaps our route home then would be along the French coast, skirting the worst excesses of the Bay... I hoped so. The idea of visiting Biarritz *(ooh-la-la)*, Bordeaux *(wine country)*, Rochelle *(history)*, and some of those lovely little islands around the Brittany coast, sounded idyllic. The fact that the ship was in Spain, also presented an opportunity to see a bit more of a country than the seventy minutes of airport lounge I had accumulated so far.

Convincing myself that these were all bonus points and that everything would work out just fine, I made ready to become a sailor...

(DAY ONE – DO YOU SPEAK BASQUE?)

Four days later, I duly arrived at Bilbao airport... which was nowhere near Bilbao. I needed a Taxi.

Wandering out of the airport terminal, I found the usual fleet of eager people-fleecers waiting patiently for a victim and made towards the first taxi in the line.

"I need to get to the Maritime Museum, please."

The reply was something unintelligible. Speaking more slowly in the assumption the taxi driver didn't understand my poor Spanish; I tried again.

(Nothing)

Motioning me to wait, he climbed out of the taxi and wandered over to the driver of the taxi behind us. Moments later, the two drivers returned and gestured in a way I assumed meant to repeat myself. This time, I elaborated somewhat...

"I'm joining a ship at the Guggenheim Museum."

(Nothing)

I gave the name of the ship and showed them a picture of it on my phone.

(Nothing)

At this point, we had a standoff. I had no idea where to go, and the taxi drivers had no idea where I had to go either.

Eventually, another taxi pulled up to unload its suitably fleeced passenger. As the driver jumped out, the two I had tried to communicate with, called him over, leaving his passenger to haul their luggage out of the taxi.

After a brief conference, the newly arrived driver encouraged me to repeat myself once more. This time I embellished my request with a few exaggerated sailing motions with my hands, and again showed him the picture on my phone.

A smile spread slowly across his face. He said something as incomprehensible as the rest, but the one word I could pick out was 'Guggenheim'. Recognising this as the location of the Maritime Museum, I repeated 'Guggenheim', and nodded furiously, pointing once more to the image on my phone. With this, the three drivers resumed their conference.

Following an impromptu election; the driver who had just arrived, picked up my kitbag and encouraged me to follow him to his taxi. I began to wonder if the rest of the taxi drivers were on some sort of European Union subsidy, and he wasn't, and therefore had to work for a living...

As we hurtled out of the airport, he explained to me in monosyllabic terms that I was in "Euskadi" - Basque country. Here, almost nobody spoke Spanish, only Basque, a language obscure in origin, and understood by only a few people outside the region. I wasn't one of them, but at least he knew of 'a' ship. I hoped the one he knew was the one I was trying to reach. It was.

Pulling up by the entrance to the Maritime Museum, I spotted the tall masts of a familiar Schooner. Somewhat relieved, I proffered a sizeable tip to my democratically elected driver and headed down to the quayside.

Not seeing anyone on board, I walked up the gangplank of the schooner, stepped onto the deck, and announced my arrival. Moments later, the First Mate appeared from below deck. Introducing myself, I offered a handshake. As he looked me up and down, I think he realised pretty quickly that I didn't do this sailing thing that often... It would not be long before he found out that I didn't do this sailing thing, ever. I followed him below deck.

At the foot of the stairs, I noted the comfort of the cabin at the stern of the ship; regrettably, that was not to be mine; while a door marked 'Captain' was definitely out of bounds too.

As the tour continued, 'Heads' I learned, were toilets, and the kitchen, a place I should refer to as the 'Galley'.

The First Mate then showed me the crew's quarters tucked under the Bow. Peering in at them, I quickly realised I would never fit into such a cramped space. Relieved to learn that I would be sleeping elsewhere, we returned to the main hold where I discovered 'elsewhere' was on top of the rope and tackle storage boxes that skirted the edge of the main hold... a place that also served as the main living area.

Tour over, it was time to 'stow' my kitbag by my makeshift bunk and report for duty.

I had no idea what I was supposed to do onboard, for I knew nothing about sailing... and definitely nothing whatsoever about crewing a three hundred ton Schooner across the Bay of Biscay. It took a tall, weatherworn member of the crew to give me a clue...

"What do you know about ropes?" he asked.

I paused and cast my mind back to the days when I used to build plastic model kits of old sailing ships. Slowly, I recalled for his benefit that I knew the difference between 'running' and 'standing' rigging, that I knew what a 'Capstan' was, that I could correctly name the three masts, that the long pointy thing sticking out the front was the Bowsprit, and that the triangular sails just behind it were 'Jibs'. I guessed correctly which side was Port and which was Starboard, and that the helm; the wheel I could see in front of me, steered the ship. I think he expected something more advanced than that...

Leading me up towards the Bowsprit, he traced the rope from one of the jibs to where it tied off at a Belay pin. He then untied it and handed the rope to me.

"Raise the Jib, and tie off."

Pulling on the rope, I watched the small triangular sail rise swiftly. To make it as taut as I could, I heaved until I could strain no more, and proceeded to wrap the rope around the pin in the figure of eight I had remembered from my modelling days. Stepping back, I waited for the inspection.

Reaching for the rope between the jib and the Belay pin, he wiggled it. It was a lot more slack than I would have expected.

"Bit slack... needs to be taut," was all the assessment I got.

I pursed my lips in disappointment. I had damn near pulled my arms out of their sockets while trying to keep the rope taut as I tied it off. If I needed more strength for this adventure, I didn't have it.

Without a word, he demonstrated how to make the rope taut by leaning back on it as he pulled the rope around the Belay pin. After smartly tying it off, he shook the rigging to show me what he meant by 'taut', then undid the rope, and handed it back to me. I took it submissively; I had been watching closely. I had to get it right; failure felt like a flight home before we'd even cast off.

Making doubly sure I'd got it right the second time, I shook the rope in front of him. It didn't seem to move as much as it had the first time. Satisfied with my efforts, I stood back for another inspection; tucking my hands behind me to hide the fact that they were already sore from the coarseness of the rope, something I dare not admit to.

My trainer didn't touch the rope, nor inspect the way I'd tied it around the pin. He had seen enough. A brief nod signified I had passed my first test.

The lesson continued...

"There are four Jibs... Stay, Inner, Outer, and Fly." As he spoke, he shook each rope and pointed to where it tied off. "When we raise sail, this is your station. Learn each Jib until you can raise and lower them, blindfolded. You need to be a lot quicker too."

As he walked off, leaving me to play with my newfound expertise, he paused.

"One last thing... never put your hand here when working the ropes, especially if it's blowing a gale."

He grabbed a rope and demonstrated the grip I'd used during my first attempt to tie the Jib off. Then, taking his hand out just in time, he pulled the rope violently. I heard the 'snap' as it pulled tight around the pin, and winced. I could visualise my hand wrapped around the pin with the rope crushing my fingers. That would hurt. He looked at me. I'd got the message, but his reinforcement removed all doubt...

"If you forget, say goodbye to your fingers..."

I spent the next hour raising and lowering the Jibs. I knew what I was doing pretty quickly, but somehow felt I had to keep practising, the watchful gaze of my trainer convinced me he was going to produce a blindfold at some point...

That evening passed in quiet reflection. I'd met the Captain and crew but already felt sure this close-knit group of seasoned crewmen, had labelled me as the Jonah aboard ship. I had much to learn, and much to prove.

I finally lay down on my makeshift bunkbed, closed my eyes, and visualised, raising and lowering those jibs repeatedly until I fell asleep.

(DAY TWO – SHORE LEAVE)

I woke to the smell of English Bacon and hurried to my morning ablutions. I was hungry. As we sat down to eat, the Captain joined us. He said only two things to the attentive audience...

"Shore leave today but make sure you return by two o'clock. We are open to the public this afternoon." He added... "There is a gale warning for the Bay (*of Biscay.*) We can't wait till it blows over else the tides will be wrong for getting into home port. So, we will run before it. We sail at ten o'clock tomorrow morning."

Statements over, he rose from the table and retired to his cabin.

The mood changed; a sense of preparation permeated the ship. Suddenly I felt nervous. Going to sea was one thing, but trying to outrun a storm was an adventure I had hoped to avoid.

Having seen nothing of Bilbao, I wanted to go ashore and have a look around before we sailed. At the very least, I hoped to take a few photographs and perhaps pick up a souvenir. I didn't dare walk off the ship without permission though, and so, approached the First Mate, who, without looking up from what he was doing, told me to be back by Noon. That was that. The ship may not have been open to the public until two that afternoon, but I still had more training to undergo. I needed no further instruction.

Grabbing my camera, I headed off along the canal towards the Guggenheim museum and arrived in time to witness the early morning light play golds, purples, and every shade in between, upon the Museum's titanium exterior.

With it being far too early for the museum to be open, I turned around and headed back past the ship, towards the heart of Bilbao, and soon arrived at what I took to be the city centre.

On one side of the river, lay the hustle and bustle of a hot and dusty shopping precinct. But it could have been any shopping precinct, anywhere in the world. Thus, I ignored it, and crossed the river to venture into the narrow streets, and faded charm of what I took to be the city's old quarters.

And yet, as I wandered among its dark alleyways, a feeling of distrust permeated the atmosphere. When peering into shops, I saw only expressionless faces stare back at me. Where I might have sat down for a coffee, I saw only e-Coli written on the menu, or perhaps it was something else... Being written in the Basque language, I didn't have a hope of ever knowing how to order a coffee, even if I really wanted one.

For all the charm of its narrow streets, the old town felt threatening... Was that a bloodstain by that doorway? Why did that man turn around and start following me...? I soon gave up on my souvenir hunting and, disappointed, headed back to the ship. My Spanish adventures now amounted to little more than four hours, despite having visited the country three times...

Returning along the opposite bank of the river, I noted the high-rise tenement blocks, derelict buildings, and industrial wastelands that littered this part of the city. I would later discover those tower blocks were the homes of the native Basque people; the more affluent parts of their city were now occupied by the Spanish...

A little further along the riverbank, I passed a billboard advertising a Will Smith film. Somehow, the translation "Yo Robot!" didn't offer the same foreboding as Asimov's masterpiece...

With nothing better to do, I boarded the ship and reported for training an hour early.

My lesson that morning could not have been more mundane, yet, as was drummed into me, more important.

There are a lot of ropes on a sailing ship, and there can be a lot of slack in those ropes. Coils of the stuff lay everywhere. My job was simple... walk around the ship and tidy them up.

My tall, weatherworn trainer carefully demonstrated the task. As was becoming the norm, he promptly undid his work and dropped it all over the deck for me to repeat the process.

Picking up the rope, I soon learned that the art of coiling a ship's rope was not dissimilar from dealing with a garden hosepipe; the rope would only coil or lay easily in one direction. Thus, by not forcing it to do something it didn't want to, I soon mastered the art. Satisfied that I could be left to continue the task unsupervised, my trainer disappeared below.

I was still diligently coiling the ropes when the visitors started to arrive. Not being delegated a role, I decided my best course of action was to carry on doing what I was doing. Nobody paid me much attention anyhow. I wasn't wearing anything to identify me with the ship, so I guess, to most, I was just someone working their passage... ironically, precisely what I hoped for.

That night the crew ventured into the high-rise tower blocks I'd passed earlier. I tagged along. They knew where they were going among the potential crime scenes, but as I was to learn, the ship's emblem on their clothing assured them of a passport to safety. Providing I assumed a position suggesting I was one of the crew, I felt sure I would make it back to the ship in one piece...

Eventually, we walked into a crowded bar where I offered to buy a round of drinks. Perhaps I saw it as an opportunity to address the crew and tell them I'd do my very best. It all sounded a bit pointless really because I didn't have a clue what my 'very best' would amount to...

Nonetheless, I approached the bar, and in my best Spanish; entirely the wrong language for our location, ordered the beers. I hoped the woman behind the bar would understand me, and not call out for someone to knife me instead. She didn't call out; she understood me perfectly... She was English...

(DAY THREE – CAST OFF)

Something stirred inside. Was it fear or excitement? I had no idea, but the morning was full of it. The sense of urgency among the crew as they checked and double-checked the ship from stem to stern was palpable too. Somewhere in the middle of all this, I made myself look busy. Nobody asked me to do anything; I just didn't want to stand out any more than I already did.

Ten o'clock arrived, and with a small group watching us from the quayside, we cast off, and slowly puttered our way towards the open sea.

As we passed through the towns that crowded the riverbanks, people gathered to bid us farewell; their spontaneous applause providing a sense of euphoria, that gradually ousted my fears of what might lie ahead. I may not have looked the part to the crew, but to the public, my position close to the Bowsprit, perhaps made them believe I was. Suitably encouraged, I picked up a coil of rope as though a film prop, and tidied it up... for the third time that morning.

We finally broke free of the river and sailed into the main harbour.

At this point, the Captain called me to the stern of the ship. Stood next to him was my trainer. This was no 'group hug' moment, just time to receive a simple instruction:

"You two will share a Watch. "We will follow the traditional Merchant Watch pattern."

I nodded, not entirely understanding what he had just said, but daring not to ask.

My trainer and now to be long-suffering 'partner' on this 'Watch Pattern', quietly made his way to the Bowsprit, and began to peer out at the mayhem of yachts and powerboats running suicidal circles around us. Not knowing quite what I was supposed to do, I remained by the Captain. I figured he would tell me at some point what that was. I hoped so, I didn't have any clues of my own...

As we left the harbour and made our way out into the open sea, the flotilla thinned and finally disappeared. I could sense the relief among the crew and wondered what would happen next. I didn't have long to wait. The Captain looked at me, and with few, but forever immortal words said...

"Andy, stand here and hold the wheel. Watch the compass in front of you. Turn the wheel GENTLY, always steering to keep her on the course heading. Remember, she will steer the opposite way to the direction you turn the wheel...."

And with that, the Captain stood aside, and the ship was suddenly in my hands. Burning our heading into my soul; I watched as the compass twitched anti-clockwise a degree. Responding, I carefully turned the wheel clockwise to bring the ship back on its heading; the Captain, all the while watching my every move.

After a few minutes, he guided my vision towards the horizon, and in a soft but firm voice, told me to fix my gaze upon it. If I spent too much time looking at the compass, I was likely to lose my bearings he said. I gulped. I would get used to it apparently. I hoped so, because, try as I might, I could find nothing on the horizon to fix my gaze upon. The sea was almost dead calm, as far as my eyes could see... it might have helped if there was a rock or lighthouse out there..."

The First Mate gave the order to raise the sails. As those around me moved like a well-oiled machine, I remained at the helm. By being unable to leave my post, I could not get in the way - an astute move by the Captain, I thought. Watching from my position, I could not help but admire the ease at which the crew went about their task; they had done it perhaps hundreds of times before. Within minutes, every inch of canvas we had, billowed in the wind as the ship took on a distinguished list to starboard.

With sails raised, the Captain cut the engine, and in an instant, the only sound I could hear was the gentle lapping of the sea against the hull as the bow dipped rhythmically through the waves.

I began to relax... we were in full sail, the sea was calm beneath a cloudless sky. As strains of classical seafaring music began to filter through my head, I rechecked the compass. A slight nudge clockwise on the wheel met with a nod of approval from the Captain. He had entrusted me with his ship, and while he was never far away, my confidence finally began to grow.

As is my wont, however, it didn't last long. The advice to look at the horizon, rather than the compass just didn't compute with my brain. I lost concentration, and the ship started to wander off its heading by more than the usual degree or two. As I tried to correct it, I panicked and began to oversteer. Within minutes, the wheel was out of my hands and back in the competent touch of the First Mate. His look said everything. If only I hadn't tried to fix my gaze on that featureless horizon, I felt sure things would have been OK, but there was no pleading my case. The matter was closed.

Thankfully, my disgrace didn't last long. I was almost at the end of my duty on the helm anyway. Thus, when my fellow Watch-stander made his way back to take his turn at the helm, I couldn't get to the Bowsprit quick enough to start my lookout duties.

The First Mate followed me. My job was simple, he said. I had to look out for two things. First, the obvious one, ships... In a matter of fact voice, he revealed that despite technology, there were ships out there that we, or they, might not see. Our human eyes were still the most reliable method of avoiding a collision.

If the first thing didn't frighten the crap out of me, then the second one did... Things floating in the sea that might risk damaging the ship... in particular, Freightliner containers. The ocean is full of metal boxes washed overboard from the numerous monster cargo vessels that ply the world's shipping lanes. Many of them stay afloat for days or even weeks. With their cargo ruined and the Insurance paid out, they roam the ocean until they sink, or wash ashore... or punch a hole in a wooden ship... like the one whose deck I was stood upon...

My heart crashed. The risk of having to abandon ship had never entered my head. I didn't even know if the crew knew I couldn't swim. I certainly hadn't told them, and now felt very foolish for not doing so. For the next two hours, I could not have strained my eyes more. I didn't spot a single ship, and thankfully, not a single metal box.

Relieved of my duty by the arrival of the next Watch, I went below to relax. In my naivety, I didn't realise that the system of Watches we were following meant that I would be on duty again in just four hours. If I had, I might have tried to grab some sleep. As it was, in little more than four hours, sleep would become a distant memory.

By the time my second Watch approached, the sea had started to swell. Regrettably, the storm we had hoped to outrun had caught up with us, and it was in a far worse mood than forecast... ideal then that I was on lookout duty for the first two hours... perhaps the most exposed task on the ship. I had waterproofs of course, but they were no match for the Atlantic Ocean. I soon needed rescuing with something more seaworthy. Thus, even before my first hour on duty had passed, I'd traded my waterproofs for a set of oilskins. If my lack of ownership of such things hadn't confirmed my complete lack of experience at sea, nothing else would... I returned to duty just as the last of the evening light faded from the sky, I could see nothing but a blackened sea, and taste only saltwater.

As my lookout duty finished, I looked decidedly worse for wear, and so did the ever more tempestuous sea around us. Nevertheless, I reported to the helm.
Perhaps saved by my earlier failings, or by the ever-worsening conditions, I was not to handle Helm duties. Instead, I had to help furl the sails. We were battening down the hatches. I began to regret my foolhardy desire to sail on the ship.
With sails furled, I returned to stand next to the helm and await further orders from the Captain, or First Mate. Alas, if there was a time when I needed to be useful, it was now. However, it was not to be. As the ship began to pitch and yaw ever more violently as it crashed through the waves, I began to turn that strange shade of green known to all who have been that shade.
The First Mate noticed it almost immediately and handed me some stem ginger to chew. This stuff is reputed to quell seasickness... but apparently not in my case. Thus, it was only a matter of minutes before one of the crew guided me down to my bunk below deck; my eyes and ears signalling my brain with all the confusion necessary, for it to decide the only possible cure was to make me violently sick. I resisted the urge as long as I could. I hoped by closing my eyes it would cut down on the feeling now whirling around inside me. Fat chance...

That night I didn't need to witness the storm from the deck above me, I could see it in the bucket in front of my face, its contents swirling as violently as the tempest surrounding the ship.

(DEATHBED RECOLLECTIONS)

I have no idea how long I continued to retch. Occasionally I would try and lie down on my makeshift bunk, only to have to prop myself up minutes later to repeat the exercise. As the engine hammered ever louder as it fought to satisfy the demands of the helm, I became lost in my own fight for survival.

At some point, I may have become delirious. I'm sure I considered jumping ship, which, in the middle of the Bay of Biscay, in the middle of a storm, is not a good idea... I'm also quite sure that my reason for doing so, was some peculiar belief that by offering my soul to the storm, Neptune would spare the ship and its crew. At the very least, I thought such an offering would end the uncontrollable chaos that churned within me; chaos I could no longer deal with.

However, unless I have been reincarnated... which might be possible... it's apparent I didn't offer my soul to Neptune that night. Perhaps I needed to stop watching old seafaring movies...

(DOUARNENEZ)

I have no idea how long I was asleep; no one ever told me. When I finally opened my eyes and turned to sit on the edge of my bunk, I didn't even know if it was the following day or whether I had missed one entirely.

While gathering my thoughts, I could still hear the engine, but it was quieter. The ship was more peaceful too. She had stopped pitching and yawing so violently and had returned to the sedate bobbing we had enjoyed as we left Bilbao. Curious as to why, and in need of some fresh air, I rose unsteadily from my deathbed, and made my way up to the main deck.

As is often the way in my life, my timing was appalling; for there, at the top of the stairs, stood the First Mate, the last person I wanted to see. Bowing my head in shame, I mumbled something about reporting for duty. He didn't say a word. Looking around at the haggard faces I should have been working with, instead of reeling in the bilges, I don't think my 'reporting for duty' cut much ice with the crew either. I wanted to say sorry, but sometimes that word is far too insignificant; this was one of those times.

We were no longer in the Bay of Biscay but slowly making our way into a large inlet somewhere along the Brittany coast. I had no idea if our destination was a planned stopover, or whether we were seeking somewhere to anchor while the ship was inspected for damage. Whatever the intention, the thought crossed my mind that the crew might ask me to leave when we made landfall. Fearing the worst, I returned below deck, found my camera and took a few photographs around the ship, I figured I might not get another chance...

Despite my regrets, when I looked back at the voyage so far, there had been moments I'd thoroughly enjoyed. Now, however, my thoughts turned to the likelihood of making my way home, not by sea, but by land...

As we rounded a small headland, the port of Douarnenez came into view. A large crowd had gathered to welcome our arrival. It felt good to know that terra firma was now only yards away, albeit that I struggled to hide the uneasy feeling that our arrival would also herald my farewell.

After we tied up, I gathered my kit together and waited for the anticipated request to leave the ship. It didn't come. Perhaps the presence of the local townsfolk now gathered several deep on the quayside, and eager to have a closer look at the ship, meant I'd won a reprieve, albeit a temporary one. I had no idea.

We spent the afternoon showing people around the ship. The sailors among them made good use of the crew, while the Engineer impressed everyone with how noisy the ship's engine could be. For my part, I spent my time trying hard to look as though I was part of the crew, but mostly just pottering around doing my housekeeping thing; lying low seemed the most appropriate task of all.

While busy with my thoughts, I hardly noticed a small group approaching. I had become the focus of their attention. When they asked what my job was, I looked up to see the First Mate catch my gaze. Taking a deep breath, I replied that it was to raise and lower the Jibs. With the merest suggestion of a raised eyebrow from the First Mate, it seemed prudent to demonstrate the task.
Following a textbook copy of the training I'd had back in Bilbao, the group moved on with a 'merci beaucoup', leaving me to return to the piles of rope I thought might need tidying again. As the First Mate turned to follow them, I thought I caught a brief nod of approval; perhaps it was my imagination.

That evening, shore leave beckoned.
Wandering among the harbourside cafes and bars, it became clear that we were the talk of the town. With many of the bar owners only too pleased to see us take a seat outside their venue, it was a cheap night. Despite how dissolute I felt; in the

eyes of the locals at least, I was a member of the ship's crew. Deep down, I already knew I would never make the grade...

(SARDINES, PEACHES, AND POTATOES)

With the crew engaged in showing yet more people around the ship the following morning, and my services not being required, I picked up my kit bag and headed into town; it seemed the best place to be. Besides, I still needed to figure out how I would get back to England.

(As an aside, I learned only some weeks after the voyage, that when I left the ship that morning, the crew had placed bets among themselves that I was already on my way home, effectively some of them thought I'd 'jumped ship'. I'll admit here that I came very close to doing so. However, if there was one thing I had learned long before this voyage, it was that I'm not the quitting type... I had proven that in France, and even more so in Morocco. Whether the crew knew it or not, they were stuck with me, unless they decided otherwise...)

Walking past the town's open-air market, the smell of freshly cooked food reminded me of how hungry I was. After recovering from seasickness, my stomach had been so sore I'd eaten only modestly the previous night. Yet despite my hunger, I could not decipher the descriptions on the hand-written menus. Fearful of another cassoulet made with horsemeat, or a nice dose of e-coli, Moroccan fashion, I decided to pass up on the risk of buying something to eat.

A little later, I spotted a small shop set incongruously among a row of private houses. The sign above the doorway simply read: 'Sardines'...

Peering through the dimly lit window, I could see someone moving around inside. Curious, I half-heartedly pushed the door, expecting the shop to be closed. To my surprise, it sprang open.

Offering a vague "Bonjour" to the old man sat behind the counter, I quickly discovered that 'Sardines' was an appropriate description of the shop. Its polished wood shelves had row upon row of carefully arranged little uniform-sized tins of them. I began to wonder if I'd stumbled upon some highly secret World Federation of Sardine tin collectors... I might have. A few of the tins even appeared to have special significance in the world of sardine tins... Was that tin found in Napoleon Bonaparte's knapsack at the Battle of Waterloo? Perhaps the one next to it dated back to Agincourt. Wow! That one looked as though it was gold-plated...

Being the only person in the shop, I had all the attention of the old man at the counter. Thus, feeling far too self-conscious, I soon made to leave. As I walked past him, I paused... In desperate need of some humour in my life, I made a joke...

"Got any haddock?" I asked.

The old man must have heard the joke a thousand times; I'm sure 'haddock' was the only English word he knew. Thus, after he completed a slow, pitying, sideways nod of the head, I bid him "adieu"' and left.

I re-joined the ship just in time to become part of a raid on the town for supplies...
Somewhere during that raid, I discovered some beautifully ripe peaches. Whether I just needed comfort food or was concerned about the risk of Scurvy, I don't know, but I was adamant we needed to buy some. It was another mistake... Peaches don't survive well in cramped ship's galleys. Later that night, I consciously helped myself to what was left of the mush they had become, while others looked on... at least I wasn't going to get scurvy.

We slipped out of port around two o'clock that afternoon. I was still on board...

My Watch didn't start till later that night, but being wide-awake and not knowing what to do with myself, I volunteered for Kitchen duties.
At the time, I had only a limited ability to cook, but I could make reasonable roast potatoes if nothing else. Somehow, peeling potatoes in a galley on a ship seemed a fitting task for my self-esteem.
With more trial and error than I would have hoped for, I produced a passable imitation of said roast potatoes; then helped as best I could with the washing-up, before returning to the deck to refine my skills once more at tidying ropes.

Now able to tidy ropes blindfolded, I turned to gaze at the crew. To a one, they all knew the ship intimately. This beautiful old Schooner was 'theirs', and they treated her with the utmost care and reverence. They were also familiar with the rigours of being on the open seas. I, on the other hand, was beginning to understand why so many of those sailors press-ganged into England's once-mighty navy, never made it back home. I felt sure I would have been one of them; lost, or buried at sea following my first encounter with a storm... Catching my erstwhile trainer's gaze, I dipped my head in respectful acknowledgement and continued with my mundane task.

(THE LONGEST NIGHT, THE LONGEST DAY)

As night fell on what I think was our sixth day, the weather deepened once more. This was not the storm from the Bay of Biscay, but it was choppy enough that helm duties fell to the Captain and First Mate alone. Thus, and having failed once already at that task, I spent my four-hour Watch looking out for anything that would mean I'd have to learn to swim...

Badly needing to salvage perhaps just one ounce of credibility, I stood firm in my responsibilities; for here, in the middle of one of the most dangerous shipping lanes in the world, I'd chosen an excellent place to claim that one ounce... and it wasn't long before my commitment began to pay off...

"Ship at two o'clock" I called out, pointing with my arm as instructed.

It seemed a bit pointless as the lights from whatever monster it was, could be seen by everyone on deck anyhow. Nevertheless, as my duty reached two bells, (one hour on Watch), I had seven ships in my sights, thankfully the same tally as the First Mate. What was disconcerting, but perhaps only to me, was that they all appeared to be converging upon us...

As the largest of them closed in on our position, I realised that despite maritime law decreeing powered vessels must give way to sail, the reality was something more akin to, 'Bollocks, we're bigger than you. Get out of our way, or you go to the bottom.' Thus, for the next two hours, we weaved and bobbed our way between an assortment of tankers, a large cruise ship, and one enormous freight carrier; no doubt responsible I thought, for its fair share of metal boxes in the ocean.

In the middle of this chaos, my fellow Watch-stander joined me at the Bowsprit. Seeing my perhaps over-exaggerated performance, he assured me that these ships would have proximity alarms blaring on the Bridge. Someone up there he continued, would be fully aware of our existence. We were close enough to the metal-box shedder that I could see its Bridge in fine detail. There was not a soul on it...

As we rolled precariously in the giant's wake, I caught sight of something in the water, not thirty feet to our starboard. Blinking through the murk and sea-spray, I looked again, focusing my eyes intently on one small spot in the black of the ocean.

There! Appearing and disappearing as it bobbed up and down in the troughs between the waves, was the tiniest of yachts; its paltry napkin of a sail flapping pointlessly in the wind.

Squinting harder, I could see its Captain and sole occupant, resplendent in bright yellow waterproofs, waving back at me in a manner reminiscent of that moment when Gregory Peck, as Captain Ahab, surfaces strapped to Moby Dick. For a moment, I wondered if this lone yachtsman had strapped himself to the mast... Stunned into action by his wave, I called out

"Ship Ahoy, three o'clock to starboard, thirty feet!"

I don't think anyone took me seriously at first. Then my fellow Watch-stander confirmed what I'd seen. With his voice, several of the crew rushed over to see for themselves. The solo yachtsman waved back once more and was gone.
(When I eventually arrived home, I spent a week or more checking and re-checking news sources for the 'Lone yachtsman lost at sea, presumed drowned' story, but never found one. Maybe he was a ghost, but then if that were the case, we'd all seen him... To this day, I've no idea if he made it.)

With a rewarding cup of cocoa in my hands, I returned to my station, a little less cold inside, and with a touch more warmth in my cheeks.

I should not have had that cocoa though, for it, the fact that I had hardly slept while crossing the Bay of Biscay, and the adrenalin rush from the chaos of the last few hours, all combined to waft the word 'sleep' over me like a thick, suffocating blanket.
I still had an hour left to serve out my Watch, but I guess my near-constant yawning, and bleary eyes, must have made it as clear-cut as the first time I tried to tie a knot, that I was once more going to fail in my duty. I didn't want to ask to be relieved, but I didn't need to. Either through expectation or resignation, the First Mate tapped me on the shoulder and sent me below. I could not have been more despondent.

When I surfaced on deck the following morning, I realised I'd slept through my Watch duty. I'd also missed the ship's rounding of the iconic Land's End, the first piece of England almost every ship sees as it approaches the British Isles from the southwest. It's something I still deeply regret.

Peering out to starboard though, my spirits rose. I could make out many of the landmarks I knew so well along the north coast of Cornwall. We were little more than a hundred miles or so from home.
Keen to set foot on dry land again, I asked the First Mate what time we would dock. The answer was not what I expected... We were coasting along because we

would not make it to port in time to catch the next high tide. In short, it would be another eighteen hours before we tied up.

Thus the day dragged ever more slowly. There were no sails to furl or unfurl; we had but one Jib aloft to aid steering. All I could do was play my part in being lookout when required, or taking the helm if asked. With no requests for my services, on either count, I began pottering around tidying up already tidy ropes, and eventually joined those on lookout duty, if only for the conversation... and there wasn't much of that.

As dusk fell, I spotted Hartland lighthouse. We were little more than ten miles from port, and yet, it would still be eight hours before my feet touched land again. I headed below for one last night in my makeshift bunk.

As I lay down, the realisation that I had not felt even the tiniest bit seasick since leaving Douarnenez, bought a wry smile to my face...

(DAY EIGHT – BUOY AHOY!)

After a week on board, I had become so familiar with the ship's motion, that even while laying on my bunk with eyes closed, I knew we had turned to starboard and entered the relative calm of a shallow estuary. We were almost home.

I raced up to the main deck in anticipation of seeing a large crowd gathered on the quayside, but was a little surprised to see not a soul on it. The reason was simple. I hadn't realised it was only six o'clock in the morning. I had learned another valuable lesson... Time, on a ship, is a way of life. Without it, the pattern of Watches can be disorientating. Through failing to manage my duties, and my time, I had completely lost track of it.

Within minutes of surfacing, the First Mate pounced. I was urgently required on lookout duties. Walking up to the bow, I could see several pairs of anxious eyes scanning the estuary. Something was amiss. My erstwhile Watch-stander debriefed me of the situation...

When the ship had left port some weeks earlier, the buoy marking the inbound port side of the channel had been observed unlit; *(black mark to those who look after such potentially lifesaving things)*. Thus, in the dim light of early morning, this dark coloured, unlit buoy, had the perfect camouflage; camouflage sufficient, that I didn't spot it until it was almost too late. If fate decreed I was to be labelled the Jonah of the voyage, then it was about to provide my pennant.

I had been asked to watch off the port bow for the buoy in question, and so, began scanning the horizon for it. However, and much to my downfall, we had taken such a wide berth coming into the estuary, that the buoy in question was already sitting almost directly beneath the starboard side of the Bow.

It was only as we swung to starboard that it suddenly lurched into view. With hardly a moment to react, I shouted in alarm. Almost immediately, several crewmen rushed forward with long poles. As they swept me aside, the roar of the engine in full reverse made it clear how dangerous the situation was.

Moments later, and with the crisis averted, the First Mate gave me a hard stare. There was no point in offering a defence for my failure to spot the buoy, no matter how unimpeachable it truly was. I had been presumed guilty, and that was that. I sighed. At least I knew it would all be over soon. Thankfully, the water was already too shallow for the crew to have me keelhauled...

As we tied up at the empty and unwelcoming quay, I couldn't wait to get off the ship. Dumping my kitbag on deck, I sat down, not quite knowing what would happen next.

"Crew cannot leave until the ship is made ready for her next voyage" was what happened next.

I turned to see the ever-watchful First Mate staring at me. Despite my sense of despair, I could not ignore his command and just walk up the gangplank, leaving the crew to clean the ship by themselves. A large part of me wanted to though, for my self-esteem had once again hit rock bottom. The question though, was just what could I do that was going to be useful to the ship? I should have known...

"Heads" was the answer.

I was to have the honour of cleaning the toilets, symbolically the task of the lowest ranks. Accepting of my assignment, I set to work.

In such mundane and often onerous tasks, one has time to think about the positives and negatives of life. I chose to think about my time on board the schooner...

On the positive side, I could tie a few knots. I knew how to steer by a compass, and I could raise and lower sails. I knew what all the various bits of a sailing ship were, and what they did, and I had, perhaps somewhat perversely, also learned, that once your brain becomes familiar with the ship's motion, seasickness will not return to haunt you on a voyage.

With some remorse, however, I had also learned how important it was to play your part as a member of a ship's crew. If one failed to uphold the task you are responsible for, as I had on several occasions, the burden you placed on the rest of the crew, was one almost impossible to redeem.

Perhaps somewhat perversely, I also realised that on board ship, sailors led a relatively clean life, despite the best attempts of Hollywood to suggest otherwise. Living in the confined space of a ship, for days or even weeks on end, teaches one that there is a need for personal hygiene. Thus, my task turned out to be not one of scraping week old shit from the porcelain with my fingernails, nor of mopping up stale urine, but one that, while unpleasant, was nowhere near as degrading as it could have been.

Satisfied I had done a thorough job, I stood back and awaited the inevitable inspection. Naturally, there were a few minor niggles, there had to be, I could not be perfect at anything, not even cleaning a toilet. Nevertheless, my efforts to do something right finally met with approval.

I climbed the stairs to the main deck one last time and grabbed my kitbag. There was just one more thing I had to do, it felt almost ceremonial, protocol if you wish, but it also felt like it was one of lasting respect. I turned and approached the Captain.

"Permission to disembark, Captain," I mumbled.

The Captain glanced at the First Mate, and with a silent nod, I was free to go. Offering my gratitude, I walked up the gangplank, and onto the quayside, knowing at that moment, my first voyage as a sailor was also going to be my last...

That week at sea was to have one last laugh at my expense; for as I walked away from the ship, it felt as though the quayside was moving, perhaps swaying side to side. It wasn't, of course; I was. After a week onboard a ship whose motion had been determined by the moods of Neptune, I had acquired the classic rolling gait so familiar of all seamen when first back on land after a voyage.

I smiled to myself. There wasn't a landlubber anywhere, who would think anything other than I had been at sea.

Privately, I knew I'd been at sea in more ways than one...

ANDY GABRIEL-POWELL

HEBRIDEAN OVERTURES

After regaining my land-legs, and realising the high seas was not the most prudent place for me to find adventure... I reverted to my love of trekking. However, after being fried alive in France, and feeling as though I'd lost some vital organs in Morocco, I chose to focus my quest among the cooler climes of Northern Europe; I'd had enough of 'pack for hot climate' instructions.

The treks that followed were enjoyable for a while, not least because I didn't need a guide, nor for that matter, did I need to work to any particularly well-planned itinerary. However, when visiting a country accustomed to dealing with thousands of back-packers traipsing over their freshly cut grass, the adventure is lost; one becomes just another Zante bound, T-shirt wearing, package tourist. Thus, it wasn't long before I decided I needed to attempt somewhere exotic again, somewhere 'out there', somewhere 'scary'.

In light of my hatred of hot climates, and places associated with poor hygiene though, quite why I decided to sign up for a trek across Mexico, I'll never know. Just uttering the word 'Mexico' was enough to convulse my still sensitive constitution into meltdown. Nevertheless, that's what I did. I should perhaps be grateful that the trek suffered the usual ignominy of cancellation; this time "for operational reasons." 'Operational reasons' turned out to be a series of earthquakes, plum in the middle of the route we were to take across a mountain range... Having never experienced an earthquake, I was somewhat disappointed... On the other hand... cue the usual fifty per cent discount...

Cancellation of the Mexican trek came only ten days before I was due to fly out. So late in fact that to go anywhere requiring a vaccination I didn't already have, was now entirely out of the question. With my only inoculation being against Yellow Fever, and in need of a trek that fitted into my already booked holiday dates, my options could not have been more limiting. The alternative though, one of spending two weeks staring at English rain from the windows of my wretched home, was unthinkable. With my fifty per cent discount code at the ready, I punched in my specific criteria, and browsed the results...

Aha! A walk through the Alpine mountains of Switzerland. That would be a great challenge... Alas no; fully booked. What about Costa Rica then? I'd always fancied something ecological. HOW much was that, AFTER discounts? That'll be a no too then. In quiet desperation, I watched as my options faded one by one.

With just forty-eight hours left before my holiday started, there was but one option left... an island-hopping trek, down the spine of one of the soggiest, most rain-soaked places on Earth... Scotland, the Outer Hebrides to be precise. It wasn't exactly exotic, but when I plotted the route to get there, it was actually further away from my home than the Swiss Alps. This gave it credibility, if not a particularly high score on the 'scary' scale.

I rang the travel company to confirm my booking. The enthusiasm of the agent who took the call was such that I wondered if she'd just won that week's bonus for selling a ticket on the company's most unpopular tour...

(DAY ONE ~ THIS WAY TO PURGATORY)

With little or no preparation time, I threw my backpack into the car, drove to the local airport, and parked my car in the long-stay car-park... I could tell it was a long-stay car-park, because it was sufficiently far enough away from the terminal, that a prudent traveller might book an extra day to allow for the walk required to get to it...

Heaving my backpack over my shoulder, I adopted the 'I've done this before' look of a seasoned traveller and followed the vapour trails of the aircraft heading towards the same airport I was.

Arriving at the terminal building, I stopped to note the sign above the door. It described the airport as an 'International' one, which, as I was to learn, applied because of its one flight a week to Canada. As I pondered the puddle-jumping capabilities of the assorted World War Two wrecks on the tarmac, and the one, hopelessly oversized plane parked next to the terminal, with 'Canada' written all over it, I wondered who'd f*cked up and thought this was the main airport for London... still at least four hours away by car...

Entering the departure terminal, the only check-in desk I could find open, was the one catering for a flight to one of those 'buy one dose of the clap and get one free' holiday destinations. The desk I wanted was, like all the remaining ones, devoid of life.

Despite signs to the contrary, it didn't take long to realise that this desk was the only one the airport planned on opening that day. Thus, having no alternative, I joined the queue; all the while doing my best to avoid any misconception that I too, wanted a sexually transmitted disease.

Twenty minutes later, it was my turn. I approached the desk, and with a smile on my face, produced my booking slip for the Aberdeen flight.

I don't think my joke about wanting a window seat, facing the direction of travel, and one preferably fitted with a parachute went down too well... The sour-faced cow behind the desk didn't laugh, and merely proceeded to blow the smile off my face with a cross-examination about what was in my luggage, where was I flying to, what time of day did I think it was, and why was I stood there smiling and joking when it was still some way short of her cigarette break...

Chastised and now minus my backpack, I walked through the security checks and started my traditional people watching fetish in the Departure Lounge.

In a small regional airport, the Departure Lounge is a microcosm of everything that exists in all major city airports. There were the usual resigned for a long wait, 'I'll read a book' types; the Zante tarts - only this time the T-Shirts described them as 'Princesses'; the screaming kids whose parent's faces read, 'God help us, we've got two weeks of this'... and the Bar crowd. For the latter, it might only have been nine-thirty in the morning, but some were already visibly close to flying unaided.

In little less than an hour, I boarded one of the wrecks on the tarmac.

Looking out of the window, I noticed I had a full view of the rotating blades of one of the plane's propellers. Jesus, I wish I hadn't watched so many disaster movies... I could visualise the propeller coming off and scything its way through the plane. Sub-consciously I withdrew my feet from the path of the blades and waited for take-off.

Twenty minutes later, we hammered down the runway, and on reaching the critical 'she canny tak no more cap'ain', lurched skyward.

We had barely gotten airborne before the cabin crew wheeled out the snack trolley. Thankfully, having already been stung by the Airline's pricing formula - Cheap flight plus baggage plus seat plus oxygen equals expensive flight; I figured a cup of tea would probably cost a second mortgage, and thus declined the persistent offer... It was to prove a financially sound decision.

Having actually sold a cup of tea to one financially naive passenger, and evidently thinking they were on a roll, the cabin crew took a chance and wheeled out the duty-frees. This seemed a bit pointless, as we never left tax-ridden British airspace...

Some while later, we crashed onto a runway vaguely nowhere near the anticipated Leeds or Bradford City the airport purported to serve. I say 'crashed' for it was unquestionably one of the roughest landings I've ever endured, the consequence of which, was to have a profound 'impact' on my return flight a week later...

Despite still being in England, those of us going forward to Aberdeen were asked to remain seated; I wondered if perhaps Scottish Immigration Officers wanted a chat? No? Was it possible that having sold one cup of tea, the cabin crew had persuaded the Pilot there was a gullible passenger onboard, and therefore a chance of selling another if they didn't let him off the plane? OK ...so I may have misread the flight-plan, but with just fifty minutes left before we were due to arrive in Aberdeen, pitching for another cup of tea was going to need a seriously hard sell.

As no sale occurred, our flight crew rewarded us on arrival at Aberdeen by taxiing the plane to a point so far from the Arrivals terminal, that if it had taxied any further, I would not have needed a train to Inverness, theoretically still eighty miles away.

The great thing about Aberdeen airport is that they never tell you just how far it is from Aberdeen. The nearest town and railway station to the airport is in fact, Dyce, about three miles distant. On realising the remoteness of the airport to anything of practical use, one is immediately hurled into a vulnerable state of mind. I was vulnerable enough to be fleeced for a ten-minute taxi ride to Dyce railway station.

Having departed with most of my holiday savings, the taxi sped out of the station, leaving me to face the barren, uninhabited wasteland that is Dyce station. Checking the train information board confirmed I had a long wait ahead of me.

Feeling hungry and with little else to do, I decided to venture into the equally barren, but inhabited wasteland, of Dyce's town centre. I found it in the form of a single shop. Taking a deep breath, I walked in.

Among the first things I noticed were the bottles of Whisky; each and every one of them sealed behind a padlocked, glass-fronted display cabinet. There were so many of them, I thought for a moment I'd walked into an off-licence instead of a grocery store. A long line of people, each clutching a bottle from one of those cabinets, stood waiting patiently for their turn to pay the overworked cashier at the nearby register.

From what I could tell, the other half of the shop possessed all that the residents of Dyce needed when they weren't drinking. This didn't appear to amount to much. Armed with a selection of botulism, e-Coli, and the all-important Tunnocks Biscuits, I looked forlornly at the lengthy Whisky queue. It may have been two hours before my train arrived, but there seemed little chance of being able to complete my purchases by then.

I was about to abandon hope when a voice behind me asked if it could help. Spinning around, I spotted another cashier sat half-hidden behind a wall of Lottery tickets in the opposite corner of the store. As she rang up my piteous selection, she seemed puzzled why I should want food and not Whisky, it was mid-afternoon after all...

Retracing my steps to the station, I discovered several people wandering aimlessly up and down its platforms. It may have been hard enough to get to Dyce, but leaving it, apparently, was also going to be a challenge... The reason manifested itself through the unusual platform arrangements at the station. *(Caution, train anorak story coming...)*

Now, something is comforting about knowing that at a traditional railway station, one platform is for trains going one way, and the other platform is for trains going the other way... In railway parlance, they call these the 'up line' and the 'down line' *(ahem)*. Sadly, for the people of Dyce, the train that arrives on the 'up' line, is not necessarily going to continue going 'up', it could go back down the way it came 'up'. The reverse is also true of the 'down' line... *(if you follow me.)* I began to think all those queueing for Whisky were the sad remains of rail passengers who'd never found their way out of Dyce...

What proceeded to occur for the next two hours then, was a merry dance of confused passengers, as they tried to work out whether the train on the 'up' line was going to continue going up the 'up' line, or whether the train that had arrived on the 'down line' was going to keep going down the 'down line'. *(Phew! Assuming the reader has not boarded the wrong train, we'll continue...)*

With no intelligible noises coming from the station's ethereal loudspeaker system, I took a gamble and boarded the train that arrived on the 'down line', praying that it would leave Dyce still heading in the same direction. The alternative had all the makings of a groundhog day, but one without a woman to win over, and only a town called purgatory to take up alcoholism in.

After what seemed like a moment of hesitation by the driver, we lurched forward in the direction I wanted to go. I could have kissed him.

I spent most of the next two hours peering out of the window while eavesdropping on two Scottish Oil workers on their way home. Of all the things they discussed, I remain fazed how people who spend twenty-four hours a day, for months on end, sitting on a toadstool in the middle of the brutal North Sea, can have golf handicaps of Four...

When they left the train at Keith, *(yes, there really is a place called Keith in Scotland... which naturally made me wonder if there was a town called Kevin or perhaps Nigel, there too)*; I turned my attention to focus on the faces at the opposite table. They were drinking heavily and appeared to be tacitly encouraged to do so by the onboard catering trolley, which had taken up an almost permanent position between us.

Now, while any amount of drinking on the train seemed to meet with approval, smoking did not. Thus, when we arrived at Nairn, some one hour and fifty minutes after leaving Dyce, the announcement of a ten-minute delay, caused the train to empty almost entirely onto the station platform. As we finally pulled out of the station, I looked back to see the stationmaster, hands on hips, surveying the dozens of cigarette ends that now littered his once tidy platform. I wondered how many times a day he did that...

After witnessing Scottish drinking and smoking culture, the culture towards having a valid ticket was equally enlightening. Shortly before our arrival at Inverness, the guard announced:

"Since Inverness station is likely to have ticket inspectors present, it might be prudent to ensure you have purchased a valid ticket for your journey today", he added... "It's just my suggestion of course". *(This is, I promise you, a verbatim quote.)*

I had to let this sink in slowly, very slowly. To my disbelief, when the guard passed through our carriage, the two drunks opposite me hailed him to buy tickets, but only to cover the journey from Nairn to Inverness... Clearly, Nairn was the new name for Dyce... where I'd seen them board the train the same time I had.

My eyes had last seen Inverness Station more than thirty years ago. Then, the train announcer was a creature from heaven, with a soft, lilting highland voice, whose home was a kiosk in the middle of the concourse. I remember her smile, a heart-warming Gaelic one, that had me gazing at her as she announced the stations each train would be stopping at. I hoped she, or perhaps her daughter, would still be there.

She wasn't, and neither was her daughter... The kiosk had gone; replaced by a sterile corporate concourse devoid of all welcome. Even the voice over the loudspeaker sounded corporate. Feeling as though I'd been robbed, I headed for the exit.

I found my lodgings for the night quickly enough and knocked on the door. An elderly woman opened it.
After escorting me to my cosy floral tainted room, she handed me a set of keys to the house and promptly declared that I could come and go as I pleased, so long as I locked the front door after me. She added that she was, "just popping across the road tonight," as it was her friend's turn to get the drinks in...

After dumping my backpack, I headed out to town in search of something to eat. Finding only Indian curry houses that had yet to open their doors, I ended up in one of those plastic corporate affairs. Consequently, it was still only eight o'clock by the time I'd eaten a forgettable meal.

Fifteen minutes later, and I had already made my way down to the imposing castle by the town's river; drawn there by a somewhere unseen, lone piper practising 'Highland Cathedral'. After listening until the evocative drone fell silent, I headed back to my lodgings.
It was an early night...

(DAY TWO ~ ROAD TO THE ISLES)

At breakfast, I was surprised to be met by three men in the dining room. What little conversation followed, centred around the North Sea oil business. I left with the impression our elderly host had quite a cosy arrangement with it...

With five hours to kill before heading back to the rendezvous point on the station concourse, I headed into town long before the shops had opened, and the streets cleared of the previous nights' drunks. I desperately needed something to pass the time.
After taking a slow wander down the high street, I reached the River Ness and turned upstream to follow a path along the riverbank, pausing only to watch a Salmon fisherman plying his art, oblivious to the traffic congestion on the bridge above him.
For a while, I found solitude amongst the footbridge connected islands in the river, discovered the endgame of the Caledonian Canal; and finally, investigated a monument to a long-forgotten battle between two Highland clans. The monument

didn't disclose what they were fighting about, probably a distillery or something I guess... Nevertheless, at three hours down, and with still two to go, I resorted to window-shopping. There really was nothing else left to do.

In those remaining hours, three shops offering tartans tried desperately to find some remnant of Scottish ancestry in my family tree; while a woman eloquently describing the two hundred whiskies in hers, damn near had me buy the lot.

Making my excuses after the sixth sample, I headed for the station, my gait and numb smile of no concern to passers-by, or to the girl at the cash register for whom I fumbled coins for the bottle of diluting water I was clutching... She had seen it all before, probably only minutes before.

Back on the station concourse, several backpackers sporting 'Jesus loves you' and 'Summer camp Lourdes' badges started to congregate around me. I pretended not to notice them, at the same time keeping a fearful eye out for any sign they were on the same trek; discovering a confirmed heathen among a 'happy-clappy' crowd, might have caused more than a few 'Hail Mary's'...

My relief was audible when they embraced two late arrivals and sodded off across the concourse. Breathing my own hallelujah, I settled down to wait for what would happen next.

At five minutes to the agreed meeting time, and with no visible sign of the guide I was expecting to meet, I became aware of the presence of a woman sidling up to me. In a broad Yorkshire dialect, she took up a conversation with my right ear.

"Excuse me, I don't normally do this, *(pause)*, but are you waiting to join a trek to the Outer Hebrides?"

My relief at finding I had not screwed up somewhere, was palpable. Moments later, several more people emerged from the shadows; presumably 'Miss Yorkshire' had drawn the short straw in the game of who would check me out.

At one minute to the appointed hour, our guide finally materialised. I noticed that despite it being a bitterly cold morning, he was wearing shorts. With boots far too big for someone of his stature, and a beard to match, he had all the appearance of someone who had just walked out of the jungle after thirty years studying lost tribes. Following the briefest of introductions, he led us to a waiting mini-bus.

As we drove from the station, 'The Beard', as I christened him, proceeded to narrate what, where, and how we were going to spend the week. As the information filtered through the minibus, it became evident there was not the vaguest of molehill or mountain, anywhere in Scotland, or possibly the World, that he didn't know intimately. For a moment, I had visions of another round of Moroccan style technical challenges beyond my capabilities. Sighing, I turned my head towards the window and soaked up the scenery.

After little more than an hour of travelling through the rugged emptiness of highland Scotland, we arrived at Ullapool, the terminus for our ferry to the Outer Hebrides. Taking up our allotted space in the vehicle waiting area, we alighted from the minibus to hear the Beard inform us:

"You have one hour, but I recommend you find food for tomorrow's lunch as the Outer Hebrides are closed on Sundays."

This sounded like a TV reality challenge, and, like most TV reality challenges, the winners had already noted the bright yellow, 'general stores this way' sign, plastered all over the wall next to the village's lone bus stop. Further clues to aid the runners-up came from the direction arrow beside it, indicating we needed to rise vertically into the air for three hundred feet to reach it...

With a pork pie, pack of sandwiches, and the Scottish staple of a four-pack of Tunnocks safely tucked into my backpack, I considered my Sunday rations adequate and headed back to the pier. There, I took out my camera and started to behave like a Japanese tourist.

Having taken a snapshot of everything I could see, I checked the ferry timetable. The potential for seasickness on the near three-hour crossing to Stornoway was all too apparent. I had been here before... I needed to find a chemist.

Like all good chemists next to flat bottomed, every chance of pitching and yawing car ferries; it was out of stock of every stomach saving remedy known to man. All they could offer was advice: Eat heartily before the ship left the shelter of the estuary they said. Looking back at the estuary, I figured I had about twenty minutes to stuff my face before the full force of seasickness would hit me...

Thus, when we boarded the ferry, I was first into the ship's restaurant, and sizing up what lead weights the menu could offer my stomach, long before the ferry had even weighed anchor.

Choosing a shepherd's pie lead weight, I sat down and began to eat; entirely unconvinced it would prevent what I feared most. Observing how full the restaurant was, I wondered if the ship had a profitable arrangement with the chemist...

As we sailed out of the estuary, and into open water, the sea lay before us like a mill-pond. There was barely a ripple upon it. Grateful for this, my stomach felt confident enough to allow me the privilege of going up on deck.

As the fresh sea-breeze bathed my face, I looked around to find just one other person sharing the deck with me. She was a student teacher from Oxford, who was moving to a University in Wales, via a friend's place on the Outer Hebrides, she said. I followed the geography of this slowly.

As the conversation flowed, she mentioned a wish to see Dolphins. Right on cue, I pointed to a pod of about twenty of them riding the ship's wake. Such was her joy; I thought she was going to kiss me.

Our arrival in Stornoway was perhaps the reality check I needed. The last few hours with a teacher from Oxford had defined all that is a brief encounter. Visions of a twosome adventure on some Hebridean Road movie faded from the mind as the minibus drove me from the opening scene.

An hour later, we arrived at Breascleit and our hotels for the night - 'Hotels' as in plural hotels... a father and son affair consisting of two adjacent houses, both with accommodation, but only one serving food... I got to stay in the food hotel...

It had been a long day. Retiring to a well-appointed, comfortable room, I crashed out. It was barely nine o'clock.

(DAY THREE ~ BUTTS & BROCHS)

For many, life revolves around time... twenty-four hours a day, seven days a week. Yet for me, when I am off on an adventure, I give time a holiday too. So, with no clock, watch, or mobile phone to remind me of it, it should come as no surprise to learn that I was awake, dressed, and hungry for breakfast, two hours before they served it.

To stave off the hunger, I decided to go for a quick wander around the village. It was quick... very quick. The wind was blowing as much of the Atlantic Ocean as it could, across the bleak landscape. With the rain working in harmony, my fleece and I were soaked through in minutes. I returned to the hotel, changed into some dry clothes and, in more hope than belief, headed once more for the Breakfast room.

I was in luck; perhaps the cook didn't have a clock either. Over a leisurely feast of eggs and bacon, cereal, fruit juice, and coffee, I spent the next hour watching the rain beat hard against the window, and the clouds descend to fog out the last remnants of the view.

Today should have been an assault on a mountain named after something to do with pigs; but it being a pig of a day, the Beard decided we would go for a walk around the Butt of Lewis instead. *(I'm not making these names up, honest!)* Thus, instead of getting soaked climbing a mountain, I presumed correctly that our soaking would now include sea spray. Back in my room, I put on a couple of extra layers of clothing and prayed that my waterproof jacket and trousers would be up to the task.

We drove through the rain for over an hour before arriving at a car-park in the small spelling mistake village of Europie. I wondered if this tiny corner of Scotland could have named an entire continent, but as we walked down to the beach, there was no one in the adjacent children's playground to tell me.

The sparkling white quartzite sand of the beach was lurid enough to make my eyes hurt, even in the enshrining murk, but within minutes of thinking I can forget the rain and enjoy some beachcombing, the Beard abruptly turned away from the sea and headed towards a nearby cliff. This was the starting point of our walk he declared. We were not going to walk to the 'Butt', but rather, we were going to circumnavigate it. Entirely why the place is referred to as the 'Butt' when it's actually at the most northerly point of the island, and nowhere near the arse end of it, god only knows; but I suspect on seeing the Scottish rain, he'd long gone on holiday to somewhere a whole lot drier and warmer...

As the Beard began to climb the modest but slippery slope, towards the cliff-top, I think he realised we were all stupid enough to follow him; for the official non-slippery path to the cliff-top, was just a few yards to our right...
On reaching the top, the weather began to demonstrate why Scottish rain is far more effective than anyone else's rain at getting through waterproofs; there was nowhere to hide from it either.

To keep our spirits up, the Beard tested our abilities further by walking up to the top of a ridge and stopping to look out into the distance. Like Lemmings, we all followed in the assumption that he'd spotted something we should see. As we got within arm's length of him, he raised his hands to stop us.

I was thankful he did, for he was stood right on the edge of a terrifying sheer-sided cliff. The thought crossed my mind that either he had glue on his boots, no nerves, or an unerring sense of balance. As one, we all backed away from him, afraid that if we had gotten any closer, we would risk accusations of foul play if he disappeared...

What the Beard was looking for, turned out to be Atlantic seals, Kittiwakes, Fulmars, and various other ocean-going creatures. As he pointed them out, several of us leaned forward just long enough to utter some "wow's" and "oh yes's," before retreating rapidly, leaving him to sway in the breeze...

Two soggy hours later, the sight of a lighthouse signalled our arrival at the Butt of Lewis. I looked forward to having a look around its cosy, warm, snug insides... but, alas, the lighthouse was closed... presumably, because even lighthouses closed for the Sabbath in the Outer Hebrides... Disappointed, I turned away to seek shelter among the surrounding rocks. It was time for elevenses.

For all his attempts to frighten the crap out of us, the Beard was at least informative. We learned from him that our damp backsides were sitting on some of the oldest rocks on the planet, three and a half billion years old to be precise. I had an overwhelming urge to break out into a round of 'Happy Birthday', but it was far too miserable to find the enthusiasm.

Twenty rain-soaked minutes later, we set off again.

Having circumnavigated the Butt, (*I really am not making this up, honest*); we turned to head south along the coastline facing mainland Scotland.

The rain, now softened by the diminishing wind, became more tolerable as the Beard stopped to point out yet more Atlantic Grey seals. As we watched them doing nothing, so they watched us doing nothing. When one of the seals started to yawn, I struggled to stifle one too. Done with the still life painting of sleeping seals, we moved on.

Ten minutes later, the Beard stopped us once again, this time to admire the site of an ancient settlement situated on a rocky promontory. Our history lesson this time involved a story of research suggesting we were looking at something Neolithic in origin. However, when the archaeologists finished work on the site, they confirmed it was actually more 'Medieval-ithic'. Well, that's what archaeologists do you know...

The Beard, evidently keen to get walking again, vaguely suggested we could take a closer look at the settlement if we wanted to. Much to his chagrin, we all decided we vaguely wanted to.

To reach it though, meant passing the Beard's test number three, the crossing of a somewhat temporary looking suspension bridge that separated the settlement from the mainland. I think he was disappointed that some at least, did not chicken out... or die in the attempt.

'Medieval-ithic' site ticked off the list, another hour of walking followed before we stumbled upon the bleak huddle of cottages and cowering harbour of Port Ness. This presented the Beard with yet another opportunity to deliver a short lecture.

Once a year, the villagers troll out to sea in search of Gannets, a protected seabird that nests on inaccessible cliffs and sea stacks. When they locate them, the villagers then conduct some death-defying climbs to cull some of the Gannets and take them back to Port Ness where they cook them for dinner. The villagers also ship the carcasses to former villagers living around the world... a sort of turkey by post if you wish. I was grateful to learn that 'Gannet' was unlikely to appear in my local supermarket anytime soon. The flavour is apparently that of rotting fish...

With the terrain now making for a more comfortable stroll, it was a quick two-mile romp through the wind and re-invigorated rain to reach the snug of our minibus.
An hour later, just as we had all dried out, we alighted for a quick look at Carloway Broch.

Brochs were the original fortified house, circular in form, and towering a good thirty feet or more high. Massive in their construction, they had a unique double-skinned outer wall, within which there was a passageway up to the second floor. The bewildering thing about these Brochs is the central heating system...
The owners kept their livestock on the ground floor. The heat generated by the animals, and presumably the pong of their cowpats; would waft up between the double-skinned walls to warm the rooms above. Ingenious, environmentally friendly state-of-the-art central heating... cow pats apart; yet Anthropologists know virtually nothing about the people who built these structures more than five thousand years ago...

Having fired up our interest in all things ancient and mysterious, the Beard bowed to group pressure for a quick look at Calanais *(Callanish)* stone circle. The circle and its achingly romantic setting, make it second only to Stonehenge in many people's, 'see before I die', Neolithic places to visit.

Calanais also gives rise to one of the most compelling arguments why our Neolithic ancestors built these stone circles. As if to demonstrate this, the Beard encouraged us to peer through the stones towards a distant ridge of hills.

Collectively, these hills form a rather beguiling outline of a naked female, with little imagination required to complete the picture. What's even more bizarre, is that once every sixteen years or so, the peculiar relationship between our planet and its sun, creates the impression that the sun is 'caressing' the outline of this female form as it transits across the sky. I could not help but mentally plot the sun's path along those hills…

Alas, despite my desire to record Calanais with a photograph, the weather, now rapidly closing in again, denied the moment. I sighed, reluctant in the knowledge that no amount of Neolithic ranting on my part would convince Mother Nature to ease up, if only just long enough for me to get the shot I wanted.

That night I created a launderette in my room. The heat from the full-on radiators, and the gentle steaming of socks, trousers, pants, T-shirt and fleece, also suggested I'd built a sauna…

(DAY FOUR ~ MEALAISBHAL AND MANGURSTADH)

Day four broke with token gestures of blue skies and promises for our first Hebridean Mountain hike.

Mealaisbhal (*"Meal-ish-val"*) is the highest point on the island of Lewis. Sadly for Lewis, (and Mealaisbhal,) its proximity to the illustrious skyline of the nearby Isle of Harris, diminishes its impact and 'right' to be as imposing as a highest point should be. Still, Mealaisbhal makes up for this by situating itself in the most remote part of Lewis, a full hour's drive from our already remote hotel.

As our minibus finally turned off the narrow tarmac road, and onto an even smaller dirt track, I could see nothing but barren hills and lonely lochs. There was not a sign of human habitation, anywhere, in any direction.

After several attempts to break an axle, and smash a few limbs against the inside of the minibus as we ground our way down the track, we pulled into what served as a car-park in this wild and uninhabited place. It came as no surprise to note that we were the only ones in it.

Having put a few joints back into their sockets, we alighted from the minibus and set off down the track.

Little more than twenty minutes later, we stopped for Elevenses. The quiet of our surroundings conveyed a feeling of unearthly presence. It was as though the mountains were sleeping. I felt it prudent not to wake them...

After scanning the horizon, I turned to see the Beard staring at the hill we had our backs too. Without further ceremony, he began to bound towards its summit. This, it turned out, was Mealaisbhal.

Scotland is renowned for its mountains, its midges ... and its bogs. Thus, it came as no surprise when, some five hundred feet up a slope so steep that each footstep burned every tendon in my knees to ash, I discovered the bogs belonging to Mealaisbhal. They had been glued to the side of the mountain. How they stayed there without sliding into the loch below, became the subject of breathless debate, as each footstep sunk into one. The piece-de-resistance of this act was to stir up a rash of midges, upset because they'd been disturbed from doing whatever midges do in Scottish bogs.

Before long, I began to think this hill wasn't some anonymous eighteen hundred foot mound, but something tenfold closer to Everest, and one laden with booby traps at that. I soon realised the only way to make headway was on all fours.

Pausing for a moments rest, I looked up to see the Beard standing perfectly upright, on what appeared to be a sixty-degree slope. With hands-on-hips, his dulcet tones informed us, that what we were doing in local parlance, was known as 'squashing a mountain'. Now I knew why.

We continued 'squashing' Mealaisbhal for over an hour before the ground below our feet turned stony, and the going eased over the saddleback of the mountain.

Reaching the cairn denoting I had arrived at the summit, I paused for breath and took in the view. I could see nothing except rugged, but achingly beautiful desolation; a desolation that man had yet to ruin. I had no doubt that a crofter from centuries past would still recognise his home. Somewhere out there, wizards and mythical beasts still roamed.

Lunchtime set in among the broken sunshine, but before I could unpack my sandwiches, so too did the fabled Scotch mist. From whence it came, I don't know, but like something out of a Stephen King novel, it moved among us, chilling to the bone, and threatening to dissolve our bodies within its wraithlike arms. Unsettled, I felt compelled to find a way off the summit, and fast. I was not the only one.

After descending little more than a hundred feet, the mist thinned and shrank back from its grasp. With the brilliance of the sun once more re-assuring my body of its warmth, I stopped to look back at the summit. Now bathed in sunlight once more, it was as though the mountain's spirits had disapproved of being 'squashed'... a place indeed for wizards.

As we made our way down through yet more Scottish bogs, I could not help but curse every minor feeling of unsteadiness, or mistrusted footfall as I slithered down the mountain; vivid memories of dislocating kneecaps, doing everything they could to create a sense of impending pain. After one too many undesired squelches, I stopped to check where everyone was.

Disconcertingly, the Beard was not among us. The mist hadn't got him though; apparently, he'd gone to rescue the minibus from its lonely vigil. In his absence, he had thoughtfully elected a new leader and given him specific instructions to follow.

Our newly elected leader did not have a beard, but the qualification of being a Scotsman with the next highest number of hills squashed, eight, against the Beard's four million and six, was enough to give him the job.

The task he had been set was a simple one... follow the line of telegraph poles we could see some way below us, and we would eventually find the road where the Beard would, should, be waiting for us with the minibus. Without further command or suggestion of leadership from our fearless new leader, we all made our own way to the nearest telegraph pole.

Arriving at the pole, we discovered the footpath we assumed would meet us there, didn't exist. What lay between us and the now mythical rendezvous, was at least another mile of a dank, smelly, midge-ridden bog.

I had forgotten that in these remote hills, there are no footpaths; one merely plotted how to get from 'A' to 'B' by using landmarks, and then guessing the safest route between them. For the next hour, twelve hapless individuals fanned out to leapfrog the impeding bogs via the sanctuary of the grassy tussocks that stood between them; all the while making their way towards Point 'B'.

We arrived at the rendezvous point just in time to see the Beard stop where he expected to find us... about half a mile from where we actually were... Despite this, and apparently satisfied we had passed his next test, he announced that our reward would be some time out on the nearby beach. Enthusiastically, we all piled into the minibus... only to alight from it less than two minutes later.

Traigh Mangurstadh *(Tray man-gur-sta)* lay half-hidden from view, behind a barrier of sand-dunes.

Having made our way through those dunes, the loneliest of beaches presented a timeless moment.

With the sky to the west, foreboding, threatening of yet more rain, and the sun behind us, the effect on Traigh Mangurstadh was one of startling contrast. While the sun gave a silvery edge to the white horses of the ocean, and the brilliant white quartzite sand sparkled our skin, the clouds above blackened the encircling cliffs to frame the picture. The only sound, the roar of the Atlantic Ocean, made its presence known on a shore, from which the next landfall was more than four thousand miles away. If I had packed my tent, my trek would have ended on that beach...

Casting my eyes to the ground, I began beachcombing; lost to the world, until a small voice urged me to check where our leader was. I looked up to see him, now barefoot, halfway up a vertical billiard table of a cliff-face. If this was another test, then bollocks, he was on his own; besides, I didn't have suckers on my feet, toe-claws or whatever it was, he was using to defy gravity with...

An hour later, and with some reluctance, I re-joined our intrepid minibus for the journey to that evening's accommodation on the Isle of Harris.

We arrived on the isle of Harris without ever crossing water. The Beard informed us that the isles of Lewis and Harris are in fact one single landmass, but retain their status as separate islands. This he continued, was entirely due to a family feud over who owned the mountains of Harris; and who owned the relatively lower-lying hills of Lewis. Neither side won, and so they went their separate ways, ne'er the two to meet, or talk, again. Lewis and Harris are thus islands of human vanity rather than physical ones.
We drove through the mountains of Harris and onward to the village of Tarbert.

Our accommodation that evening was renowned for the encampment of spoiled celebrity nobodies who absconded from the nearby island of Taransay during the making of a dross TV reality series. Less well known perhaps is that my room was past its sell-by date, something I discovered when the weight of my towel caused the towel-rail to break free from the wall, and collapse to the floor...

(DAY FIVE ~ AN CLISHAM)

Tarbert provides everything the Islanders need... in a pint-sized pot. It does this squeezed between formidable hills while lying perched on the smallest of Isthmus between the Atlantic Ocean and the relative shelter of The Minch, a turbulent stretch of water that separates the islands from the mainland. The modest of tidal waves could sweep the entire village to oblivion in a matter of seconds...

ADVENTURES OF A MIDDLE-AGED FART

Today we were to take on 'An Clisham', the highest point on Harris, and at twenty-six hundred feet, the highest point in the Outer Hebrides.

Our minibus duly climbed back up the road between Tarbert and Stornoway, and promptly disappeared into a mist so thick it needed a consensus vote among us to agree where it had gone... Thankfully, we were all on board it at the time...

We finally pitched up at the only flat piece of land that wasn't in the middle of the road and disembarked to find the cloud closing in still further. This didn't seem to worry the Beard, who assured us it was an easy track up to the summit... Reluctantly we made to follow him. We didn't have much choice really; he had the keys to the minibus...

Within yards of setting out, we began the now-familiar routine of bog-hopping. But as the ground steepened, we realised the bogs of Harris, unlike those on Lewis, hadn't learned to glue themselves to slopes. Instead, they just covered the ground with a primaeval goo that provided all the grip of an ice-skating rink...

The Beard, who evidently not only had toe-claws but webbed feet, soon strode off into the distance, leaving us to negotiate our own way forward. It was not long before he had completely vanished into the mist.

Little more than thirty minutes later, the ground levelled off. It was a good place to take stock of our surroundings. Somehow we had all become separated. Rather than call out for voices to follow, I kept going in what I assumed was the right direction. Somewhere out there, I hoped to find a summit, except there was no one in front, or behind me, to confirm where it was. As the mist enveloped everything in a sweat of ice-cold crystalline droplets, an unnerving sense of being lost crept over me.

With some relief, I finally spotted the unmistakable shadowy figure of the Beard stood astride a stone cairn. I could tell it was him from the profile of the beard... and the angular way his shorts jutted out just above the knees. I knew then that I had made it to the summit.

As my eyes became accustomed to the murk, several of the huddled boulders nearby, morphed into huddled trekkers. I promptly joined them to sit, like they were, with feet dangling over a small ledge, and began to munch thoughtfully on my sandwiches. In front of me, the grey blanket of nothingness was all-consuming.

A few minutes passed before the Beard started to speak slowly, and with that measured calm of Doctors when the news is not good...

"Can I suggest you chaps don't do that thing where you push yourself off of a ledge to stand up...? It would create an awful lot of paperwork..."

Stopping mid-chew, I turned instinctively towards my neighbour for some form of analysis. He'd also stopped chewing, and was looking back at me; our minds combining in the slow assessment of the Beard's words.

With a sense that our feet were dangling over a cliff-edge, hundreds of feet above the ground below, and that they were about to be sucked over it, we recoiled our feet violently away, and frantically shuffled backwards as fast as we could. I finally stopped shuffling only when the feeling of pissing myself, finally abated. A similar backward scrabbling from the rest of the group soon followed as the Beard's words filtered through the mist.

That mist had made the ledge seem benign, but the sensation in the pit of my stomach assured me that I had potentially just avoided the end of my life. I now understood entirely, why the best advice of seasoned mountaineers when you cannot see where you are going, is to camp down and wait until things clear up. I didn't know whether to curse the Beard for being reckless, or trust that he had a sixth sense that could read the intentions of our minds...

Before long, the icy fingers of the mist began to claw their way through my clothing once again. No longer having a desire to finish the sandwich in my hand, I hurled it over the unseen cliff-edge, half expecting someone or some 'thing' to throw it back.

With a sense of urgency, I stood up and followed the Beard back down the mountain towards the Minibus, lost somewhere below us.

If yesterday's descent was at times hairy, today's was going to twist every joint in my legs, clean out of their sockets. With the phantom sense of pain from so many past falls plaguing me, I crept down that hill like an old codger who'd lost his Zimmer frame. After slipping for the fourth time, and cursing loudly in the process, the Beard materialised from the mist to reveal the secret of bog-hopping to me.

"The trick," he said, "is to be nimble, and dab quickly with the toes, barely touching the ground before you spring to the next step."

This seemed an odds-on way to remove a kneecap to me, so with deep foreboding, I tried a few steps according to his advice... It worked, although I was grateful to the mist for hiding my ungainly ballet.

After several appallingly executed grand jetés, I made it to the more accessible slopes with both legs still intact. Sometimes the simplest of things can earn the greatest of respect... From wondering if the Beard was trying to kill me, I now considered I owed him a pint...

Hotel food is always expensive. So that night, some of us headed for the half-the-cost bar across the road. As we walked in, the Dartboard action stopped in mid-flight, and the beer froze in mid-flow.

Our Scottish colleague, he of the temporary leader status back at Mealaisbhal, approached the bar while the rest of us remained close enough to the entrance to effect an escape with minimal casualties. After a tense stand-off, he ordered a pint and asked if we could all get a beer and some food.

To our relief we Sassenachs from south of the border, 'the auld enemy' of centuries past, were permitted to stay and eat... so long as we brought beer and made no reference to any sport we had beaten Scotland at lately. Since haggis-tossing is not a sport I am familiar with but appeared to be the only one we hadn't beaten them at, I prudently remained silent while waiting for my fish and chips to arrive.
Having collected them from the bar with head bowed in subservient acknowledgement, I made my way outside to join the others.

During the short walk back to the hotel, I looked skyward. So far as I could tell in the pitch black of a highland night, the mist had finally lifted...

(DAY SIX ~ IT'S ALL A BIT TWEE'D)

Morning woke up wet, but thankfully, it wasn't me... so I made my way down to breakfast.

Our mountain today would have to wait. First, we were off to visit one of Harris's legendary weavers of tweed, an almost bulletproof fabric worn by everyone from Antarctic explorers, to famous pop stars, the Beatles among them.

I walked into the workshop to be humbled by the skill of the eighty-something woman, and her two daughters, but saddened to learn that better money could be made by holding one's hand out for unemployment benefit... Even so, pride and good old-fashioned Scottish stubbornness had ensured the art would still be practised for one more generation at least. They also had one of the best sales pitches I'd heard since Mohammed's in Morocco...

On spying a small piece of tweed woven with a purple dye made from the local heather, I picked it up to examine it. Seeing my interest, the mother sidled up to me, and in a soothing Gaelic lilt, assured me that purple was being phased out as it was too expensive to make. She added that purple also happened to be the most popular colour among the rich and famous, but by that time, my hand was already rummaging for my wallet...

Emerging from the tiny workshop, I stopped to look at my purchase in the broad light of day. Within seconds, I was set upon by a posse of Scotland's resident population of midges. As the first one sunk its fangs into my skin, I pondered the justification for their existence.

Hearing my curses, the Beard chose the moment to advise everyone that midges are weak flyers, and even the simple act of swaying from side to side is usually enough to prevent them from landing on you. He also suggested that black clothing tended to attract them. For one particularly unfortunate sod, this was a rather late piece of news on the colour front...

The workshop, being on a rather flat area though, was clearly not challenging enough for the Beard. Thus, we were soon hurtling towards our rendezvous with the ferry for North Uist, and our next mountain.

Realising that we would be over an hour early for the ferry, the Beard chose to stop for a look-see at one of the most exquisite beaches few ever set eyes upon... Luskantyre. The brilliant white 'Machair' that makes up the beach is comprised of tiny fragments of seashells, which, when crushed underfoot, or swept along by the incessant wind, create an eerie high-pitched sound. It's almost as though someone is singing.

For a while, the rain and mist, and whatever ailed the deepest parts of my soul, were washed away by the sound of the sea, and the caress of the Machair between my toes. Offshore, the island of Taransay provided a backdrop, while to my right Harris's dressing of mountains soft-focused the eyes. I could imagine that on a dark and windy night, Luskantyre gave birth to legends of Mermaids...

For the second time that week, I'd wandered alone on a beach so mesmerising, that I could have just sat down, grown old, and faded contentedly into the sand...

We arrived at the ferry terminal just as the sun finally began to put in a genuine attempt at brightening the scenery; it hadn't done this since its momentary appearance on the beach at Traigh Mangurstadh. I climbed out of the bus to encourage it...

Finding that I was stood next to the Beard, I followed his gaze. In the distance, I could discern a small molehill in the middle of the island just across the sound; the Beard had his eyes firmly fixed upon it. I felt like telling him to take some deep breaths, while I massaged his shoulders in a desperate attempt to calm his withdrawal symptoms from not having climbed something since yesterday...

It was not the longest of ferry rides, and just thirty minutes later, we disembarked. Twenty minutes after that we were staring at Li a'Tuath *(Lee-uh-too-a)*, the molehill the Beard had been salivating over for most of the last two hours.

The hill resembled little more than something one might attempt during a Sunday afternoon stroll, but to access it made up for what it lacked in the challenge to reach its summit. The Beard, as keen as ever for his vertical fix, soon had our group strung out over several hundred yards of Scottish bog, as we made our way to the mountain's base.

Pausing for breath, my eyes mentally plotted the easy route to the summit; nevertheless, the Beard had already determined we would take the North Face of the Eiger approach. Like everyone else, I duly followed him.

We finally reached the summit and sat down for lunch, just in time to witness the mist roll in once more. I began to wonder if it was following us... It didn't stay long though, for as the wind gently nudged it away, there, behind it, and very much heading our way, were some particularly dark and menacing clouds... menacing enough to cause the Beard to stop eating, rise from his seat, and set off down the other side of Li a'Tuath with some purpose. I sighed heavily; and, once more, rose to follow him...

Chasing after the Beard, I noted the tussocks on this side of the mountain appeared to be further apart than those we'd negotiated before climbing Li a'Tuath. I wasn't the only one with this perception. I wondered what the ghost of a crofter might have thought, had they witnessed our attempts to leap between the tussocks while trying desperately not to fall into the bogs...

Personally speaking, I chose 'Option one'... the 'step quickly and lightly' method the Beard had demonstrated on An Clisham. Unfortunately, I soon learned that Scottish bogs react like water-beds... if you are rather heavy and 'bounce' on them long enough, they eventually give way...

Some elected for 'Option two'... the 'giant leap for mankind' method, which, because this is not the moon, usually resulted in gravity playing its part to soak several body parts besides the victim's boots, as they fell short of their target.

Those failing both these options merely elected to take the 'sod it, I've already got soggy boots' approach and took the most direct route... irrespective of the consequences. ...Meanwhile, the Beard, already a long way ahead of us, remained bone-dry...

When we finally made it back to the Minibus, the Beard informed us that our achievement had been to cross an area about as "off-piste" as Scotland gets...

Thus, with some pride, we set off for our hotel; decorum pervading the interior of the minibus, as no-one made any comment on the tidemarks or the smells of those less fortunate in their choice of bog-hopping method...

Our hotel that night was in the small village of Carinish. When we arrived, the Beard surprised us with the information that he had a date with, we presumed, Mrs Beard, and that he would therefore not be joining us for the evening meal.

With backpacks slung over shoulders, we walked up to the reception desk to be greeted by a blind steaming drunk... He was so drunk that he couldn't read the room numbers writ large upon the piece of paper in his hands. Snatching it from him, we figured out the rest for ourselves.

Opening the door to my room, and longing for a hot shower, I turned the tap on full blast. Finding the water still cold five minutes later, and then discovering there was no heating in the room either, I stormed back to the Reception Desk.

By the time I arrived, several of our group had already gathered there to make polite rumblings, while they waited for our blind steaming drunk to reappear. When he finally tottered out of the kitchen to face us, I cut straight to the point:

"Where's the Owner, please?" I demanded.

"I AM the owner!" he replied, with his hand clutched American like to his chest.

"Who else is here?" I asked, in the hope that there was a more cohesive member of staff present.

"The Chef!" he replied.

"Go and get him, please."

"I AM the chef!" he declared still clutching his chest but now swaying violently.

I gave up. No hot water and no heating is one thing to tolerate, but clearly, there was to be no dinner either. Even if our drunken host had attempted to cook something, events in Morocco still haunted me sufficient to remove all desire to eat it, and this without consideration of the potential for a gas explosion, if our inebriated chef cum owner's breath had caught the pilot light on the burner...

Frustrated, I wandered out of the hotel to set eyes on a modest-sized building a short walk down the road. There was a small car-park in front of it. If I hadn't just found the local community centre, then I'd discovered the village pub.

To the bewilderment of the two meals a night restaurant that made up a quiet corner of the pub, twelve of us thundered in and ordered food. We were in no hurry and would eat whatever they could provide us with. It didn't take long for the waitress to work out that we were staying at the hotel up the road...
The beer flowed freely that night. Not since Torres Del Paine had I relaxed and enjoyed company so much.

Our enjoyment, however, was curtailed rather abruptly around ten o'clock, when somebody suggested that our decision to abandon the food at the hotel might have resulted in our being locked out. With visions of backpacks strewn across the bog infested fields surrounding the village, we headed back to the hotel with some haste. Thankfully, the door was unlocked; the hotel appeared to be deserted.

We thoughtfully locked the door behind us that night... despite not checking to see if the owner was asleep in the flowerbeds...

(DAY SEVEN ~ UISGE GU LEOR / WHISKY GALORE)

As usual, I was first to rise for breakfast.
Walking into the dining room, I found a lad from the Czech Republic laying out the tables. After a polite 'Good morning', 'Anton' revealed that he was working the summer at the hotel, and planned to return to college in Prague in a couple of weeks. I felt for him when he admitted it had been three weeks since he had last received any wages. I left the hotel that morning wanting to physically wring Anton's wages out of the owner, cum cook, cum alcoholic, but on seeing all the empty bottles behind the bar, suspected the only thing I might have wrung out of him, would have been whisky...

Today, was to be an assault on the giddy and technical heights of Ben More on South Uist, but with seventy miles per hour winds, and the surprising knowledge that even the Beard wasn't convinced he could achieve the climb in those conditions, there was a change of plan.

After searching in earnest for something else to satisfy his vertical needs, the Beard finally decided to take us to the island of Benbecula. This was interesting because the island appeared to be dead flat, and primarily made up of water.

As it turned out, it did have a high point. 'Rueval', at a mere three hundred and sixty feet above sea level, was perceptible as little more than a bulge in the landscape. Nevertheless, it was the highest point on the island, and thus, the Beard had to climb it, and we, no choice but to follow him once more.

Before attempting the mighty mound, however, I expressed concern that I was fresh out of Tunnocks biscuits and that nobody had a packed lunch either. Personally, I suspect had we asked for one from our inebriated hotel owner, it would have resulted in another Culloden... or at least several whiskies.

After taking a deep breath, the Beard bowed to our famished conditions and drove past the sign for Rueval, and on towards the incongruous Armed forces base at Baile Mhanuich *(Bali-van-ich)*. Here, we visited our first and only supermarket on the trek.

This was no corporate affair, however; this was a traditional family-owned business. Its mission, a simple one... to stock one of everything each person on the island required. I was grateful that everyone on the island appeared to require Tunnocks biscuits, for they had an entire shelf to themselves... Restocked, we made our way back to Rueval.

With a ready-made mini-bus sized track right up to its flanks, the Beard spoiled the fun by pulling into a lay-by, to allow us the jollity of a short trek in the wind and driving rain.

With our short trek over, soaked, but still only two hours into the day by the time of conquest; I asked if we could take a trip down to the island of Eriskay. To my jubilation, the Beard agreed, partly I suspect, on account that he had never been there either. I sincerely hoped Eriskay didn't have any mountains on it...

I couldn't believe my luck. When I signed up for the trek, I'd wondered if there would be time to make a personal visit to Eriskay. I no longer needed to wonder, for that wish was now a reality.

If you've spent your life on another planet, or watched too many television reality shows, you will not know the fateful story of twenty-eight thousand cases of whisky, courtesy of the S.S. Politician... So, for the sake of explaining my enthusiasm at our impending visit, indulge me if you will...

Back in the days of World War Two, as America shipped food and armaments to the British, so we sent them whisky. Unfortunately, one of these shipments ran aground on the rocky shores of the island of Eriskay. Fortunately for the Islanders who had been devoid of whisky for some months, however, the wreck was close enough inshore to allow them to stock up... duty-free. Official estimates state that over two thousand cases; twenty-four thousand bottles; of that whisky, vanished from the wreck. Quite what happened to them is conjecture, but from reports that followed, visitors to the island claimed to have found many of the island's four hundred residents incoherent. The story became a book, and later, a much-loved piece of film noir.

We rattled through the mist and rain of South Uist for almost an hour, before rounding a bend to see a causeway stretching a tarmac finger towards the tiny island on my 'see before I die' list. I noted a sign on the causeway warning us to look out for otters... From what I could see of the weather, they would have had better sense to be on holiday in Zante...

The tiny island of Eriskay, one that you could walk around in only a few hours, not only had a legendary cargo to its name, but also played host to Bonnie Prince Charlie when he landed there in his attempt to claim the English throne. The event was the start of the Jacobite Rebellion, a rebellion that ended catastrophically for many a Highland Clan, less than a year later, at the Battle of Culloden Moor.

The beach where he landed; 'Coilleag a'phrionnsa' - which poetically translates as 'the Prince's cockleshell strand'; is easy to find; the clue being the appearance of a small pink flower which grows there. Legend has it that the flower secured its foothold on the beach after Bonnie Prince Charlie cast its seed from his hand, as a gesture of his homecoming. When it's not flowering, there's also a towering monument to the event, perched incongruously on the dunes above the beach to aid identification...

As I alighted from the minibus to take my fill of history, I sensed there were few more evocative places on this Earth. I could have been waiting for Bonnie Prince Charlie's arrival myself...

Soaked by the ever-increasing wind and rain, we soon jumped back on the minibus. My heart sank; I would have loved to explore more of the island, not least because of the romantic notion that I might discover a bottle of the fabled whisky from the S. S. Politician, hidden down some long-disused rabbit hole.

With the day still young, and most of us now visibly soaked to the skin, the Beard decided we had time to stop for a warming drink at the island pub, the aptly named 'An Politician'. I could not restrain my delight.

Walking up to the bar, I ordered a 'wee' dram of Uisge Beatha *('oosh-kee ba-har' - 'Water of Life')*... but you might call it Whisky, as a celebration of this brief utopian moment in my life.

After a short respite involving at least two more whiskies, the Beard stood up and began to gaze out of the window. I should have known... he'd spotted a hill, one he evidently hadn't climbed before. Thus, he proceeded to announce that he was going to climb it, but, and to my relief, declared that the trek to the summit was "optional". This was a good thing because I wasn't moving... for now at least.

With the rain now lashing horizontally across the island, the Beard, assisted by a few brave souls, set out for the assault.

Within minutes, our elected second in command decided to open up the pool table. The inevitable 'Scotland v England' match that followed, was liberally encouraged by several more drams of whisky.

Each time I approached the bar, I would, much to the amusement of the barmaid, try to pronounce the name on the bottle of my next whisky. After more drams than is recommended to make public, the thought occurred to me. I had to ask the obvious question...

"Has anyone ever found one of those missing bottles from the S. S. Politician?" I slurred to the barmaid.

She smiled and replied with an astonishing, "Sure, someone found this one down a rabbit hole last week."

Removing the bottle from the shelf behind her, she handed it to me. I sank slowly onto a nearby barstool, the bottle cradled carefully in both hands; my eyes glazing over as the hubbub of the crowded bar faded into the background. Caressing the bottle with my fingers, I noted the cork was still in it. Naturally, I asked if I could volunteer to try the contents, but, apparently, I could not... Nevertheless, for a moment at least, there was just that bottle, and me, together in our own little world.

It was a moment I will never forget. I just wish I'd been a little less inebriated; I might then have remembered to get a photograph...

Carefully passing the fabled bottle back to the barmaid with great appreciation, I sighed heavily and ordered one of its lesser mortals for consolation.

By mutual agreement, we finally declared the game of pool an honourable draw, although the whisky sloshing around inside me, had my soul favouring a Scottish victory, or perhaps an Eriskay one.

When the hill-climbing heroes finally returned, the Beard hastened us to move on. I sighed. I could have stayed, stayed forever... My last chance to claim asylum on Eriskay occurred while buying more Tunnocks biscuits at the island's store; I blew it.

We were soon driving back across the causeway, and with indecent haste heading into the reality that our holiday would soon be over. Tomorrow we would leave the Outer Hebrides for the island of Skye and one last ascent. Tonight though was all about memories, whisky, good company ... and more whisky.

Euphoria and melancholy, finally set in long after midnight...

(DAY EIGHT ~ OVER THE SEA TO SKYE)

Our last full day woke to a clear blue sky, a stiff breeze, and still no sign of our alcoholic host.
Breakfast a-la-Czech, ended with a whip-round to present the young lad with enough cash to get him a lot nearer Prague than the hotel owner ever seemed likely to.

As I waited for the others to gather themselves before we headed for the ferry to the Isle of Skye, I crossed the road to the field opposite to take a closer look at the remains of a small Kirk *(church)*. The information board next to it contained enough history to humble the mightiest of English churches. The hand-carved Gaelic inscriptions, indecipherable upon the tombstones, told their story to only those who mattered.
The Beard hurried our minibus across the island of North Uist that morning with enough spare time to visit a chambered tomb; the entrance to which would suit any Tolkiensian storyline. He followed this with a short route march up to the summit of another mound, 'Langais', and then down to a small stone circle, sat amongst the heather showing its colours for the first time that week.
The photogenic circle continued the Tolkiensian theme, with a story of people dancing on the Sabbath, and being; as they are in every Neolithic circle, turned to

stone. The unlucky souls here danced for Finn MacCuil, who lords over them today as the largest of the monoliths.

When visiting these mysterious places, time is all too easily lost. Thus, when caught off-guard by this fact, the Beard, concerned we would miss our ferry, route-marched us to the minibus, and then demonstrated its Turbo-charged go-faster stripes, as we broke most of the local speed limits to reach the terminal in time. We arrived just as our ferry to Skye was swinging expertly into the bay.

I spent the time aboard that ferry looking back towards the Outer Hebrides with a longing no amount of accompanying wildlife could distract. It was not home, but my heart tugged for it. One day, perhaps...

The ferry duly arrived at the village of Uig on the Isle of Skye and, minutes later, with no chance to sample the efforts of the nearby brewery, we headed for the hinterland of the Trotternish peninsula, and our final trek of the week.

Our objective was a pinnacle of rock oddly named 'The Old Man of Storr'. The Beard, however, decided to go one better and headed for something less pronounceable, the 'Quiraing'.

After rounding a sudden and precipitous hairpin in the road, our goal appeared high to our left. I can only describe the scene before my eyes, as the crumbs of what might be left if someone had taken a giant bite out of the plateau we had just crossed. Those crumbs also had names - the 'Needle', the 'Table', and the 'Prison', among others.

We walked out across the sheep nibbled grassland, and up towards the cliff face to take a look at 'The Prison', which, as its name suggested, gave an excellent impression as somewhere suitable to produce a remake of 'The Count of Monte Christo'.

Soon after, we reached an almost vertical ascent. Looking up, I concluded it was only suitable for goats... and Beards. Disappointingly, our Beard was already two hundred vertical leaps up it by the time I'd contemplated this fact. With a wry smile on my face, I leaned forward and began my ungainly 'on all fours' ascent.

Reaching the top of the slope, I paused for a moment to gawp at the equally well-named 'Needle'. It looked unassailable; yet, as the Beard informed us, two boy scouts had climbed it only a few years previously. I had visions of two spotty teenagers in shorts, armed only with a pack of Tunnocks, and a penknife. I looked at the Beard suspiciously... and wondered if he had any offspring...

After another short climb, the Beard declared it was time for Elevenses.

From our rocky perch, we looked down upon the 'Table', a sheer-sided plug of volcanic rock left over from a time when the Atlantic Ocean thought it would part the continents of Europe and America through Skye, rather than its ultimate choice, Iceland.

To accompany the view, the Beard related a bizarre story of inter-village football that took place on the 'Table' every year. Given its lofty perch, I wondered just what happened if someone kicked the ball off the 'Table'. From my position above it, I calculated the ball would roll at least seven hundred feet down the hill to the car-park below if they did... This left me wondering if the job of 'Ball-boy' was filled by conscription...

Following a circuitous route back to the minibus, we headed inevitably towards our last night's accommodation in the village of Edinbane.

Despite the chill wind, the rain, the mist, and the disappointment of being locked out of the local lock-in at the village hostelry that night, I climbed into bed, concluding that the trek had ended in high spirits... albeit mainly whisky spirits...

(DAY NINE ~ LONG ROAD HOME)

The solemn breakfast that morning, announced our departure from the Isle of Skye across the new bridge connecting it to the mainland. As we crossed, strains of the 'Skye Boat Song' flashed through my mind; I mentally registered the island for a return visit one day.

Once on the mainland, our faithful Minibus cut loose, and with an open road, nuked its way past Mach One in its indecent haste to shed us and find an excuse to return to the Outer Hebrides. I couldn't blame it... there was a lot more to see over there... especially if the mist ever decided to leave.

At Inverness Station, the Beard, whose ever-smiling face failed to hide the need to seek the nearest vertical challenge as soon as possible, said his goodbyes and evaporated as mysteriously as he had arrived a week ago. The temporary friendships formed during the last week also disappeared to board trains heading in all directions south. I alone joined the train back to the purgatory of Dyce.

I arrived at the dreaded Dyce station and wondered if it was possible to walk to Aberdeen airport. I didn't have time to consider the idea further before the only other passenger to alight at the station, figured the airport was my destination too and offered to share a taxi with me. Even better, he was an oil-worker, and on expenses. This one, he declared, was on him.

We arrived at Aberdeen Airport, our brief encounter ending with him walking off to find some hair-raising flight in a helicopter to one of those toadstools in the North Sea. I'd learned just enough about him to know his golf handicap was 'One'...

Crossing the concourse to the check-in desk for my flight home, I discovered that 'sour-faced cow' from Exeter had moved to Aberdeen; either that or she had a twin sister... Whichever version she was, she certainly enjoyed herself informing everyone that our flight had been cancelled... due to 'technical difficulties,' she said. From my outbound flight experience, I deduced this to mean the plane had crashed somewhere. With rather too much flippancy, 'sour-faced cow' concluded her announcement by suggesting there "might" be a flight tomorrow...

If this were Stornoway airport on the Outer Hebrides, I would have suffered that delay gladly, but we were still too near Dyce to contemplate the idea of finding a hotel for the night... Visions of becoming one of those I'd seen in the shop queueing for whisky, were all too real. Thus, I had to find another way home, at any cost...

Wandering back across the concourse, I approached the Hire-Car desk and discovered to my surprise, that I could trade in the 'return' part of my airline ticket, for a hire car. Even better... they had run out of 'economy class' vehicles, so offered me an 'executive hire' for the same price. With keys in hand, I re-crossed the concourse, pausing only to jingle them at 'Sour-faced cow', before heading out of the terminal for the drive home.

Ten hours had passed since waking on the Isle of Skye that morning; ahead of me lay an eleven-hour drive, but 'cruise control', leather seats, and an amazingly powerful 'in-car' hi-fi system, ensured I arrived home safe...

As the sun began to break the night sky, I crawled into my bed and closed my eyes. With memories of pristine beaches, Eriskay, and the warmth of a phantom whisky inside, I slept like a baby.

ADVENTURES OF A MIDDLE-AGED FART

THE UNDISCOVERED COUNTRY

As the world discovered adventurers like me, so it made it harder to find those 'white bits' on the map we all sought. It also tended to use a pricing formula along the lines of 'think of a number, and double it' if we wanted to go there. Then, one day, something almost miraculous happened...

With little fanfare, one of the smallest of European enclaves, one, once firmly behind communist iron doors, declared its independence; and did so without the expected fight for freedom. Here then, was a genuinely undiscovered country, one still relatively naïve to the money it could make from being a 'white bit' on the map, but one that was ready for business nonetheless.

Getting there proved to be tougher than I thought. I could find no information about visa requirements whatsoever; the country's main airport had yet to re-open, and even if I planned to get there by being seasick on a ferry, there wasn't one of those either. For all my efforts then, I was very quickly back to 'square one'.

A few weeks later, however, I was surprised to receive an email from one of my connections, alerting me to a trek in a 'new' country. That 'new' country turned out to be the very one I was trying to get to... Thus, with little regard for knowing how they'd achieved what I'd failed to, I clicked on the link and booked my place. At last, I was bound for 'Crna Gora'... Montenegro.

(DAY ONE ~ CULTURAL NOTES)

Have you ever found yourself looking furtively at luggage labels while queuing at an airport check-in? While waiting my turn for the flight to Dubrovnik, I confess I was no exception. From what I could see, this was going to be a very popular flight.

With nothing better to do, I struck up the obligatory idle-talk with my next queued in line and quickly learned they were going on holiday to Croatia. They didn't know precisely where in Croatia they were going, even though it was written on their luggage tags. If they needed a further clue, the flight they were queueing for was bound for the same city... As is wont with these sort of inane conversations, though, they wanted to know where I was heading too. Recognising their holiday destination, half of me wanted to say the same place, but I knew I was heading somewhere with far greater kudos... or so I thought...

"Oh, Montenegro," I blithely replied.

I didn't exactly get an 'ooh' or 'ah', more of an 'oh'; I could tell they didn't have a clue where Montenegro was, let alone Croatia, which, as I was fast becoming sympathetic towards, would be their hosts. I smiled benignly at their ignorance, and secretly wished holiday tummy on them. Perhaps next year that holiday hotel in Benidorm they thought they'd booked would turn out to be a brothel halfway up the Congo...

After following the usual human degrading process through the time-tunnel, aka security check, I melted into the departure lounge for the obligatory two-hour wait for the boarding call, and began my people watching observations...

No Zante crowd this time, but inevitably for an English Bank holiday, there was a large assemblage of package tourists bound for Marbella. They were easy to spot, distinguishable by the beer bellies, Hawaiian shirts, straw hats, 'Eau du sun-cream', sunglasses - worn in a moderately lit airport lounge with polarised windows... and their six tons of carry-on luggage. I watched one such Social Security profiled family buy a ticket to win a Ferrari; or rather, watched the father buy one, while the rest of the family berated him for spending all the fish & chip money.

There were also the familiar massage chairs, one complete with a victim, whose comatose grin suggested he'd actually got his five pounds worth of de-stressing. I hoped that by the time he woke, the chair had prepared him for the sudden onrush of stress he would endure when he realised it was long past his scheduled boarding time.

Getting airborne that morning was one of the more hairy versions I've endured. With zero visibility, sudden glimpses of other planes through the murk, and lots of banking and twisting, I wondered if our haphazard climb occurred because the pilot was using sonar to find his way out of the greyness that engulfed us... Nevertheless, by the time we broke free of the cloud, we had already climbed twenty thousand feet.

As we levelled out, our pilot, evidently relieved at not hitting anything, informed us we would be travelling across northern France, then via Stuttgart, before turning south to fly down the Adriatic coast. The information was all rather pointless though, as the cloud cover below us remained featureless, punctuated only by the occasional vapour trail, which we regularly dissected on our way over wherever.

Following a less than subtle turn right, presumably, to avoid denting the plane on one of the Alps, we descended through the grey, to reveal a coastline of shattered slivers of land... the Adriatic coast had finally pierced the gloom. Despite the ugly truth that the Mediterranean is among the most polluted seas in the world, the arm of it that lay below us, was making an excellent impression of blueness... perhaps it was just the dye...

Dubrovnik airport was a long time coming. The descent, laborious if meticulous, as we ducked and dived between islands and mountain peaks on our way to land proved a unique experience, for I had yet to land at an airport where the natives could sit on their porches, and look down on you as flew past. But this was that landing...

Not for the first time in my life, we alighted onto the tarmac. I had no desire to wave or kiss the tarmac this time though. If I had, the steaming package tour mob behind me would probably have made use of me as a carpet... Instead, I headed straight for the terminal building.

Immigration control was the traditional small country stamp without a word or look. On collecting my backpack, I headed out into the entrance lobby.

Seeing two sporty looking women, I latched onto them and followed them towards a man wielding a card with the correct company name on it.

"Cycling tour Sir?"

Sod it. No. What is it with this cycling thing, anyhow? Nevertheless, the bevvy of beauties surrounding the Eddie Merckx lookalike sign wielder had me sorely tempted to try it...

There were plenty of other boards to peer at, though, but it was the sound of laughter coming from one board-toter I'd ignored while following the cycling beauties, that finally attracted me back to inquire.

After several enthusiastic handshakes, and derisory comments about the Welsh and Scottish contingents present - followed by the traditional retaliatory strikes against the English, it became clear I'd found the right group. Evidently, this trek was also going to be a lot more fun than France...

As the laughter died down and international frontiers were re-secured, our board-toter proudly declared that he was Serbian... There followed a long silence.

Serbia had been the aggressor in both Bosnia and in Montenegro... precisely where we were heading. Nobody quite knew how to react. Even so, like sheep to the slaughter, we followed him to the car-park where he proudly revealed the traditional trekking sized minibus, and yes, it was complete with an equally traditional oversized trailer.

As we approached it, I thought I heard a woman scream. It could have been, for what emerged from the driver's seat had all the appearance of a nine-foot ex-Russian Shot putter, with twenty years of steroids down his throat. But no, our driver was actually Herzegovinian, and the proud owner of a small fleet of minibuses. I noted he had the eyes of someone who drove his minibus for twenty-three out of every twenty-four hours...

We had driven little more than twenty minutes out of the airport when we reached the customs post for Bosnia and Herzegovina. Looking behind us, I could still see Dubrovnik. I now understood how the Serbians managed to destroy the place with such impunity during the Bosnian war; they could hit it without ever leaving Bosnia.

Several anxious moments later, a flash of the furry eyebrows our guide possessed, suggested we could enter Bosnia, possibly I thought because we appeared to be hostages.

Like all stamp collectors, I examined my passport to find a vague inky box with the letters "B&H" inscribed upon it. Since I could not think of any other country which could describe itself as 'B&H', and the likewise branded cigarettes were now out of fashion, I settled that the passport stamp had kudos. With a knowing smile, I tucked it back into my trouser pocket.

Little more than five miles later, we drove past a bullet-ridden sign. We had been welcomed to 'Republika Srpska'.

Within yards, a Ford Transit van of indeterminate vintage with paint slapped scrawl declaring that it belonged to the local police force, pulled across our path. The doors opened, and two gun-toting individuals stepped out. At this point, our driver thought it prudent to stop.

One of the gunmen walked up to the minibus and tapped on the door with the tip of his rifle. Our driver opened it. A short conversation followed between the gunman and our Serbian eyebrows. Things deteriorated with the news that the gunmen wanted our passports...

As the smile spread across the gunman's face... and that of our Serbian Eyebrows... the thought occurred to me that perhaps we really were hostages.

Reluctantly, I dug out my passport. After all, there's no point arguing with someone who clearly knew how to use the Kalashnikov in his hands. Assuming the worst, we duly followed them back to the nearby town of Trebinje.

The one f'd 'NATO fuck of' graffiti sign on the wall of the only shop in town, was enough to dispel any thoughts of camera snapping as we pulled up next to it. The gunmen ushered us inside the shop.

In times of war, any place will serve as somewhere to execute people or hold them hostage, but while the war was still fresh in people's mind, Bosnia was now officially at peace... we hoped.

With untold relief, the only hostage-taking done in Trebinje was that of the American ten-dollar bill I handed over the counter, for the one-dollar bar of chocolate I purchased from the shop. This proved sufficient to ensure I could return to the minibus. Others followed my lead.

A few minutes later, and with all hostages back in the bus and accounted for, the gunmen motioned us to follow them out of the town. At this point, I could tell that our Serbian's eyebrows were sweating a little, and our driver, despite his large frame, was decidedly tense. I felt helpless but strangely calm; there is, after all, nothing one can do in these circumstances.

We eventually reached a steep-sided valley where the van stopped. One of the gunmen, now with his rifle casually slung over his shoulder, walked back to our minibus and hopped up onto the step. In his hands were our passports. He then proceeded to call out the names on the passports, trying his best at English pronunciation. One by one, we deduced who he had mispronounced, identified ourselves, and walked up to the front of the bus to collect our passport; not one of us being stupid enough to correct him. When my turn came, I nodded respectfully towards the gunman and turned to walk back to my seat. I don't mind admitting I half-expected to fall to the floor with a bullet in my back...

Passports returned, our would-be captors jumped back into their van, turned it around, and headed back to Trebinje. We were free to go.

Once confident we were out of danger, I opened my passport to reveal a single 'Republika Srpska' stamp; something that was to cause consternation later that year when I travelled to the United States of America. I couldn't quite work out whether the immigration officer at Newark airport thought I'd made it up, or considered that I must have been some kind of covert specialist during the Bosnian War. After a minute or two staring at it, he handed my passport back across the counter in an almost slow-motion fashion... He didn't question the stamp, and I didn't offer any explanation...

I lost count of the hairpins we negotiated as we climbed out of the Trebinje valley, and climb we did. According to a GPS device in the clutches of one of our group, we were more than four thousand feet above sea level by the time we reached a border post. With some relief, I realised we were about to leave Bosnia.

A few yards further on my passport acquired another suspiciously amateur mark. This time, I was hoping for 'Montenegro'; what I got was 'Crna Gora', which, at the time, had no meaning whatsoever.

We finally stopped for a well-deserved beer at a mountainside shack. With the feeling that we had arrived at our destination, everyone began to settle in for the evening. It was not to be. It might have been eight o'clock, but the Eyebrows apologetically informed us, there was still another two hours' drive ahead of us.

With heavy sighs, we re-joined the bus and headed down the mountain to the town of Niksic, where we stopped again, this time for the bus's sake. Refuelled we set off once more.

Almost an hour later, we reached the town of Savnik, which turned out to be a derelict eyesore; an open festering wound set in a deep valley in the middle of stunning mountain scenery. The entire town appeared to be rotting its way down to the Earth's core. With the only visible industrial buildings, clearly long defunct, and the many locals we saw, giving seasoned impressions of unemployment, it came as no surprise to learn that Radovan Karadzic, the butcher of Srebrenica, was raised here...

Some miles further on, someone spotted a sign announcing the way to Zabljak, *(zja-blick)* our intended destination. To our surprise though, our driver reversed back past it and turned to head up what appeared to be a narrow dirt track. By now, night had fallen.

As we drove up the track, I could gauge how much we had climbed every time the cliff-edge on my side of the bus became visible in the moonlight glinting off the river below us... With its giant potholes, and narrow bridges with no safety barriers to prevent you falling off them, this last stretch of our journey, joined a very exclusive list of 'Greatest arse-twitching journeys I have known'.

We finally broke out onto a high plateau, and twenty minutes later, sighed with relief as we pulled up outside our hotel. It was almost midnight. The journey had taken eight hours from Dubrovnik, but as the owner of the GPS confirmed, we had travelled just one hundred and eighty miles...

As we regrouped in the lobby of the hotel, the owner proffered a box full of keys and disappeared back to his television in the adjacent room. I didn't get lucky and picked a key to the same room as one of my male colleagues...

The owner, now clearly having done his bit for customer services, ignored the question of where the rooms actually were, for it was patently obvious they could not be in the building we were standing in. It took a group of men smoking and drinking something questionable in the hotel's tiny bar, to provide the answer. After a brief conversation with the Eyebrows, one of them, cigarette in hand, motioned towards the hotel entrance. Our guide returned, walked past us, and out into the car-park. We followed. The accommodation block was on the opposite side of the road...

I opened the door to my room and looked around. Making a mental note of the shower and washbasin, I propped my backpack against the wall at the foot of one of the beds and moved to the window to draw the curtains. There weren't any. I looked for a Venetian blind. There wasn't one of those either. Giving up, and with only a rudimentary 'Good Night' to my roommate, I crawled into bed, drew the covers over my head, and fell into a deep sleep.

(DAY TWO ~ THE BEARS ARE WEARING UNIFORMS)

Early morning investigations of the bathroom, revealed the one-time tradition of all foreign destinations... no plugs. Being plugless, I lathered my face and stepped into the shower to shave while washing away yesterday's grime.

I had not been stood in the shower for more than a minute when I discovered it had a unique feature...

The showerhead sat in its holder innocuously enough, while, with eyes closed, I tipped my head back to allow the water to dribble over my face. Seeing me at my most vulnerable, the showerhead then wilted viciously. My nose caught the full force of the impact. Promptly questioning the shower's parentage, I leapt out to inspect the damage. There was a small but neat cut across the bridge of my nose.

I pondered warning my roommate about the risk but considered it far too early in the trek to establish whether he had any annoying habits. I said nothing.

Wandering out of the apartment block, I allowed my eyes to rest on a snow-patched mountain, incongruously set as the backdrop to a road full of building sites.

Zabljak it seemed was already well aware of its potential as the new tourist capital of Europe.

Crossing the road to the hotel, I entered the dining room. It may only have been seven in the morning, but the air was already thick with cigarette smoke. Glancing at the source; I wasn't entirely convinced any of them had left the bar since we arrived last night... Cutting my way through the fog, I made towards the table set aside for our group. The Eyebrows joined me a few minutes later.

During my adventures abroad, I have always made an effort to learn some essential words and phrases in the local language. The language of Montenegro, however, is one complicated by a Cyrillic alphabet. Thus, however much I might have liked to offer the Eyebrows a 'Good Morning' in Montenegrin, I was way out of my depth.

Nevertheless, following the usual English pleasantries, I broached the subject of learning those basics. The Eyebrows smiled, and from under his trekking notes *(yes he had them too, I wondered if he had ever met Clipboard Man)*; he handed me a crib sheet of Montenegrin words with their English counterpart... the Montenegrin had also been thoughtfully italicised in the phonetic language.

Venturing to tangle my tongue around the Montenegrin for 'Please' & 'Thank you', I finally uttered something that registered a smile of understanding, *(or pity,)* from our now table-setting waitress. A personal target of learning one Montenegrin word a day was clearly going to be a tough challenge.

Breakfast was that strange brew of eastern European fare: Strong flavoured smoked meats, smoked cheeses, and rustic bread; but at least I could be comforted by the appearance of those little white plastic tubs of marmalade, that taste like apricot jam, or was it banana? Passionfruit maybe..? Perhaps today it was peanut butter fudge...

With breakfast all but finished, the cook arrived with a large platter of what she proudly declared as the national dish of Montenegro. 'Priganice', are small ball-shaped pieces of what appeared to be something fried.

In front of my nervous colleagues, I took one and bit deeply into it. In an instant, I realised what Montenegro's national dish would be described as in the western world. Hiding the urge to smile, I kept up the show with a doubtful look on my face. When asked what it tasted like, I merely replied that I wasn't sure. The game was up when I couldn't stop smiling as I hurriedly stuffed a second one into my mouth. Montenegro's national dish turned out to be deep-fried doughnuts...

A little after eight o'clock *(and several deep-fried doughnuts later,)* our guide stood up to issue plans for the day's trek. As we acknowledged the instructions, I noted our chain-smoking breakfast fellows listening intently. One wonders what they made of our plans to go for a picnic at a mountain lake...

Twenty minutes later, we set forth. Walking down the road towards the mountains revealed more building sites than morning glances had first suggested. Yet, there was nothing but a deathly hush from every single one of them. Late starters I thought, but not according to the Eyebrows. Everyone in town had more than one job; apparently; being a builder was not today's job.

Entering the main street in Zjablick, the first four shops we passed, all sold haberdashery. The fifth one, however, displayed the magic trekking word 'Cola' on its door. Thus, a dozen of us burst in to shatter the morning peace of the woman behind the counter.

Armed with my purchases, it dawned on me that while I had learned Montenegrin for 'please' and 'thank you', I had not learned any Montenegrin numbers yet. Not understanding a word of what the cashier was asking for, my eyes hunted for the cash register in search of some clues. I couldn't see it, and so gambled that ten euros would cover whatever it was she had just said. It did. I received enough currency back to make it embarrassingly obvious I had just cleared out the shop of a weeks' worth of change.

A short distance after the cola shop, we turned sharply off the road and headed for the mountains.

The unfenced boundary of Durmitor National Park appeared to be defined by a one-man kiosk. We could have stormed the kiosk and won easily, or quietly walked around the back of it without its occupant ever knowing, but at two euros a permit for the entire week, it would have been a new record for penny-pinching if we had. Nevertheless, the park guard who processed our permits was wearing a gun, suggesting perhaps, that he had encountered some who thought two euro's a bit excessive...

To the diminishing accompaniment of several thousand randy green frogs trying to find a one-night stand in the nearby swamp, we trooped into the ever-darkening pine forest and made our way to the 'Black' Lake.

The lake was not so much 'black', as mosquito-infested, and they were large enough that I had to duck to avoid getting my head cuffed by their wings. Thankfully, the crescendo of their dive-bombing attempts in search of our blood was an adequate warning of an impending attack. There were many fatalities on their part...

While conducting some strange oriental dance with the mosquitoes, I noticed the advance of Generalissimo 'Ivor Gunn' - which he appeared to be removing from its holster. He had emerged from the nearby restaurant.

With no wars to fight, it was evident that the National Park was his new front line. It also appeared that we had transgressed it by not paying the correct entrance fee. A lively debate about permit charges ensued. Two Euros only covered a day said Generalissimo, but not according to the Eyebrows.

Waiting tensely for the gunshot, several of us discreetly sidled into the restaurant and waited for the arrival of Henry Kissinger. He didn't show up. However, spending money in the restaurant was to prove a smart move. Evidently, Generalissimo protected it for the going rate. With this week's down payment secured, the gun was re-holstered, and permission granted to enter the park as often as we wished.

A tree-darkened track led us to the edge of a clearing. In the middle of it sat a restored water mill, pondering its stream. We disturbed its pondering, and it responded by absorbing us into its.

As adult children paddled their feet, while others basked in the sun, and the scent of a riverside meadow tickled the senses, the scene dressed my mind with memories of halcyon times. I could have spent all day there. It was idyllic.

It could have been anytime, sometime, before the Eyebrows brought us back to the present day. We rose and ambled off after him somewhat reluctantly, remembering that this was, in fact, a trekking holiday.

A little while later, we stopped at a memorial provoking memories of heroes past. Standing among the dense forest, I found it difficult to conceive that its tranquil location marked the site of a bloody battle. Nevertheless, these things are never erected in places of no consequence, and wars make no allowance for places which only peace deserves. I listened intently to the Eyebrows as he related the story.

Eventually, we stepped down through the forest and arrived at the shores of another lake. This was our destination for today.

For his part, the Eyebrows sat down at a nearby picnic bench and began to produce something of a feast from a rucksack half the size of what came out of it.

The glorified picnic that followed could not have been more enchanting. Sitting among the tree canopy with not a soul to disturb the peace, time once more faded from importance.

Our leisurely walk back to the hotel avoided another Balkan war by making a circuitous route behind the one-man, and now probably heavily armed kiosk we had encountered at the entrance to the park.

The evening meal was something forgettable though, and a little while later, fearful of asphyxiation by cigarette smoke, the day melted into an early night.

(DAY THREE ~ THERE'S MORE SNOW THAN I THOUGHT)

Today's breakfast variation was fried eggs. The cook served them as though someone, having recently read up on the theory of how to make them, now sought confirmation they'd got it right. With approving nods of heads, she returned to the kitchen to reward our verdict with a second batch. Meanwhile, my senses continued to struggle with the concept of passive chain-smoking at seven in the morning; the source of which, so far as I could tell, had still not left the bar since our arrival three days ago...

Today was to be one of the week's highlights... We were to climb up one side of a giant pinnacle of rock called 'Medved' (*The Bear*), walk over the pass behind it, and return down the other side to complete a full circle around its base.

Arriving once more at the entrance to Durmitor Park, we ventured cautiously past the kiosk, paying little heed to the militant mutterings from within. After passing the Generalissimo's hideout, we turned away from the main path and once more entered the dark forest.

Barely a few yards further on, we stopped to stare at a cave surrounded by trees, into whose trunks had been hammered hundreds, if not thousands of coins. Here, the Eyebrows offered a short history lesson, which began with the surprising news, that the cave had once been the home of the man who became President of Yugoslavia, one Josip Broz Tito...
Peering inside I could see the inspiration for wanting something better... like a palace or two.
The mystery of the coins in the tree-trunks was solved with the news that they represented prayers left by his disciples. Judging by the number of empty slots where the coins had once been, quite a few must have obtained a refund when Tito's Yugoslavia collapsed...

Durmitor is that rare thing in crowded Europe; a place where the waters of streams are pure enough to drink. That morning, the minute dribble seeping from the muddy ground, and running along an ancient wooden trough provided our refills.

Durmitor is also a place where one has to give way to oxen hauling logs down the hillside... Seeing that we were tourists, the owner of the Oxen brought them to a standstill, so we could take photographs. We offered him a few Euros, but he would not accept them. I doubted it would be long before he would be arranging this spectacle on a fee-only basis.

Not long after we passed the oxen, we began ploughing through deep troughs of snow, something the Eyebrows had not expected.

"There's more snow than I thought," he said for the third time as our boots sank ever further into it as we climbed ever higher.

As the trees cleared, we stopped to admire a large patch of mountain crocus, the vivid pink of their blooms, striking against the whiteness of the snow; snow that according to the Eyebrows was still not supposed to be there. Nevertheless, we ploughed on, and finally crested the ridge that heralded the entrance to the hidden valley around the base of Medved.

Making our way into the valley, the Eyebrows informed us that somewhere beneath the snow on the valley floor was a lake that for generations had kept an almost terrifying secret. Each summer the water level in the lake would slowly recede until the snowmelt filled the lake once again in the winter. For a long time, nobody knew where the water went, until one day, an enterprising scientist poured dye into the lake and discovered that it ran through an underground fissure in the limestone, before emptying out into the depths of the Black lake far below us.

The Eyebrow's story left me feeling that to fall through the snow and into that lake, was to fall to certain death, sucked through a crack in the rocks by the force of the water, never to be seen again, until the day one's remains reappeared as mosquito food in the Black Lake. I shuddered as I considered this while we edged our way along a faint depression in the snow; the only indication for the track we were supposed to be following, far above the lake.

We hadn't gotten far when the Eyebrows produced a rope from his backpack. I'd never been roped together on a trek before, yet the Eyebrow's insistence would have had grave consequences if I'd refused...

Sure enough, within minutes, one of my colleagues lost their footing and slid feet first down the slope towards the hidden lake. In an instinctive move, I fell back against the snow and dug my heels in, taking all the strain on the rope I could muster, heels all the time treading back hard against the surface. Sheer terror can give one the strength of Hercules, and right now, I needed to be Hercules, as three more followed down the slope.

The Eyebrows shouted out to them to kick hard with their feet, but even after they had stopped sliding, the fear within me would not let up my grip. It was several minutes before everyone had managed to regain the track, and I finally relaxed.

Our guide, grateful that I had apparently saved the day... or his job, made me out to be some kind of hero, but since I am not one for hero-worship, my uncoordinated feet soon demonstrated this fact, by promptly losing their footing and sending me likewise down the slope. I'd been here before...

Instinctively, I rolled over onto my face and slammed my feet as hard down into the snow as I could. Cursing, I clambered back up, and passed the hero tag to the next in line, just in time to see him take his turn at repeating my performance. With snow-packed nostrils and bent sunglasses, I finally joined the earlier fallers for lunch.

At this point, the Eyebrows, contemplating the snow that surrounded us *(of which he thought there was more than there should be,)* reconsidered our prospects for rounding the pass behind Medved, still some distance above us. There weren't any. Admitting defeat, he set us on a course to retrace our steps... all the way back to Zabljak.

We arrived back in town to discover a bar undergoing refurbishment. It was evidently targeting the tourist cash that was surely coming to town. We gave it all the encouragement we could by buying twelve pints of beer.

As we chilled out around the bar's brand new tables, the owners approached us to announce that they had also just installed a new set of restrooms, something that only in an undiscovered country would people make a point of telling you. Since we were their first customers, and not wishing to disappoint, many of us duly christened them...

We ate out that night. Whatever the pie on my plate consisted of, it tasted good. There was not a hint of smoked ham, cheese... or cigarette ash in it.

(DAY FOUR ~ TRIPPING OUT)

The early morning sun finally drove me to desperation for a way of blocking out the light in our room.

I grabbed the piece of string our first night's investigations had presumed to be the remains of some long-gone Venetian blinds and began tying my towel to it. As I tugged at the string, I caught sight of something moving outside the window. The more I toyed with the string, the more whatever was outside the window, moved. Puzzled, I stopped tying my towel and gave the string a deliberate tug. Night descended into the room as the blind slowly unfurled... It was on the OUTSIDE of the window...

Having created night, I was now fully awake from my efforts to do so. With my roommate now stirring from the commotion I'd been making, I pulled the blind back up. As he sat on the end of his bed blinking in the sunlight, I tugged the string, and with a loud "ta-dah" fanfare, night once more descended into the room. As he offered something akin to a polite 'golf-clap', I hauled the string back up to secure the daylight...

That morning I was on a roll for I also discovered how to take a shower without risking several stitches. By using a bar of the hotel soap to wedge the showerhead, I was able to counter-balance it sufficient to risk diving beneath it. The soap bar wrapper also made an excellent plug for the washbasin. Now, at last, I could also have a decent shave.

Ablutions completed, I walked out of the accommodation block to breathe in another glorious day of blue skies, warm sun, fried doughnuts, and cigarette smoke.

Breakfast's main conversation that morning, centred on the subject of blisters. Yet, while all trekkers carry the full range of concoctions and potions to combat them, the latest cures are always something of keen interest. Thus, it was no surprise to see breakfast enlivened by the discrete passing of various packets of these cures, over and under the table. Why in such discreet manner I had no idea, but at least it gave the bar-crowd something to talk about... I wondered if they thought this trekking thing of ours was just a cover-up for a meeting of British drug smugglers...

As the Eyebrows changed the subject to the details of the day's trek, the Tara Canyon; second only to the Grand Canyon in depth, I could see the resident smoking crew listening more intently than usual... So the drop was taking place at the Canyon then? As we left the dining room, I glanced back to see them doing their best to ignore us for the first time since we had arrived at the Hotel.

Walking back out into the sunshine, I was suddenly roused from my thoughts by a cacophony of Lorries, cranes, jackhammer drills, and numerous banging and crashing noises. They were coming from every single one of the building sites that lay strewn along the road to the town centre... I could only conclude that the locals had woken up that morning, and unanimously declared:

"Today... we build Zabljak!"

It was a quick march into town for the usual rations. Quick, because any lingering would have resulted in our becoming a construction casualty. As excavators shuffled back and forth, without the merest suggestion of looking where they were going, and scaffold poles swung blithely across the pavement, the people of Zabljak industriously urged their bricks and mortar ever upward... apparently at whatever human cost.

At the cola shop *(just past the four haberdashers)*, the owner appeared relieved to see that I had learnt enough about Montenegrin numbers to hand over the right amount of coins, either that, or the re-emergence of the cash register from behind the tomatoes, had been deliberate in order to give me a clue...

As we left town that morning, we passed a ramshackle assortment of tents and stalls. It was not only construction day in Zabljak; it was also market day.

A cursory glance past the stalls selling haberdashery revealed one offering a rusty wing from an old Yugoslavian built car; clearly business would be brisk today I thought. I longed for a closer look, though, for the market had a pervasive atmosphere of discovery about it. Maybe there were pieces of Soyuz spacecraft on offer, perhaps even the odd Nuclear Warhead?

Feeling more than a little conspicuous, probably because everybody had heard the rumour about our drug deal, I turned to see our group heading off through someone's garden and hurried after them. The potential for buying spare parts for Sputnik would have to wait.

Glancing back one last time, I heard someone shouting something unintelligible in my direction while waving something in the air. It might have been a missile guidance system... Maybe they were on special today... 'Buy one get one free' perhaps...

For the next hour or so, we traipsed along a small country lane, one shrouded in pine trees that deadened all but the sound of our boots echoing on the tarmac. I wondered if we should break step...

The Eyebrows eventually brought us to a halt; the puzzled frown on his face causing his eyebrows to merge, *(either that or they were planning on having a baby eyebrow.)*

He was looking at a makeshift wooden sign, lying by the side of the road. Evidently, it had some critical information on it. Unfortunately, even he couldn't discern its Cyrillic scrawl.

Eventually, he decided to plunge into the surrounding scrub. He was looking for the path to a lookout point above the Tara canyon he told us.

Accepting our offer to fan out and look for it, we broke into small pockets of trekkers, each following the advice of several, 'it's this way', no, 'it's that way' advisors. The track I elected to follow, twisted and turned with no discernible direction, until suddenly, the scrub I had been thrashing my way through, finally peeled back to reveal the successful 'that ways' group sat on top of a rocky promontory just ahead of me.

I strode purposely up, only to halt with a lurching sensation in the pit of my stomach as the path vaporised over the cliff edge just in front of them. Regaining my composure, I gingerly leaned forward to take in the view.

The Tara Canyon may only be a third of the depth of the Grand Canyon, but nevertheless, it was still comfortably within the 'Shit, that's a long way down' category... Sitting as near to the cliff edge as my bladder would allow, I took out my sandwiches.

It was not long before some enormous butterflies appeared. Someone called them 'Apollo's'... I think they could have made it to the moon and back. Hurriedly finishing my sandwiches, I grabbed my camera and began photographing them.

At this point, I feel it prudent to offer a word of advice about using a zoom lens near a cliff edge. I don't recommend it. Focusing on one of the Apollo butterflies, I felt strangely aware that I should not take another step back...

Making our way back to the hotel, we took a leisurely ramble through an endless assortment of pine-fringed fields. With the ever-present mountains as a backdrop, and the rolling fields surrounding us filled with alpine flowers, and picturesque dilapidated barns, I had an overwhelming sense that Julie Andrews was about to appear, running towards us with arms outstretched...

Little more than an hour had passed since we'd left the Tara Canyon, but it was long enough for the Eyebrows to decide to stop and sit down beneath the trees on the edge of one of those fields. We didn't need any further hints.

As some dozed in the afternoon sun, and others read, I sat empty-minded, tripping out on the utopia before me... All I needed was a little cash to fix up one of the cedar wood barns I could see, build a big fence around the edge of the field it was in, and erect some enormous 'Sod off, it's all mine' signs, - life would then be complete...

It was an early night again. As I dozed off, my mind was still in that field, watching out for Julie...

(DAY FIVE ~ A WALK ON THE WILD SIDE)

This morning, I breakfasted with options on my mind. Option 'A' was a white-water rafting expedition down the Tara Canyon.

Having seen the rapids from the top of the canyon, it looked rather tame... OK, I'm lying... It actually looked impressive, even from four thousand feet, but since I'd already seen enough water in my life, this was a 'No'.

Option 'B' was another trek to another lake; only this time, the lake was further away. This sounded promising until I learned that the Eyebrows was taking a day off, and had arranged a new leader for this trek, someone who didn't speak a word of English. Having learned my lesson in Morocco, I chose not to ignore the spirits this time and declined this option too. As I was to learn later, I'm glad I did.

Option 'C', then, was a day off to do my own thing. Being a little footsore, I wanted to take things at a more leisurely pace. What could be better then, than creating my own adventure, one in which I could spend as much time as I wanted, enjoying Mother Nature's offerings in Durmitor National Park?

Thus, as everyone sounded off his or her options, I called out "Option C". I wasn't sure whether anyone considered my announcement with gravitas or derision. As it happened, if I had hoped for some company on my sojourn, I wasn't going to get any.

The announcement of "Proja!" from our ever-innovative cook interrupted the conversation. 'Proja' turned out to be Cornbread... with bits of real sweetcorn in it...

Breakfast over, I wandered back to my room and collected my backpack. As I put together the day's essentials, it dawned on me that I had seen a notice by the park entrance, advising visitors that the area was one of the last places in Europe where you could see bears and wildcats. Suddenly, all concerns about what sort of 'Deliverance' country I might encounter, paled into insignificance.

With thoughts of bears and wildcats already troubling my mind, things didn't get any better when I emerged from the hotel.

In the sunlight that greeted me, the first thing I noticed was the free-range cattle roaming the streets... and they all had enormous horns. Looking around for an open gate, or perhaps their owner, I saw nobody. All the building sites had fallen silent again, and even the hotel bar was now smokeless. The scene could not have been more reminiscent of a spaghetti western if it had tried.

As the opening bars of 'The Good, Bad, and the Ugly' ran through my head, I made my way slowly down the street, all the while keeping a wary eye on the cattle. I just wished they didn't have a look in their eyes suggesting the grass they were chewing, might have gotten them a jail sentence...

My overactive imagination was already busy creating the headline... 'English tourist killed in Montenegro', it read; the cause of death not from being munched down to half a leg by a bear, but by being processed into cowpat by a man-eating bovine, halfway down the main street of a would-be tourist haven...

Above the cacophony of randy green frogs still trying to find a one-night stand in the nearby swamp, I approached the guard's telephone kiosk at the entrance to Durmitor Park with some trepidation.

Somewhat taken aback to see the Generalissimo standing there waiting for me, I sincerely hoped our contretemps a few days ago had not resulted in his demotion; if it had; he was likely to be out for revenge on those responsible... me being one of them. I proffered my permit with little hope of it being accepted. He looked at it and announced something in Montenegrin I didn't understand but knew full well what it meant - my pass was out of date.

Fortunately, being British, my response was to do that typical British thing of shrugging shoulders and feigning a lack of comprehension. Long past caring, the Generalissimo gave a tired wave of the hand and disappeared back into his box. Submissively offering a "Kvala", I walked briskly past him, and into the Park, all the while hoping he didn't have a change of heart and start using me for target practice.

On my way to the Black Lake, a Squirrel showed me his nuts. Realising that if he stood there long enough, I would get a photograph of the moment, he melted back into the pine forest before I could get my camera out...

Turning right at the Black Lake, I soon found the enchanted Mill we had discovered a few days ago. Pleased with my navigation so far, I took off my backpack and lay down upon the grass. Time for a little sunbathing.

As I soaked up the morning sun, I turned my head to take a closer look at the alpine flowers surrounding me. I could tell they were doing their best to convey a feeling that Julie Andrews was correct; the hills were indeed alive... Perhaps that was the problem though, for the absolute silence became a little unsettling. I had to move on.

Not long after, I reached one of those places where paths left, right, and vaguely straight on presented their options. I decided to keep the stream to my left and eventually arrived at the War Memorial again.

This was all well and good, but I wanted to see what else was here in the forest. It was time to be brave... to seek out new worlds... to boldly go where ... Okay, to walk up the hill that I could see a mile or so in front of me at least...

Climbing over its lowly summit, I spotted a large pile of cedar loosely arranged into a mountain chalet. Either I had found a previously undiscovered second home prospect, or some bastard had been living there, in this perfect idyll for the last hundred years... Seeing a lone bench, somewhat incongruously placed by the side of the trail leading up to the chalet, I sat down to unpack my lunch.

With my back cradled in the comfort of a warm bench; I looked over to the cedar wood chalet fading quietly in the sun. In front of it, haystacks peppered a million-flowered meadow in the way only sepia tint photographs can define. Above, in a sky painted the blue of childhood drawings, a lark sang unseen. As if to complete the picture, behind me, the forest had chosen to stand far enough away to ensure that, if I spotted a man-eating bear... or cow... charging from beneath its cover, I still had enough time to finish lunch before having to flee...

Peace descended. I began to trip out... Julie was running across the field in front of me again... I just wish she'd mind the flowers...

How long I sat there, I really don't know. When I eventually rose, devoid of all sense of time, I figured it would be best to head back to town. With no signposts to guide me, I made off in a direction away from Medved, the mountain we had attempted to circumnavigate two days ago.

Not long after, a wizened old man appeared. He was ambling slowly towards me, his head bowed deep in thought. As we passed, I proffered a greeting, but his expressionless gaze and the lost look in his eyes said nothing. Perhaps this place did that to people. I wondered if the chalet I desired was his. If it was, I doubt money meant anything at all to him.

Continuing to plough down through the trees, I finally discovered a track I recognised. This, I knew, would lead me back to Generalissimo's kiosk.

Quickening my pace, I scampered past the kiosk. No shot rang out; presumably, either the Generalissimo was asleep, or had been demoted to Janitor for allowing me into the park with an out of date pass... for the second time in a week.

I arrived back in town somewhat earlier than expected; time then, to find some tourist trappings, a postcard or two perhaps.

The town of Zabljak couldn't offer any postcards or at least nothing to remind me of Medved, Tara Canyon... or Julie Andrews. Thus, I had little choice but to select from a range of dog-eared photographs, that looked identical to the dog-eared concrete blocks I was standing among. Reluctantly I bought a couple of these and headed for the post office.

There, the Postmistress smiled as she watched me stick the stamps on the back of the photographs, scribble a few 'wish you were here's', and then hand them back across the counter. As I gave a 'No Postcards' shrug of the shoulders, she responded by turning her palms up and pursing her lips... I don't think she was offering sex, but I'll never know, for despite handing her a couple of euros, I turned and walked out. The photographs arrived home two weeks after I did...

A beer and a spell of people watching followed, but the people I was watching out for never arrived. Thus, it was a long and silent walk home, but at least the cattle had gone; presumably, they were now either back in their field, or in someone's freezer...

Dinner that night took place at the best restaurant in town. The menu was impressive; what was available, less so...

"I'll have the beef please."

"Not available, sorry."

"OK. I'll have the Lamb, thank you."

"Sorry, we do not have any lamb."

" What about Chicken?"

(Shake of head)

"Fish?"

"No"

However, they did have several types of smoked hams, and some smoked Pork that was sort of like smoked ham... and some smoked cheese. I sighed and elected to have what everyone else was having. I can't even recall what it was.

The inevitable dinner conversation declared my day as the most uneventful, but certainly the most chilled. On hearing the other's exploits, I half-wished, I had taken up one of the alternatives. On the other hand, I'd had a secret rendezvous with Julie, dealt with a psychotic squirrel, fended off, *(run away from,)* some drug-crazed bovines, risked being shot at by a thoroughly fed up Generalissimo, and met someone whose facial expression suggested he'd smoked a few with Jerry Garcia... What adventure could be better than that?

(DAY SIX ~ PILGRIMAGE)

The morning woke to my last look at Medved. We were moving on today. Despite the warm days of sunshine we had enjoyed, it was still as snow-capped now as it was when we had first arrived. I wondered if I would ever return to complete the circuit around its base.

With a succession of fried doughnuts attempting to prove that smoked meats were now a thing of the past in Montenegro, and still no sign of the local smoke pollution team; breakfast lasted a whole lot longer than it should have done.

Reluctantly, I rose to grab my backpack and head for the minibus. It was already mid-morning; our Olympian driver had been waiting patiently for us since six o'clock. He had driven through most of the night to get there...

In preparation for a long and tiring journey today, the Eyebrows advised us to stock up at the supermarket when we stopped for fuel in the town centre.

The supermarket, housed in what I had previously mistaken for being a derelict communist headquarters; offered a surprising array of western delicacies. The price on much of it though was evidently well beyond the reach of the locals; most of whom were waiting patiently at the one-loafed bakery counter.

I prudently avoided buying the last loaf, and instead filled my basket with crisps, chocolate, and cola... all the essentials our western lives would be intolerable, but healthier without. An hour later and Zabljak was vague in mind; we were heading for the coast by way of a brief pilgrimage to Ostrog.

Ostrog is famous for its built-in-the-cliff monastery, but what they don't tell you is that Ostrog is not one, but five monasteries, the built-in version merely being the one highest up the cliff face. As we swerved our way along the precipitous mountain roads, I considered whether the five monasteries had each been built to honour a busload of tourists who'd plunged over a cliff on their way to Ostrog.

For the ghoulish, Ostrog and its churches, and monasteries also sport an excellent selection of body parts. They belong to those who sacrificed a hand or two, in the belief such an act would deliver them from the Ottoman Empire's Islamic indoctrination. For the most part, rather than be delivered, they all just seem to have died for their belief...

The gradual climb up the hillside to visit each of the churches and monasteries was worth it for the cultural intake alone. But on reaching the highest monastery, I could quite see why the solitary monk involved in building it, chose to set up home there; the views were breathtaking.

With a slightly mawkish desire, I had hoped to see the tomb of the intrepid builder. Alas, it was not to be. A local priest had taken up residence by the entrance to the monks' tomb and was busy advising a woman on her knees before him that, in this male-dominated country, it was entirely her fault that her husband didn't love her anymore. Discrete voyeurism suggested that the furious bobbing up and down of her head in front of him, was her admission that she needed to pray for plastic surgery... Either that or they were auditioning for a Montenegrin blue movie...

The other show I had to see while up here, was the miracle of the single grapevine growing out of what was no more than a bucketful of apparently highly blessed, no doubt with fertiliser, soil. Back at the shop a thousand steps below, the number of bottles of wine claiming pedigree from its grapes was clearly also a miracle...

Three hours later and we were back on the bus and heading for the bright lights, big city.... and traffic jams.

Watching how Montenegrins deal with traffic jams was definitely a cultural highlight of the trek. We Brits tend to sit silently doing that British thing of waiting forever for someone to move an inch, or two forward. Here in Montenegro, the approach was a little more direct...

I, like everyone else in the minibus, craned forward in the expectation that blood was about to be shed, as we watched while a lorry, by attempting to insert itself into the traffic flow from a side street, had been subjected to a tirade of abuse by a posse of angry drivers. To a one, those drivers remonstrated with fists waved from car windows, amid a cacophony of car horns. Wisely, the lorry driver diplomatically reversed back to whence he had come from. With fists withdrawn, the traffic began to move once more. I have a vision the lorry driver is still there, waiting for a break in the traffic... either that, or he and his lorry are at the bottom of a Montenegrin cliff...

An hour after our disappointment at the lack of blood-spilling, the Adriatic broke through the mountains to reveal the town of Budva. As the newfound wealth of Powerboats played offshore, the polluted streets of the city and 'don't drink the water' soviet style hotels made for a drab setting.

Some miles later we eventually burst through a tunnel and into the wondrous City of Kotor; a Dubrovnik before the tourists if you like. Before we could utter some appropriate 'oohs' and 'ah's' however, our driver veered left to skirt the lagoon on the opposite side to where the city stood. Looking across the water, it was difficult to believe such a place could still exist undiscovered on this over-discovered coast.

We finally arrived at our hotel just as dusk began to settle in.

The village of Prcanj, from where our hotel revelled in its bougainvillaea terraces, had a view worth millions on the French Riviera, but in the land of plug-less showers, and cat urinated corridors, it was still trekking grade affordable.

That night, I elected for an unadventurous pasta dish but complimented it with audacious consumption of the local wine. The laughter from our table shattered the warm night air long into the small hours before mutual agreement reluctantly ended the festivities.

I returned to my room only to experience the rather novel concept of booting the cat out before turning off the light...

(DAY SEVEN ~ I LOVE MONTENEGRO)

This morning woke to become one of those days which life, occasional perfects... I found a new champion pizza house; one where stone-baked meant the pizza was actually baked on a stone and enjoyed the luxury of having our own boat on which to potter around the Kotor lagoon. Sometimes, a trek is not all about the walk...

The sun blazed its clear blue sky as our minibus took us back to the city of Kotor. On reaching the city gates, we alighted, and made our way through the early morning quiet up onto the ramparts of the citadel walls; we were heading for the vantage point afforded by a lookout, far above the city.

Following a slow, unhurried plod up the many steps to the lookout, our guide disappointed us for the first and only time... He wanted a group photograph...

Having carefully marshalled us below a flagpole bearing the Montenegrin flag, the Eyebrows walked back to take the picture. After twenty yards, he turned and looked through the viewfinder. Not satisfied with what he could see, he encouraged us to squeeze together a little more. Still not happy, he proceeded to walk back another twenty yards and try again. With another motion to squeeze even closer together, and another ten yards or so of back-pedalling, he finally got the picture he wanted.

When we got to see the image later that evening, we understood why he had walked so far back... He wanted to get the Montenegrin flag at the top of the pole, into the frame. The resulting image thus became one of a dozen dwarfs, apparently supporting a two hundred foot flagpole as it punctured the sun... Nevertheless, here was a man proud of his work. Our smiles left him to his treasure; he had already provided riches enough for us...

Making our way down the other side of the citadel, I spotted a tiny chapel set among Van Gogh styled cypress trees. Curious, I walked over to investigate...

The chapel's doors hung open to reveal a long-neglected ruin; the hand-carved inscription on the lintel over the entrance was indecipherable. Yet, just inside the doorway, someone had placed a small box marked with a plea for donations. Taped to the front of the box, a handwritten note described the ruin, as the church of 'St George and St Marie –C.1224'. Taken aback by the revelation that this tiny chapel was almost eight hundred years old, I took a photograph, and with some appreciation, placed a twenty Euro note in the box. What has become of that chapel, I have no idea...

Back in the old city, I rediscovered the pizza restaurant I'd spotted when we first arrived. Being hungry, this was an easy win.

From my table, I could see directly into the kitchen. There, a small boy tended to a roaring log fire beneath a large stone slab. In the background, someone of perhaps teen age spent his time spinning pizza dough acrobatically into the air, before catching it, and throwing it to land perfectly flat on the stone slab. There, the third member of the show transformed the pale disc into a feast, that only minutes later, arrived at my table on the end of a long-handled wooden paddle. Without further ceremony, the chef slid the wafer-thin pizza onto the rotating platter in the middle of the table, and left me to it... no cutlery, and no pizza-cutter... because this really was the perfect pizza for 'tearing and sharing'... except it was so good, I wasn't sharing.

Tottering back through the streets under the weight of pizza, I discovered the shops within the city walls had already become aware of the tourist potential for Kotor. My vanity to own a T-shirt proclaiming that I had been to Montenegro, made me easy prey for them. Parting with far more money than the T-shirt was worth, I wandered suitably impoverished, out of the main gate to meet the rest of the group.

When I found them, I was a little surprised to see the Eyebrows standing there, resplendent with his equally well eye-browed family in tow. After a courteous introduction, he pointed to our next trek... it was onto a boat, our own exclusive boat...

Pulling away from the jetty, I dangled my fingers over the side, as the sun continued to blaze in its cloudless sky, and mirror itself upon the lagoon. With little concern for speed, we puttered slowly towards an island, sat postcard-like in the middle of the lagoon.

When we disembarked at its jetty, the Eyebrows offer a tour around the island's church. I opted out; for the lagoon's water looked far too inviting to be denied the pleasure of my feet...

Sitting on the edge of the jetty, I removed my shoes and socks and dipped my feet into the ice-cold waters. Closing my eyes and breathing deeply, my ears began to hear the serenade of a gentle soprano voice. It was coming from the courtyard behind me. I haven't a clue what it was singing about, but the warmth of the sun, the ice-cold waters, and the gentlest of caressing sea breezes, didn't require a visit to a church for me to hope that, if heaven truly existed, *(and it wasn't on a beach in the Outer Hebrides,)* it would be like this.

Perhaps an hour later, the village I had been ogling at from the jetty, became a lot clearer as we drew alongside one of its piers.

In the necklace of jewels that surround the Kotor lagoon, Perast is the teardrop centrepiece; a centrepiece that inspired the Montenegrin people to defend it (*successfully,*) against the marauding Ottoman Empire. Drifting through its streets and along the narrow quay, I had little doubt its stunning beauty would one day make it the hottest real estate on the Adriatic coast; perhaps the Ottomans knew what they were losing out on...

We had only a short stay in Perast, but it was enough to add a great photograph to my collection and witness a Russian film crew shooting something that had all the look of a Hollywood 'B' movie about it.

The movie, so far as I could make out, involved a lot of scantily clad girls swooning around a handful of Olympians; one of whom, evidently a swimming Olympian, dived into the lagoon and ploughed like a shark towards one of the scantily clads, doing the helpless damsel bit. He was back on the quay with scantily clad over shoulder, more or less before the film crew had cranked up the camera. I got the impression there was to be a retake when he threw the scantily clad several hundred yards back out into the lagoon...

Making our way back across the lagoon, we arrived at the venue for our evening meal.

Approaching the quayside, I noted several boys fishing from it. Each time one of them caught something; it was duly inspected, then thrown into one of several large plastic tubs that stood behind them. As the scene continued to play out, I watched a man in a waiter's uniform, walk over to one of the tubs, grab a still flapping fish, and wave it at a table set a few feet further back on the quay. Its diner, nodding approvingly, signed the fish's death warrant. We ate similarly, although I was thankful that our host had already chosen the fish.

To get back to our hotel that night, meant taking an overlong walk under the influence of excessive amounts of the local wine. Walking down the narrow street, I vaguely remember thanking the alcohol content for providing the necessary swagger, by which to avoid the equally influenced Montenegrin drivers sharing the road...

(DAY EIGHT ~ ROOM WITH A VIEW)

Today we paid homage to King Peter, who lies in his tomb on top of Mount Lovcen... Yes, that's right he's dead. He's been gone a long time, but to Montenegrins, he's the hero that saved the country from the Ottoman Empire and gave them their first attempt at Independence.

As usual with heroic kings, he was a man of the people and upon his death decreed that he should be buried in a simple grave, on top of the mountain he'd found so inspiring. He was... except that, despite being something of a visionary, he didn't pick up on the coming of President Tito, and the all-consuming desire of

Communism to turn heroes of the people, into their heroes, by providing them with facilities befitting that of communist ideology.

Consequently, King Peter's simple tomb was simplified further, by the application of hundreds of tons of marble, a tunnel full of pilgrim-sized steps, a permanent guard, and a viewing balcony, which he, now buried deep inside his marbled mausoleum, would never be able to look out from.

To get to his mausoleum meant another ride in the minibus. It was without its trailer this time but still possessed its nine-foot giant.

Our climb out of Kotor to reach King Peter is one I will never forget. We took the scenic route... up something we learned the locals referred to as 'the ladder'. This involved a gravity-defying first gear ascent, all the way up the side of a mountain, and, just for fun, required our minibus to negotiate no less than twenty-seven hairpins.

At first, the scenery was impressive, and the view spectacular. However, as the swerving around each bend appeared to take us ever nearer the edge, I consciously began shifting my weight towards the centre of the bus. I hoped it would be enough to save me if we re-enacted the finish to the original 'Italian Job'. I wasn't the only one...

Sometime after I'd lost count, or perhaps reached the point where the torture of seeing my life flash before me for the umpteenth time, had finally worn me to the 'I don't want to live any more' point; we stopped. We'd reached the top, and while the view was a photographic certainty, most of us headed for the strategically placed mobile bar, in the hope of finding a stiff drink.

Once over the summit, I expected an equally death-defying descent, but no, here, there was a sweeping Alpine vista of such beauty, that I realised why Julie Andrews was not up at Durmitor. Here too was the smell of the Montenegrin version of Prosciutto ham; at a quarter of the price of the Italian version... and it tasted better.

The guided tour of the smokehouse was pre-health & safety period, but as our eyes got used to the darkness and the beechwood smoke; I finally stopped apologising to all the hams I kept bumping into.

The smoked ham and cheese taster that followed was successful enough to ensure several hams, and various bike-wheel sized blocks of cheeses would make their way back to England. Getting them past the sniffer dogs of English customs officers, though, would clearly be a challenge. Having already pushed my luck when returning from Morocco, I regrettably declined the attempt.

The walk up Mount Lovcen to see King Peter was pleasant enough, but I understood why he would be a bit miffed when I saw the communist version of his grave. Lenin however, would have been very envious indeed.

We stayed long enough to enjoy our own picnic on King Peter's Balcony and then headed down through the mountain to the tunnel entrance, where we re-joined our minibus for the journey to Cetinje.

Podgorica might well be the modern-day capital of Montenegro, but on arrival in the old capital, Cetinje, it was apparent they would have to fight to retain that claim. This ancient city, filled with the trappings of having once held court to numerous embassies, and royalties, sat quietly waiting its moment, while money from the European Union lavished its grandiose buildings with wedding cake standards of décor. Noting that European beer and ice cream prices, had also arrived, it was not long before our minibus headed back to the hotel in Prcanj; lured perhaps, by the thought of a sunset dinner on the terrace...

With the local Vranac *('Vranesh')* wine costing only five euros a bottle, it would not be prudent to reveal how much of it was consumed on the terrace that last night. Suffice to say, that as Kotor lagoon reflected in the evening sun, so I reflected back on the adventure.

Crna Gora, as I now knew Montenegro, had been a revelation, one I felt sure at the time, would, in just a year or two, be a revelation only to the privileged few who could afford it. For now, though, we were its millionaires.

(DAY NINE ~ THE TOURIST TRAP)

A quiet, unhurried and reluctant breakfast, woke the morning. Despite the frantic efforts of the Eyebrows and our Olympian driver, we did our best to leave late enough for them to worry about missing the ferry.

As we were to discover, there were no bridges across the Kotor Lagoon. Instead, two worn-out car ferries plied a monotonous ten-minute crossing of it at its narrowest point. Despite the ten-minute trip, however, they only ran every ninety minutes, regardless of however much traffic wanted to use them... No, I couldn't work that out either.

Boarding the ferry felt like saying good-bye to Montenegro, although in reality we still had an hour or more of it to drive through. Our arrival on the far shore, though, re-introduced us to a sense of urgency we had not felt for more than a week. Clearly, the invasion by the rest of the world was beginning to succeed where the Ottoman Empire had failed.

For the next hour, we ploughed on through an almost continuous ribbon of nameless towns and villages, all, rapidly being swallowed up by new hotel developments.

All too soon, we were back where we had started, Dubrovnik, Croatia.
With time to spare before our flight home, we made a brief visit to the walled city.

As the gates opened for business that morning, I catapulted my way through them in search of Dubrovnik before the rest of the world arrived. I found enough people-free alleyways to create a photographic record to prove I achieved just that...

Mission accomplished, I returned to the main thoroughfare, to discover that the tourist trap had indeed been sprung; its camera totting prey now well and truly ensnared, as the city picked their pockets clean.

Finding a seat by the harbour, I sat down to watch the pleasure-cruisers return from their tours, in half the time they had taken two hours ago. While a guided walk along the city walls above me took on the pace of a keep-fit class. After witnessing ice-cream cones shrink as the queues to buy them lengthened, I declared I'd seen enough and headed back towards the city gates; pausing only to stop and listen to one of the city's Venetian Guards discuss the history of Dubrovnik with a distinctly American gap year twang.
Somewhere deep within me lay the sad regret that this would be the fate of Kotor soon enough.

It was a short drive back to the airport, and following some fond farewells, I boarded my flight home. I think I was asleep before we even took off. It had been a quite extraordinary week.

I woke just as we began our descent. The murk of nine days did not appear to have ever left. I hoped our pilot not only had sonar but X-ray eyes. This was, after all, the same airport where another aircraft on the runway, had caused the aborted landing at the end of my French adventure a few years previously...

After passing through immigration, I made my way down to the station and boarded the train home.

As we cantered our way through the English countryside, my mind drifted back to Montenegro.

What struck me most about our time there was the relative innocence of the people. They had yet to understand how mass tourism would change them or how it would impact their culture and their country. I felt sure the days of the smoking crew at Zabljak, would end the moment a snotty tourist posted a bad review on social media, and wondered how Generalissimo would handle the first package tour groupie who dropped litter in his pristine Durmitor Park, a place where I'd not seen a single piece all the time I was there.

Ostrog's miracle vine really would need a miracle to cater for the demand too. As for Kotor, where I had witnessed the first inklings of the invasion; while it was still a long way short of becoming a Dubrovnik, I suspect what I'd seen, had already been tainted by their presence.

As for King Peter, his mausoleum had been peaceful enough during our visit, but with the steaming hoards expected of mass tourism, I hoped he'd made arrangements to find another mountain.

I sighed. Montenegro and its people had been kind enough to grant me a vision of what a truly white bit on the map looked like. In fact, Montenegro wasn't even white; according to my mobile phone, it didn't exist...

DRINKING THE KOOL-AID

When I came home from Montenegro, life took a different path. I met and fell in love with a beautiful woman, and suddenly, life became a twenty-four hour a day adventure as we explored the road of life together.

Alas, tragedy struck in the most brutal way possible, just twenty-two months later; after which things went into a bit of a downward spiral. I lost much of my zest for life and became something of a recluse.

Rattling around in the home I'd shared with my late wife, it became all too apparent that something needed to change. In short, I needed a new adventure. What that would be, I honestly didn't know for a very long time. Then, during one long and lonely night, spent only in the company of a good bottle of wine, I decided to go with the wildest of ideas... Maybe I could restart my life, *(and begin a new adventure,)* in the United States of America, the former home of my late wife.

There would be challenges, that, I knew for certain, but I'd spent time in the country already, and knew people who knew my story; our story, and who had a kindness and generosity I would come to define as beyond measure.

Reasoning that if the US embassy declined me, I would not have to go through the rest of my life, wondering if I'd missed an opportunity, I duly filled out the online enquiry form and hit the 'submit' button; perhaps more in hope than expectation.

Hope, almost stalled at the first hurdle... for two weeks after I'd submitted my enquiry, the embassy wrote back declining my application on the basis that I'd not been married long enough to qualify. The letter also said there was no appeal.

Remembering that my late wife never took 'No' for an answer, I appealed... I had reason to... the so-called 'Widow's Penalty' by which I had been refused, had been repealed three years earlier. In politest possible terms, I referred them to their own website for confirmation of this.

Just forty-eight hours later, and without apology, the briefest of letters dropped through the letterbox, confirming I could formally apply to settle in the United States of America.

(ONE GIANT LEAP)

Six months after receiving that letter, I was duly granted the right to settle in America as a 'Lawful Permanent Resident'. Two months after that, I flew to America to see my late wife's parents. We had planned this trip long before I knew whether I would be allowed to settle. Regardless of this fact, however, the US Embassy's instructions made it clear that this, my first trip to America after being granted settlement, was to be recorded as my official immigration.

Thus, when I arrived at Orlando airport, clutching the 'Do not open' envelope the US Embassy had sent me, I was directed by the Immigration officer to a small waiting room. There, a few anxious minutes later, an agent formally welcomed me to America. That was it. I had become a street-legal resident... even if the only thing I had arrived with, was a suitcase containing just one week's worth of clothing... and my mind wasn't totally convinced I was doing the right thing.

Nevertheless, I duly returned to England a week later, secured with the knowledge that I had established a base from which to start my new life. All I had to do now was decide if I really was ready to take such a giant leap, something, that after living in the same country all one's life, was not as easy a decision to make as it might seem.

For the next couple of weeks, life felt a little strange. Here was I, going about my usual business, yet, all the while, knowing I could up sticks any time I wanted and emigrate to America... On the other hand, I could just forget about the whole thing and remain in England, or perhaps move to the Outer Hebrides of Scotland, a place I had fallen in love with a few years previously. A Christmas party finally made the decision for me.

On the night in question, I spent most of the time looking into a stiff glass of whisky... Perhaps that was all it took. Understanding that loneliness can be a killer, I swallowed the last dram and headed for an early night. I'd made my decision. I was going to America. I had concluded that if I'd stayed in England, I'd probably never make it through another year... What a candid confession that is...

Over the next few weeks, I sold everything I owned. It wasn't much, but it was a life. When you do such things, it's interesting to note what becomes precious, and what does not. Things I'd owned all my life I sold or gave away. Yet I carefully packed every pebble, and fragments of pottery my late wife had accumulated from our walks... all ten pounds of them. I also dismantled and packed the tiny table and two chairs we had shared during our twenty-two months of happiness; it was coming with me, no matter the cost of shipping would far exceed its value.

The day finally arrived when I said my farewells to the people I'd known for almost half my life and headed to my mother's house, some two hundred miles distant, and where I would spend my last few weeks in England. The countdown was most definitely now on.

During those final weeks, I arranged the despatch of my possessions to America, and spent as much time as possible, saying my goodbyes to a country that had been home for all fifty-six years of my life.

On a mild and insignificant February morning, armed only with a one-way ticket, I boarded a plane bound for America...

(WELCOME TO AMERICA, WELL ALMOST)

When I arrived at JFK airport, New York, it felt bizarre indeed to head for the American Resident section, rather than the 'alien' section of the Immigration Hall. I didn't get that far. An officer stopped me and declared that I couldn't go through immigration the American way, even after I showed her my 'visa approved' stamp. Instead, she directed me to another officer who proceeded to remove several barriers and guide me to a short queue of about ten people. It didn't take long to realise this was the queue for those who, for whatever reason, United States immigration didn't seem happy about allowing entry to America.

If that was the feeling I got while waiting my turn for interrogation, then my worst fears became all too apparent when a Chinese girl in front of me, began to kick off about why she was in the same queue.
Despite being lost in my own questions, she interrupted them to show me, and everyone else, her visa and passport. I spotted the problem almost straight away, for, despite her strong American accent; I didn't have the heart to tell her that her hair

was about five microns shorter than it was in the picture on her Visa... I sighed... After all, my hairline had receded years ago...

A few minutes later, the Immigration Officer called me forward. As he sifted through my passport, I explained to him that I was already a 'Lawful Permanent Resident' of America, so wasn't quite sure why I was in his queue. I told him that my social security number, and official Green Card, were at my mother-in-law's place in North Carolina, and pointed to the big blue 'approved' stamp on my visa; something I hoped would suffice. He looked at the visa and then at the computer and declared:

"Yup, I can see that right here."

Yet, despite seeing it 'right there', what I hoped he would do didn't happen. Instead, he decided the best course of action was to get me "Verified". I wasn't sure what he meant by that, but in the same sentence, he told me not to move. This seemed like a sensible instruction... he had a gun... and so had every other officer I could see...

While waiting on my fate, the officer spent his time slowly reviewing my Customs Declaration. I began to wonder if the two packets of hobnob biscuits I'd declared, were being considered a lethal cargo. Finally, he scrawled something across the declaration with a thick blue pen and handed the form back to me. Moments later, another officer arrived, and with little more than a nod, directed me to follow him.

We crossed the back of the Immigration Hall and entered a dingy 'abandon hope all ye who enter here' office, where I was directed to take a seat. There were six other people in the room, each of whom with a face suggesting they were facing immediate execution.

I watched the officer take my passport up to the high altar... a raised bench with three officers sat behind it. Purposefully strutting up and down behind them, was a female officer, her hair tied tight at the back of her head. She had all the appearance of someone who could sentence you to death with a slight twitch of her head. The lack of emotion on her face was equally chilling. Behind her, two more officers stood to attention, each with some sort of pump action rifle held across their chest... one hand was firmly on the 'pump' bit.

One of the officers sat at the bench proceeded to look back and forth between my Passport and a computer screen. He had the same puzzled look on his face as the agent in the Immigration hall had. Things were not going well.

Finally, he decided to hold court with the officer who had brought me to the room. I could see fingers pointing at the 'approved' stamp in my passport.

At the end of the conversation, I witnessed them nod in agreement. Either that was an approval for the firing squad, or there was hope yet. The officer who'd brought me in then left; presumably to be deactivated for agreeing I had a legitimate immigration visa...

The officer in possession of my life, looked once again at the computer screen and, still frowning, slowly raised a large ink stamp. With ink stamp raised, he paused long enough to audition as a quiz show host about to tell a contestant they were wrong; before a brief 'twitch' from the female officer behind him, sanctioned the downward thump of the stamp onto my passport. Closing it, he called me forward and handed my passport back to me. Hesitating to make for the door, I looked back for some sort of approval to leave. Without a word, another nod confirmed I was free to go. Almost running out of the room, I tried to pace myself as best I could... I thought I'd heard the 'pump' of one of those rifles...

As I reached the door I came in through, the woman guarding it, stepped purposefully in front of me, and held out her hand. There was no way past. She wanted to see my passport. I handed it to her with a feeling of total rejection.

After looking at it briefly, she handed it back, and stood aside with a "Welcome to America" acknowledgement... At this point, I wasn't so sure about the 'welcome', but I thanked her anyway.

I guess they were just doing their job, but one of their colleagues had already done their job for them, by approving my residency more than two months previously, and with an awful lot less terror involved...

Walking towards the luggage hall, I stifled an overwhelming urge to run as fast as I could. The fear of hearing my name called back had become very real, indeed.

In the luggage hall, I collected my belongings with remarkable ease; they were, after all, the only things left on the carousel, piteously going around and around with a 'poor bastard never made it' label on them.

I headed for the final check with the agricultural people; knowing that beyond them, lay America.

I could not have looked more conspicuous with my three suitcases; one large enough to hide someone in, a backpack slung over my shoulder, and a guitar case balanced precariously on top of the smallest suitcase.

I approached the checkpoint. I could see one of the customs officers focusing on me. There was no point trying to avoid him, it would only have raised suspicion that I really was trying to smuggle someone into America. On the other hand, I wondered if my cargo of Hobnob biscuits had made it onto Fox News, and they'd broadcast that

I was going to be gunned down for trying to bring them into the country. I had no idea, but by now, I was past caring.

Feeling my shoulders sag in resignation, I handed over the declaration for the hobnob biscuits and waited nervously. The customs officer looked at the form, now illegible due to the scribblings and bullet holes in it, and, perhaps taking pity on me, filed it without a second glance. His attention then turned to the visa in my passport. I watched as a puzzled look spread across his face.

"I've never seen an 'I' 'W' category before. What is that?" He asked.

I so badly wanted to make it into something top secret but prudently capitulated. I told the truth; I had been admitted as an 'International Widower'. I don't think it was what he expected. With a humbled offer of condolence, he waved me through.

More than two hours after arriving at JFK, I finally stepped out onto the airport concourse. I was, at last, a free man in the United States of America.

To get to my hotel in Times Square, I decided to make the journey in one of New York's iconic Yellow Cabs; it seemed a fitting introduction to the city. Looking around at the manic comings and goings, I realised I had no idea how to get one.

For a moment, I just stood there, taking everything in, until my ears honed in on someone shouting and whistling to my right. There, hidden among the chaos, was a pint-sized woman who appeared to be controlling the entire fleet of New York's yellow cabs with her voice... I walked up to her, and in an almost apologetic way, asked how I could get one of the yellow cabs to take me to Times Square.

Her response was to command me to "wait right there", pointing to a particular spot on the sidewalk... (That's 'pavement' for my English friends, but if I'd written that here without explanation, half of America would quite correctly assume I was standing in the middle of the road. I'll leave them to explain that to you...). I moved purposefully to where she had pointed and waited.

With a shrill whistle and a wave of white gloves, a yellow cab screeched to a halt in front of me. I was in the back of it and hurtling out of the airport less than a minute later.

As we drove towards the city, I tried hard to look ahead at the skyline, but could not help noticing that my driver didn't appear to be paying much attention to traffic lights, or even other traffic. Thus, the focus of my attention faded from the skyline and moved rapidly to look for possible escape routes, in the event he hit something...

Somewhere on the way downtown, we zoomed past a fire truck. Regardless of its flashing blue lights and frenetic blowing of horns, it was stuck behind someone fastidiously driving at about half the speed limit. I figured the driver of that car must have been deaf and blind... Therefore, on behalf of the fire department of New York City, I'd like to apologise to the people whose house burned down that night; but I'd also like to suggest to the fire department that, next time they get a call; they should take a Yellow cab...

We sped down Madison Avenue, and then Fifth Avenue, or at least I think we did... for I spent most of my time doing that thing where you crouch down low and try to peer upwards through the top of the window, in the hope of seeing something you might recognise. By this logic, I reason that I must have seen at least five floors of the Empire State Building; assuming I was looking out the right side of the cab...

Minutes later, as we passed through a set of traffic lights, I finally caught sight of one of the skyscrapers I'd longed to see. In a fleeting moment, the Chrysler Building's crowning lights provided a smile for my tired face. Two minutes later, we came to a halt outside my hotel.

Despite a most generous arrangement through family and friends, the hotel pillaged me for a deposit of one hundred and fifty dollars ... to cover "incidentals" they said. When the receptionist finally handed me the key to my room, she added to the shock by telling me it was on the THIRTIETH floor... The last time I'd slept that high, was on the side of a mountain...

Why the hell my brain suddenly recalled watching 'Towering Inferno' as the elevator rose to heights I didn't know it could, I don't know, I just wish it hadn't...

Finding my room among the maze of corridors, I unlocked the door and collapsed angel-wing fashion onto the bed - Peace at last.

After a minute or two of coming to my senses, I sat up to survey the room. Tucked beneath the television, I found a cupboard containing a tiny fridge. I was starving and felt sure it could provide life-sustaining food, and, with luck, something alcoholic with which to celebrate my arrival in America. However, I was equally sure it had tamperproof seals on it that would set off an alarm at the reception desk.

There was also a whole list of extras available too, according to the hotel information pack... Shoes shined...? Suits pressed...? Just call! I touched nothing and called nobody... I had a distinct feeling they were all 'incidentals'.

After unpacking the basics, I paused to look at my passport. There, next to the original 'visa approved' stamp on my immigration visa, was another 'visa approved' stamp... if you follow me...

It was about this time that I became aware of what I was convinced was a slight swaying motion. For a moment, I wondered if my sense of balance was still stabilising after the hair-raising taxi journey. It wasn't. The building was swaying slightly. I could hear a stiff breeze swirling around outside, and realised that every time a gust slammed into the building, the whole structure, well, wobbled. Just a slight tremble you understand, but enough for one who had never experienced the sensation before, to be able to detect. I wondered if the motion would make me seasick... I'd been there before...

Doing my best to ignore the sensation of movement, I fired up my laptop and connected to the hotel's 'Wi-Fi'. I had a promise to keep; to send an email to expectant family back in England confirming I had arrived safely. As I hit the 'connect' button, a message appeared on the screen informing me that 'Free Wi-Fi' would cost me twenty dollars for ONE DAY... Sighing dejectedly and aware that immigration had already used up all the available space on my arse for new holes, I closed my laptop and resigned myself to sleep.

Lying there, eyes closed, my mind vividly recalled the day's events. What with the terror of almost being thrown out of the country, the hair-raising journey in a taxi cab, hotel 'incidentals'... and yet not a bite to eat... it concluded that on my first day as an American resident, I had become roadkill...

(CLASS ACTIONS)

I woke at five-thirty and checked out. The girl on reception looked to see if I had triggered any of the tamper alarms in my room. Disappointed, she then duly attempted to get my 'incidentals' deposit back. I say 'attempted' because, as she hit the magic button, their system crashed. Powerless, she apologised and offered that the cheque would be in the post... *(Yes, for a while I thought that too, but it did indeed arrive a few days later... with an apology).*

I'd been told that Penn station was only two blocks away, but not knowing how big a 'block' was, and it being painfully obvious I didn't have a clue about New York City, I'd made an arrangement the previous night with the taxicab driver who delivered me to the hotel.

Sure enough, and to my relief, he was waiting for me as I walked out the hotel door. I've no idea if it's customary to make bookings direct with a Yellow cab driver, but nonetheless, within a minute, my luggage and I were speeding towards Penn Station.

ADVENTURES OF A MIDDLE-AGED FART

There were so many 'one-way' signs pointing the wrong way to where I needed to get to, that by the time we arrived, I realised I could have walked it quicker; now I understood the term 'Blocks'. Still, I was grateful to 'Angelo' for getting me to the station with plenty of time to spare. I had learned enough about him to know he'd been working all night, and I was his last fare before finishing his shift. I gave him a very generous tip; he'd earned it.

Turning to look around for something I assumed would look like Grand Central Station, I was not a little perplexed to find there wasn't one. Penn Station, I discovered, wasn't grand at all, it was underground. I finally figured this out when I spotted an escalator heading down into the bowels of the Earth beneath the assortment of buildings that surrounded me. It also helped that a large number of people kept disappearing down it.

Peering down that escalator, it astonished me how fast it moved. I wasn't entirely sure at that point how I was going to get three suitcases, a guitar case, and me, down it in one piece, especially since there didn't appear to be an accompanying 'up' escalator, that would have allowed me the option of leaving a suitcase at the top, and coming back up for it.

In London, getting everything down an escalator in one operation is not that difficult, for they tend to operate at a very stately pace. They are actually slow enough to allow you time to read the small print on all the advertising panels that line the escalator walls. Not so in New York... Here, everyone, and everything, including escalators, appeared to live in a perpetual state of urgency, one singularly intent on getting to where they, or it, needed to go.

I glanced down the escalator again and calculated that if I got it wrong, I, and my luggage, would be catapulted halfway across the concourse. The risk of injuring myself, and for that matter, the fifty people I would probably skittle out in the process, had me wondering if there was an elevator somewhere.

With people climbing all over and around me, trying to get to said escalator, there was nothing else for it. Clutching everything, I stepped onto it, jolting violently as my body accelerated from nought to perhaps seventy miles per hour in a split second.

When the escalator reached the bottom, I stepped off, only to move like an out of control spinning top for several feet, before regaining my balance and coming to a halt on the concourse. It still amazes me that I didn't fall and break my neck...

Having saved fifty people's health insurance premiums without a thank you... not to mention the lawsuits, I gathered my scattered belongings and looked around for signs of what to do next.

It's at this point I have to give thanks to all those American films, and TV shows I'd seen involving train travel. Had I not seen them, I wouldn't have had a clue what to do with my suitcases. Sure enough; there it was... a place to 'check' my luggage.

In England, you're on your own, so far as getting your luggage onto a train is concerned. If you're lucky, you might even find somewhere to stow it. Yet, more than a hundred years after steam first powered its way across America, nearly all long-distance trains here, still have a carriage set aside exclusively for luggage, and a whole industry of people based on getting it into that carriage, and back out of it at the end of your journey.

I handed over my guitar and the two largest suitcases, and in return received a tiny fragment of brown card... my only proof of ownership to a quarter of everything I owned.

With luggage dealt with, hunger resurfaced. I headed across the concourse in search of breakfast.

I'd already heard that when in New York, it is impossible to leave without trying a Bagel... Seeing one such 'family-owned' bagel shop, I made straight for it.

The complexity of the menu was bewildering, yet I was the only one trying to decipher it. Around me, everyone moved in that well-oiled routine way that big-city rush-hours do.

Eventually, the gaze of one of the women behind the counter prompted me into action. Giving up on the menu, I pointed to a bagel in the display case. The sign read 'French Toasted', whatever that meant. It appeared to have what I thought was a crystallised cinnamon sugar coating on top of it. The woman then exposed my naivety by asking me what I wanted on it. I didn't have a clue. With a "What do you recommend" question, the woman suggested cream cheese; lots of cream cheese as it happened. Adding a medium-sized bucket of coffee to my order, I headed off to discover the waiting room for my train, and twenty minutes later, followed a small crowd of passengers down a corridor to it.

When I reached the platform, I was not a little surprised to hear the typical 'fizzing' sound that undeniably meant overhead power cables. This may be a nerdy thing to report, but it came as a considerable shock to learn that America had discovered Electric Locomotion. Like the rest of the world, I had long thought the best American railways would provide for my journey, would be something built in the 1930s; something that might, at best, achieve a death-defying thirty miles per hour, on rickety tracks laid by Chinese navvies a century ago. I was wrong... well, almost...

We pulled out of Penn Station to the still traditional summons of "All aboard" and made our way slowly out of New York City, and across the Hudson River into New Jersey.

Somewhere between New York and Washington D.C., *(mustn't forget the 'D.C.' bit... they get twitchy about that)*, our train reached something approaching one hundred miles per hour. This was a little hair-raising as the tracks were clearly not up to the job. Each time we hit a kink in them, everything in the overhead racks moved or leapt out to land on tables, and in the aisle. One jolt, in particular, was so violent, it threw one hapless passenger into the laps of two elderly women. They seemed quite pleased about it...

Nevertheless, the driver's enthusiasm from achieving the magic 'ton-up', combined with the shake, rock, and roll of the carriages, all made for an exhilarating ride. I just wish they'd fitted seatbelts...

We arrived at Washington only to promptly lose our electrifying image. Our new engine was a diesel, from the circa 1930 period I had expected to see in New York. It also had a snowplough fitted to it... a fact that is important to register, as it will come in use later in this story.

Some thirty minutes passed before we eventually crawled from the station and crossed the Potomac River. We were heading into Dixieland, the south, a place I hoped would become my home, and where my new life would begin. What struck me most about that moment, was the stark difference between the affluence of Washington, and the relative poverty I witnessed within yards of entering the state of Virginia. The sedate speed of the train, however, was now much more in keeping with what I had expected back in New York.

In need of more bagel, I made my way to the Buffet car, only to be disappointed with the fayre on offer. Hungry and in urgent need of something to eat, I purchased a large amount of salt, fat, and sugar, that had been arranged into some sort of food; I say some 'sort of food' for it tasted nothing like the food I had been eating for most of my life. Thinking I was going to need something to wash my mouth out with afterwards, I elected to buy another 'bucket' of coffee. However, by the time I got back to my seat, I understood why the Buffet car served coffee in buckets... the rough motion of the carriages as we made our way through the Virginian countryside, ensured that what was left in my bucket, constituted the 'medium' I had hoped for in the first place...

Amazingly, we arrived at the border of North Carolina on time. 'Amazingly' because, after nine hours, still being 'on time' would be impossible in England... British Rail has enough trouble staying 'on time' after five minutes... However, it was at this point things started to go wrong...

Having crawled into a town called Rocky Mount, we slowed to a stop in the station. So far, so good. Twenty minutes later, we were still there. Seeing the conductor walk through our carriage, I asked him about the delay. The answer came as a surprise. In almost anywhere else in the world, freight takes second place to passenger rail services, but here in America, that's rarely the case, because the freight companies apparently 'own' the track.

For the next hour, we crawled through the North Carolinian countryside, as we followed the all more important freight train that had destroyed our timekeeping. Despite the timetable informing me that the journey between Rocky Mount and Raleigh would take about an hour, we had lost two hours before arriving anywhere near Raleigh. In fact, it soon became apparent, there was a real possibility we might not arrive in Raleigh at all...

After coming to a stop still some distance outside the city, I asked our now despondent conductor, what the delay was this time.

"Tornado" he replied...

I wanted to give him an award for the best excuse I'd ever heard. Nonetheless, twenty minutes later, we finally pulled into Raleigh station. The tornado, I learned, had crossed the tracks in front of the train shortly before we arrived...

Ten minutes later, and as the train driver cranked up the engine to leave, there was an enthusiastic announcement over the speaker system alluding to the hope of clawing back some of the lost time over the remainder of the journey. As if to endorse this, we hit eighty miles an hour a few minutes later... It was at this point; those heading for the Buffet car gave up all hope of returning with anything still in one piece, or containing any liquid whatsoever...

The enthusiasm of our driver lasted barely thirty minutes before news filtered through the carriage that we were once more stuck behind a freight train. It would only be a "very short stop" according to our now psychologically disturbed conductor, but it lasted another twenty minutes...

For the next hour, the journey became little more than a gentle plod through the North Carolinian countryside; at times, it would have been quicker to walk.

Sometime past caring, there was a sudden jolt. We lurched to a stop. There was no explanation. A couple of minutes passed before the train restarted. When it did, it crept almost apologetically into the nearby station at Kannapolis.

Something was most definitely wrong, but I had no idea what. In my naivety I assumed if there were a problem with the train, Amtrak would have a relief locomotive available at Charlotte, just twenty minutes away, that would be sent to rescue us. Thus, with nothing better to do, and presuming I was right about the rescue, I packed my laptop away and cleared the table in front of me of thirteen hours of food detritus.

We spent almost ten minutes at Kannapolis station, before our conductor, now on his way to a padded cell, quietly informed everyone within earshot, that we were going to be running to Charlotte, our next and final stop, under a "Slow Order" (quote/unquote,) because we had hit a tree on the track... However, a few miles later, our 'Slow Order' became a 'Stop Order', as we ground to a halt once more.

The conductor duly reappeared to inform us that they had stopped because, every time the engine passed over a road crossing, the driver claimed he could feel the front of the engine 'lifting' off the tracks. Apparently, the tree we had hit was still wedged beneath the front of the engine. Worse than that, it had bent the snow plough blades sufficient to force them under the engine's leading set of wheels... Hence why the driver could feel the train 'lifting'...

Nevertheless, all would soon be well, said the conductor, as he had radioed ahead for someone to send a big hammer, with which to fix the problem... At least that's what I think he said... he was beginning to show signs of delirium.

Another hour passed before the man with the big hammer arrived. Alas, he soon discovered that what he really needed, was a bloody big hammer; and preferably one with an oxy-acetylene cutting torch attachment, *(and presumably, a massive trolley jack to lift up the engine, while he removed the tree and fixed the snowplough...)*

We were now running FOUR hours late. Time then for the voice of authority, a lunatic, to take charge of the situation.

Standing up; he immediately began to talk about a Class Action lawsuit against the beleaguered train crew... Personally, I felt sorry for them. Long since abandoned by anyone with decision-making authority, or customer services, our situation had rapidly deteriorated into farce.

Mr. 'Class Action', – he kept repeating this, so I assumed it was his name, continued to whip up an audience, which as one might expect, only led to more confrontation, and a subsequent decrease in the information flow from the train crew.

Since I had only slept for two of the last fifty-something hours, and not having an AK47 to end the Class Action with, I resigned myself to muttering "shut the **** up" under my breath. However, with the voice of authority continuing to berate and threaten the train crew, without actually achieving anything constructive, I finally exhaled loudly, and rose to confront the situation, summoning all the patient diplomacy I had left in me... it wasn't much.

Seeing me rise, the conductor turned to face me. I noted his eyes had that, 'I'm going to kill someone in a minute' look about them. Thus, on taking a deep breath, I asked him, in a calm, unemotional voice, what the latest news was, and what our options were.

Since I had not affiliated myself with Mr Class Action, he opened up to me by revealing the bad news that we could have been derailed. I thanked him for the prudent decision to stop... Lightening up, he continued with the really bad news... The train company had no contingency planning for train failure. This, we had no choice but to somehow get the train moving again.

At this point, I looked out of the carriage windows to see passengers jumping off the train and walking along the track. Since this is considered damn near suicide in England, I pointed them out to the conductor. Unbelievably, he informed me that he had no jurisdiction to stop anybody from doing just that... even if that meant people risked walking into the path of an oncoming freight train while crossing the tracks.

About this time, 'Class Action' began asking everyone to sign up to his litigation plans. He wanted their name, address, and every other personal detail he could think to ask for. Unsurprisingly he didn't get a single response. Disappointed, he then offered some verbal doubt about our being right in the head and decided he too was going to join those jumping off the train.

Sadly for us, he got off on the right side of the train; sadly, because I was looking forward to seeing him start a Class Action with the freight train, now thundering past us on the other track...

Shortly after 'Class Action's' departure, our conductor, the buffet staff, and the train assistants, also fled. I was not even convinced we had a driver any more.

Cue the arrival of Mr 'T'.

ADVENTURES OF A MIDDLE-AGED FART

I shall call him Mr T, because he had that kind of attitude, and look, that suggested he could build us a new train out of what was left of the old one. The tool-belt around his waist had such an assortment of various weapons dangling from it, I believed he could do just that.

Since I had become the elected spokesman of those still left on the train, I approached him with the obvious questions. He revealed that the Rail Company had managed to convince him, as one of their off-duty employees, to get out of bed... it was well past midnight by now... and sort things out. I could tell he wasn't happy about this... If only 'Class Action' had remained behind, I would have liked to have seen how short and bloody his discussion with Mr T would have been...

Within an hour, Mr T had summoned, a bloody big hammer, with, I assume, an oxy-acetylene cutting torch attachment, four police cars, a fire truck, and spotlights so bright, that half the population of the nearby town must have thought there'd been a jailbreak. There was also at least one helicopter flying overhead, adding its searchlight to the drama.

After no more than thirty minutes, Mr T returned to inform us that we would proceed to Charlotte, and arrive there in twenty minutes. At this point, I figured he must have removed the snowplough, and the tree, presumably while propping the engine up with his spare hand... The Rail Company clearly needed more off-duty employees...

We finally arrived at Charlotte, where it still took the Rail Company another fifteen minutes to unload the luggage... I wondered if Mr 'T' had been asked to remove a snowplough from the luggage truck too...

So there you have it...

I had arrived in America, Tuesday night. By the early hours of Thursday morning, I had survived being 'immigrated' twice, had a near-death experience in a taxicab, been pillaged by a computer crash, saved the lives of fifty people by sacrificing myself on Penn Station's escalators, dodged at least one tornado, avoided a train derailment, ...and witnessed a Class Action against a tree.

That night, I closed my eyes to the realisation that I had just done something REALLY scary... Perhaps I should tell my Doctor...

CPSIA information can be obtained
at www.ICGtesting.com
Printed in the USA
LVHW041119111119
636959LV00006B/2193